THE CAPTAIN'S RUN

THE CAPTAIN'S RUN

GREGOR PAUL

HarperCollins*Publishers*

HarperCollins*Publishers*

Australia • Brazil • Canada • France • Germany • Holland • Hungary
India • Italy • Japan • Mexico • New Zealand • Poland • Spain • Sweden
Switzerland • United Kingdom • United States of America

First published in 2020
by HarperCollins*Publishers* (New Zealand) Limited
Unit D1, 63 Apollo Drive, Rosedale, Auckland 0632, New Zealand
harpercollins.co.nz

A catalogue record for this book is available from the National Library of New Zealand.

ISBN 978 1 7755 4164 6 (pbk)
ISBN 978 1 7754 9195 8 (ebook)

Cover design by George Saad, HarperCollins Design Studio
Cover image by James Coleman on Unsplash
Typeset in Minion Pro By Kelli Lonergan
Printed and bound by CPI Group (UK) Ltd, Croydon CR0 4YY

CONTENTS

'Enjoy, which is not easy. I think it's really important to embrace, and I wish I knew at the beginning what I knew at the end, because I would have enjoyed it more. I wouldn't seek the job, I wouldn't go trying to be the All Blacks captain; if it's meant to be it's meant to be, and be inclusive. There are so many people around, especially with the All Blacks today, who have great ideas, and to be honest, the All Blacks captain is about building an environment and creating a team that makes decisions.'

—SEAN FITZPATRICK

'Don't worry about the stars, they'll help you. Worry about the guys that are coming on, the guys that might have a bit of pressure on them. Look after them, because the good guys in the team, they'll be your assistants, they'll help you. That's the nature of the Kiwi, I think. The last guys I ever had to worry about were Bryan Williams and Ian Kirkpatrick. I needed them and I spoke to them — they were great. But the guys who might be getting a bit of stuff poked at them through the press — you know, this modern media sort of stuff — they're the guys to go to give your shoulder to if you want.'

—ANDY LESLIE

'Focus on playing well first, don't hold back. I think subconsciously at times I held back from my natural game just because you didn't want to give away penalties or be overly aggressive. I think subconsciously I did pull back on that side of my game a little bit. So play well first and then the other thing is ask for help, or get people around you who can help you that you trust. You don't have to do everything on your own, that's probably the big thing.'

—REUBEN THORNE

'Remember that the captain is the main conduit between players and management and to make sure that that role is well done and when you start to dig into that, it opens up into everything from player welfare, strategy, selection, making sure management are doing the right thing. So I guess that understanding that you are the conduit — you know, the senior player — so understanding that role and making sure that balance is right.'

—GRAHAM MOURIE

'Always lead from the front. You need to listen to your senior people around you and if you feel you are under a lot of pressure, real pressure, don't be afraid to change the game plan, no matter what the coaches say. You can wear it if it fails. That's your choice you have to make. The question you have to ask yourself is whether I am big enough to go outside the game plan and do something different.'

—BUCK SHELFORD

24 NOVEMBER 2013

IT'S HOPELESS. ALL over. It has to be. Not even the All Blacks could escape from the hole in which they currently find themselves. Not even this All Blacks side, which has won all 13 of its tests in 2013, can be seriously thinking they can still win their fourteenth and become the first professional team to go through a calendar year undefeated. It's too late and the 52,000 people packed into the Aviva Stadium in Dublin know it.

Ireland, after 108 years of trying, are finally going to beat the All Blacks. They are within 60 seconds of the final whistle and they lead 22–17. The crowd, having seen their golden boy, Johnny Sexton, push a penalty wide six minutes earlier to leave the door ajar for the All Blacks, have regained their confidence that it's all over. They aren't fretting that Sexton's miss will be costly. How could it be? The Irish have the ball and they are well inside New Zealand's territory. Ireland can't lose it from here.

They get 10 seconds closer to victory when No. 8 Jamie Heaslip smashes another metre to create a ruck. Another 10 seconds disappear when, after a laboured recycle, halfback

Conor Murray passes to lock Mike McCarthy, who chugs into the throng of black shirts desperate to strip him of possession. They aren't able to and Murray once again has the ball, this time opting to pass right to flanker Kevin McLaughlin. He charges into the All Blacks in the hope more time will be eaten up. There are 28 seconds left when the ball becomes available for Murray, but before he can pass it, referee Nigel Owens has blown for a penalty. It's to the All Blacks. Owens is signalling that the Irish sealed off the ball and says: 'Number 17 … straight off your feet.' Ireland prop Jack McGrath has handed the All Blacks the faintest lifeline.

The All Blacks have possession, but their position is still mostly hopeless. They have less than 30 seconds to conjure a converted try from midway inside their own half. It's a near-impossible mission, but obviously captain Richie McCaw doesn't think so. He grabbed the ball as soon as Owens awarded the penalty, tapped it and took off. He'd made a full 10 metres before Owens blew again to bring him back. The captain hadn't taken the penalty from the mark and another 10 seconds have been wasted. But McCaw doesn't remonstrate at Owens' pedantry. There's no reaction from the skipper, no sense of frustration or panic. He turns and throws the ball to Aaron Smith, who is standing on the mark and calmly tells the halfback to tap and pass to someone.

Ben Smith is that someone and he makes it to almost halfway. The recycle is quick and two passes later Kieran Read is crashing into the Irish. Another quick recycle has Beauden Barrett probing the right touchline, before he's tackled and the ball is moved to lock Sam Whitelock, who smashes another few metres. The tension is incredible. The noise is deafening. The clock has turned red, signalling the 80 minutes are up and that the All Blacks can't afford even the tiniest error. One mistake and the game is over.

The All Blacks give no sign that they are feeling the tension. Their fifth-phase play sees Ma'a Nonu push a wide pass to Ben Smith, who comes back infield. The All Blacks forwards are there in a flash, protecting the possession. Aaron Smith looks to his right and doesn't flinch when he sees that it will be Owen Franks taking possession, with his brother Ben the next available recipient. The Franks brothers are brilliant scrummagers and tough men — but this is not their scene. Pass and catch isn't their natural game but Owen has his hands out, takes the ball and passes nicely to Ben, who crashes into the tackler. Owen makes sure the ball comes back. Hope is maybe rising as the All Blacks are now on Ireland's 10-metre line. And Ireland are wilting.

Smith fires left to Aaron Cruden, who himself makes a long pass to Ben Smith. One more pass leaves Kieran Read in space and he charges into the nearest defender but flips the ball back to Smith as he does so. The All Blacks are up to Ireland's 22 and then Nonu, playing at halfback, takes them well inside it when he sneaks down the blindside. The Irish crowd are losing their confidence. Not their voice, though, but the noise is now aimed at willing their team to hang on.

The All Blacks can maybe sniff blood and another charge by Ben Franks leaves space on the right to explore on their eighth phase of attack. Julian Savea has come off his wing to create confusion in the Irish defence. He passes to Liam Messam, who runs strongly, bringing the All Blacks to within five metres of the tryline. Whatever momentum has been built, though, is stalled by a wobbly pass by Smith, which sees Nonu have to gather a bouncing ball back on the 22. The crowd lifts, their roar suggesting they believe it's the mistake they have been waiting for. But Nonu has an acre of space, takes off and makes good ground before he's stopped.

What was once unthinkable is now a probability. If the All Blacks attack left, they have a chance to score. And that's what they do. Cruden fires a flat pass to Dane Coles and the reserve hooker somehow, with two Irish defenders on him, slips the ball to Ryan Crotty, who flops over the line. Dublin is stunned. And then the Irish are heartbroken when Cruden — who is given a second attempt due to an early charge-down attempt — lands the winning conversion. The All Blacks produced 11 immaculate phases in 95 seconds to pull off the greatest escape ever witnessed in a test match.

It is the best example of pressure rugby that anyone will ever witness, and while there were heroes in black everywhere, the victory would never have been possible had it not been for the calm and belief permeating from McCaw. The All Blacks were 19–0 down after 17 minutes. They were 22–7 down with just 13 minutes left. They were facing the prospect of going 25–17 behind on 73 minutes when Sexton was kicking for goal. And despite always being behind and never in control of the game, McCaw didn't give any hint of victory not being possible.

His body language never deviated. His head was up, his shoulders back, and his voice strong and calm. He refrained from any emotional rants and continued to preach the same thing to his players — to only focus on doing the next task well. He was desperate to not be the first captain of an All Blacks side that lost to Ireland, but his desperation was channelled, focused and inspiring. His players would all say after the game that they were periodically riddled with doubt — had plenty of moments when they really didn't believe they could win. And then they would see McCaw, so poised and certain that the victory was achievable, that he exorcised their demons.

As McCaw explained after the game: 'When I was a young player and first started in the provincial game our captain taught me something pretty important. We were down by a similar margin, 29 to very little. I thought the game was over and he said "believe", and we got home in that game. Since then, I've never, ever given up, and always been proud of All Blacks teams, that no matter whether you're behind, seemingly out of the game, you never stop believing there's a chance.'

In a cauldron of noise and emotion, he remained dispassionate, and such was the strength of his demeanour and conviction, and such was the respect in which he was held by his peers, that he

'When I was a young player and first started in the provincial game our captain taught me something pretty important. We were down by a similar margin, 29 to very little. I thought the game was over and he said "believe", and we got home in that game. Since then, I've never, ever given up, and always been proud of All Blacks teams, that no matter whether you're behind, seemingly out of the game, you never stop believing there's a chance.'

— RICHIE McCAW

instilled a similar belief in them. The All Blacks would never have won without such brilliant captaincy. If the captain had shown even a hint of vulnerability, Ireland would have won.

An hour after the final whistle, Aaron Smith, still a little stunned at what had happened, says he's never experienced anything like those closing minutes. He says he was gasping for air, desperate to stop running, but had been able to keep going because he had been convinced by McCaw that the game was still theirs to win. He admits to being in awe of his captain — unable to comprehend how the skipper had retained such a cool head and been able to give such precise instructions about what he wanted.

Smith had started to think midway through the second half that victory was beyond the All Blacks, but McCaw convinced him otherwise. McCaw inspired him to see what was possible. It's the greatest piece of captaincy Smith has ever seen. It's the greatest piece of captaincy anyone has ever seen.

CHAPTER ONE

THE PIONEER CAPTAINS

ANDY LESLIE KNEW he was fighting a losing battle to keep his breakfast down. The rising tide of anxiety inside him was going to result in a tsunami, where everything solid would be caught in its path and hurled out. Try as he might, he couldn't stop the enormity of the last 24 hours overwhelming him. It shouldn't have been like this: this should have been a day of pride, excitement and optimism. A day spent receiving pats on the back from those he did and didn't know. A day spent gripped by the warm glow of having achieved something special.

But it wasn't going to be like that. It was going to be a day spent gripped by fear, panicking almost, at the turn of events which had seen this perennial provincial battler somewhat randomly named as captain of the All Blacks.

Leslie had played in more All Blacks trials than he could remember but never had he been selected for the national team. In 1974, he was 30 — an age which said he wasn't without hope but that if he wasn't selected now, he most likely never would be. The occasional press report in the past had bandied his name around as a possibility, but not in 1974. So, when he and a few others sat under the grandstand at Athletic Park in Wellington waiting for the team announcement, Leslie was barely even half listening. 'I know I was sitting with Ian Stevens, who was a halfback in the trials, and that's when Jack Sullivan named the team,' recalls Leslie.

'I was always used to hearing A.R. Sutherland come out and in this case it was A.R. Leslie. I was picked in the team and I didn't hear it at all. Ian Stevens actually gave me a whack on the back, saying, "Shit, you're the captain as well." And that's how I found out under the stand, sitting there on the steps. All of a sudden, you've probably got the most responsible job in New Zealand being the captain of the All Blacks and you've got to set standards. Whether you like it or not, people look up to you and they expect standards. People expect a wee bit more of you and you've got to live up to that.'

A bit like Newton's third law, that for every action there is an equal and opposite reaction, Leslie found out he was captain of the All Blacks at precisely the same time as Ian Kirkpatrick discovered he no longer was. Recognised at the time as arguably the world's best rugby player, Kirkpatrick, a fearless and dynamic loose forward, had taken over the captaincy in 1972. By 1974, after a difficult and largely unsuccessful tour of the UK and France in 1972–73, Kirkpatrick was no longer the preferred choice to lead the side, despite continuing to be a world-class player.

His dignity was not considered worth protecting by those picking the team. No one pre-warned him what might be coming. No one sat him down and explained before the public announcement what was going to happen and why. He was dumped as captain without a word being said, yet still picked in the team, leaving him and Leslie to awkwardly find a way to work together.

'All of a sudden, you've probably got the most responsible job in New Zealand being the captain of the All Blacks and you've got to set standards. Whether you like it or not, people look up to you and they expect standards. People expect a wee bit more of you and you've got to live up to that.'

— ANDY LESLIE

'I remember quite vividly that at breakfast time the next morning — and it wasn't through excess drink — I couldn't hold my breakfast down,' says Leslie. 'Everything just caught up with me. The magnitude of the responsibility of replacing Kirky, who I thought, well, who I knew was the best rugby player on the planet, hit me. Kirky hadn't been told beforehand that he was losing the job. He wasn't supported and there was a camp of guys who thought that Kirky had been badly done by so I had that to handle as well. Those other guys who had missed out on the captaincy, I have no doubt many of them were thinking, *Who's this guy Leslie?* That was one of my hardest jobs, to get the confidence. The most traumatic thing was dealing with that, with the honour. You weren't taught how to make speeches, you weren't taught how to run anything. Everything was assumed that you would take the mantle on.'

* * *

It was, if nothing else, entirely consistent that Kirkpatrick should hear he was no longer the All Blacks captain in the same manner that he learned he was. Two years prior to being dumped, he was at home, tuned to the radio to hear the team that had been picked to play Australia for a three-test series. He'd made his debut in 1967 against France, and while he was initially a surprise choice, his performances were of such quality that he went on to win a further 16 test caps and was one of the few players almost certain of his place in the team.

Still, despite his standing and experience, he never took selection for granted and felt the usual elation that came with hearing he had once again been picked. But what threw him was that he had also been named captain. 'I never wanted the captaincy as a real yearning,' he says. 'Just being part of the All Blacks was enough for me. You play in the All Blacks to be as good as you can and you don't want to get too far ahead of yourself.'

Like Leslie, and probably like every All Blacks captain before him, Kirkpatrick had to accept the honour and find a way to do the job. There wasn't an opportunity to say no. There was no discussion or negotiation, and it would have been almost treasonous, certainly unpatriotic, to reject the captaincy. This was how things were in the amateur era — you were asked, so you did, and those named captain of the All Blacks had to wear the title the best they could. If the responsibility didn't sit well with them, they would have to find a way to live with it; to be able to carry it without the burden weighing them down. It was an era of stoicism and gritty determination where the pioneering spirit lived a little closer to the surface, and if someone wasn't sure what they were doing as captain, they were expected to be resourceful and adaptable until they did.

New Zealand had been built by problem-solvers, people with resilience who didn't feel dismay at the enormous challenges they faced. These, without ever being put in such direct terms, were the qualities expected of an All Blacks captain. There was no manual from which they could learn. There was no one particular way the job should be done, and so the captain had to learn as he went, working off gut instinct most of the time and being guided by common sense the rest.

No one, it seems, ever set out to win the role. Players fell into the captaincy more than anything else. There were those like Kirkpatrick who were deemed to have earned the right to be captain by dint of their performances, their longevity, and the respect in which they were held. And then there was someone such as Leslie, who was asked to be captain on debut, winning the role on the basis that the All Blacks coach of the time liked the way the Wellington captain operated as a No. 8.

Understandably, given the lack of clarity about how the job should be done and what, in specific terms, was expected, captaincy came with little or no job security. And, given that resilience and resourcefulness were deemed integral qualities to possess, it was considered that deposed captains had all the necessary skills to deal with their fate and hence there was no need to spare them from the inevitable hurt they would feel on being dropped in full view of their peers.

Towards the end of the last millennium, those asked to be best man at a wedding in the UK would often start their speech by saying they considered their role to be similar to having sex with the Queen Mother. The joke being that it was a great honour to be asked, but that they didn't actually want to do it. The same sentiment applied to the All Blacks captaincy.

* * *

The rain was pelting in horizontally, driven by a ferocious wind that few locals in Sydney had ever experienced. It made for almost impossible conditions, but there was no chance the first of three tests between the Wallabies and the All Blacks was ever going to be called off or abandoned in 1974. The weather was just one more thing with which Leslie had to contend. He was in the unique position of being captain yet also making his test debut. Before the game, he'd met with referee Roger Vanderfield, who had told Leslie not to hesitate to ask if there were any decisions about which he required clarification. When the Wallabies won a penalty at a lineout in the first minute, Leslie asked what it was for and was promptly told by the referee to 'piss off'. Test football was not panning out as he had imagined.

That fear he'd felt the day after being named captain didn't seem misplaced in Sydney. The All Blacks were 6–3 down after 40 minutes, and the conditions were so dire there was no obvious tactical lever to pull to change the nature of the test. The game had been reduced to farce and it was effectively a lottery situation in terms of what might happen. The first half had flown by so quickly and with no real shape or pattern, that when it came to half-time, Leslie didn't have a cohesive thought in his head. Like many captains before him, he had that moment of being consumed by self-doubt. Every All Blacks captain has been there — uncertain about their ability to lead and unsure whether they are the right person to stand in front of their peers and do the whole Henry V, 'Once more unto the breach' thing.

But as he battled to get his head around what was required to bring the All Blacks victory, Kirkpatrick stepped into the void. 'The weather conditions that day were abysmal. Some of the worst I have ever played in,' recalls All Blacks wing Bryan Williams, who was one of the senior players in Sydney. 'Kirky virtually took control of that game. He got the ball in his hands frequently and took us forward. Andy was in a situation where he had never played a test match and he was being asked to get over the nerves of that and captain the team at the same time.'

The All Blacks won 11–6, the winning try being scored by Kirkpatrick, and while Leslie may have felt underprepared and ultimately a little lost at times, it didn't do his reputation any harm. This wasn't an age of micro-analysis or neurotic media dissecting each and every decision. A victory was all that mattered and it could paper over any number of cracks — obvious or otherwise — in an All Blacks performance.

Nor was it an era of overstating the role and influence of the captain. Blame was not often squarely laid at their door in the wake of a defeat, and likewise, a victory was rarely heralded as a triumph of one man's leadership. There was greater appreciation of the concept of team and the various roles everyone played within it.

Perhaps, too, there was less expectation about performance and there was none of the modern obsession about the style of rugby played. All anyone cared about was winning — how it came hardly mattered, and that may have been because preparation for test football in the amateur era came with major time constraints and stringent rules. Back then, rugby had to fit around life, and not the other way round. The game was genuinely amateur, and the law-makers acknowledged that by insisting that the earliest international teams could assemble was the Wednesday night before a Saturday-afternoon test.

An All Blacks test in New Zealand created an almost conflicting dynamic where it was such a major event for the nation and yet the team had so little time to prepare for it. New Zealand was not awash with entertainment options in the 1960s and 1970s. Those not fortunate enough to have tickets would be huddled around the radio and, later, the TV. Rugby was still the best way for New Zealand to make its presence felt on the global stage: still the preferred lens through which to see its colonial relationship. There was an intensity of pressure and expectation but a paucity of time, which strangely, to some extent, made life less complicated for captains. There wasn't enough time to overthink things.

'I saw my role as making sure we were all on the same page and well organised prior to each test match and that we knew what we are all doing,' says Kirkpatrick. 'It was nothing like it is now. We had no time to get specific about how we wanted to play. We would train on Thursday morning and there were photographs in the afternoon. Then there was a light captain's run on Friday. Our preparation was pretty limited to say the least. We just didn't have the time and that's what the rules were. You couldn't assemble any earlier so you had to hope that we could put something together that was going to be good enough to win — because when you became an All Black you didn't lose. The whole purpose was to win and we just had to prepare as best we could in the time we had.'

What also helped immeasurably was the nature of provincial rugby. New Zealand's best players were spread across the country back then. None of the clustering of talent in the urban centres that exists today was happening and so a typical All Blacks team would contain a handful of men with provincial captaincy experience. There were leaders throughout most All Blacks teams: grizzled types who knew their way around the bottom of a ruck and didn't lack for taking the initiative.

'I saw my role as making sure we were all on the same page and well organised prior to each test match and that we knew what we are all doing. It was nothing like it is now. We had no time to get specific about how we wanted to play. We would train on Thursday morning and there were photographs in the afternoon. Then there was a light captain's run on Friday. Our preparation was pretty limited to say the least.'

— IAN KIRKPATRICK

An All Blacks captain didn't need to be overly prescriptive about his expectations and most weren't. Instead, they mostly assumed that the players around them were not only self-motivated, but that they fully understood their responsibilities, because that's how rugby teams worked at all levels.

'I remember my first game of senior rugby at Petone and I was playing No. 8 and I was an 18-year-old and Ken Graham was my captain,' says Leslie. 'We had won the scrum against the head and we were on the goal line. We were attacking and something happened and Ken turned around and the conversation was more or less, "You're the No. 8, you're in charge of that situation, you should have had a call on that. I'm the front-row forward, I don't know what's going on there." That was my first game of senior rugby and I learned from that stage to take responsibility for your position, and that's what I think we all used to do then, take responsibility for our positions.'

To a large extent, the job of captaincy in that period was essentially being chief orchestrator. It wasn't about being chief strategist or motivator. It wasn't about being a public figurehead, or a statesmanlike figure operating in the public domain. There was little media coverage other than the live broadcasts and analysis pieces that journalists of the time generated from their own observations. There was no cult of personality or sit-down interviews to shape in the public mind the deeper nature of the captain or the culture of the team.

The captain was there to toss a coin, decide whether to kick for goal or not, and to try to ensure that everyone understood what was usually a simple game plan. It was a system that also relied heavily on trust — that each player would know their individual role and be brave enough and determined enough to take responsibility for doing it — and arguably, as much as individual empowerment was the All Blacks' greatest strength, there were times perhaps when it was their greatest weakness.

There was, as Kirkpatrick can see now, times when it would have been better not to have assumed that every player knew the full extent of their responsibilities. Or that even if they did, it shouldn't always have been taken as read that they were in the right head space to deliver. This was particularly the case when the

All Blacks were offshore, as the captain's job changed markedly on tour in comparison with a home test.

* * *

Lansdowne Road crackled with the obligatory excitement and hope that came whenever Ireland played the All Blacks. It was 20 January 1973 and the Irish, who would celebrate their centenary the following year, had an inkling they were finally going to post the coveted victory against the All Blacks that had eluded them in 68 years of trying. Their side contained genuine legends of the game such as Willie John McBride, Mike Gibson and Fergus Slattery, and while fullback and captain Tom Kiernan was in the last throes of a memorable career, he still had something left.

For all that Dublin was enveloped by hope, it was hard to maintain through the first 60 minutes as the All Blacks were in control. The visitors had ascendancy in all the key areas and appeared destined to secure the Grand Slam they were after. Previous victories against Wales, Scotland and England had left the All Blacks on the verge of making history. One more win in Dublin and they would become the first All Blacks side to complete a clean sweep against the Home Unions in one tour — and back then, that sat alongside a series win in South Africa as the Holy Grail.

When Alex 'Grizz' Wyllie crashed over to make the score 10–3 early in the second half, the All Blacks looked poised to ease out to a comfortable victory. Ireland weren't dead and buried, but they had conjured so little despite their energy and intent that it was hard to see how they could score the points they needed.

That was certainly the view of Bryan Williams and no doubt other All Blacks, and it was ultimately what left them vulnerable when first-five Bob Burgess hoofed the ball down the field from a scrum inside his 22. 'We were leading 10–3 which required Ireland to score a try,' says Williams, who, along with fullback Joe Karam, chased Burgess's kick. 'They had Tom Kiernan playing at fullback, who was at the absolute end of his career, and we probably hung off him a bit thinking he wasn't going to run and of course he dummied and ran. Ireland ended up maybe 30 metres out.'

From there the Irish won a penalty to make it 10–6, and when the ensuing kick-off was put out on the full, Ireland attacked right and wing Tom Grace chipped ahead into the All Blacks' dead-ball area. 'Grant Batty and I were haring back,' says Williams, 'but Grace was a bit faster than myself and he scored. That made it 10-all. And you know, up until then Ireland hadn't looked like scoring a try. We were in control.'

Grace had killed the Grand Slam dream, and while that final quarter could have been seen as just reward for Irish resilience combined with a temporary lack of concentration and focus from the All Blacks, it was actually symptomatic of something deeper. The All Blacks, had they been properly focused, would never have drawn in Dublin.

But that All Blacks side was not glued together as it should have been. They had played their first game of that tour in Canada on 19 October, and by the time they had arrived in Dublin the combination of too much time together and too much time away from home had impacted.

This was barely even an analogue age. The world didn't have instant communication forms that touched every corner of the globe. Even phoning home was expensive and at times laborious and the role of the captain on these long tours changed. With, typically, just one coach and a manager travelling with the squad, pastoral care became a major part of the captain's brief. Anyone and everyone was vulnerable to frustration and negativity setting in given the length of time the squad spent away from home, but often the most vulnerable were those who were playing the least.

Despite the fact that a tour could range from 18 games to as many as 32, which was the case in 1972–73, it didn't always mean there was a fair or logical allocation for individuals. It wasn't uncommon for some players to go weeks without being involved while their rivals vying for the same position were playing all the time. The absurdity was hard to understand, and those rejected could potentially become disheartened to the point of being disruptive.

'I guess in 1978, for example, it wasn't a particularly well-selected team,' says Graham Mourie, who captained the All Blacks on that tour. 'If you take into account that there were six loose forwards and I think one of them played three games, one played four and one played five out of 18, which is a total of 12. Leicester Rutledge and I played 26 between us. So you've got to manage those guys who were obviously frustrated that they weren't getting the games. They were the most important members of the team because they were the ones that were most likely to drag the team down and cause issues in other areas.'

It was the skipper who was mostly responsible for maintaining morale and keeping the troops on task. But while he could pick up a few low-hanging bottom lips with a cup of coffee, an attentive ear and some kind words, he needed his senior players to do their part in holding everyone to account.

On the 1972–73 Grand Slam tour, the senior players didn't do their part. The culture of self-responsibility may have been there at the start of the tour, but it wasn't by the time the All Blacks arrived in Ireland, and Kirkpatrick, with the benefit of hindsight, regrets that he didn't do more to impress upon others that they needed to regain their hunger to be at their best. He assumed too much, he says, believing that because he had been driven and relentlessly disciplined as a player, that such traits came readily and easily to everyone else.

Knowing how much to say and how much to get involved in the lives of others was a constant balancing act for captains of that era. Saying too much carried the risk of belittling players who would often have more test experience. Don't say enough and a Grand Slam that was there for the taking slips away. 'It was always in the back of my mind. That wonder whether it was all going to pan out,' says Kirkpatrick. 'So you had to rely on your team-mates to do their part. Although it was a team game, it was still lonely. You had your job and if you didn't do it and half the team were the same, then you weren't going to win. You just had to hope that all the players had their own motivation.

'It was up to the individuals to do what they were supposed to be doing. I knew that when I was a player, I had a job to do and I pretty much just wanted to get on with it and do it. That was what I expected of all the experienced guys that were around me when I was captain, without having to tell them. I knew they knew that, so that wasn't a big deal really, but it didn't always work out that way.

'Looking back, that's probably where I made a few mistakes. I thought that the guys didn't need me to rev them up other than to make sure we were organised. I probably didn't hit that home enough in general, I am talking about — knowing that I expected senior players who were captains of their unions to stand up and do their thing. Once you get on the paddock it is too late to say something behind the goalposts. The team has got to be onto it before they get on the paddock. If they are not, then they are going to come second and that is why we drew that game in Dublin. Ireland played bloody well and we didn't play as well as we should have. You can say something [during the game] but I think it is too late then. The guys have to be onto it before the start, not switch on halfway through.'

CHAPTER TWO

GAME OF THRONES

THE HASTINGS BROTHERS, world-class players and among the most experienced in the Scottish team playing the All Blacks at Eden Park in 1990, appeared to have got themselves in a muddle midway through the first half. Scott, playing at centre, took a long pass from his first-five Craig Chalmers and then appeared to lose his bearings, turning his back as the All Blacks' defence advanced. It looked like he might clatter into his brother Gavin by mistake, until he released the ball at the perfect moment. The confusion was a well-planned illusion and Gavin, having charged through the hole his brother had made with the deception, kicked ahead for wing Alex Moore to score in the corner and put the Scots 18–9 ahead.

The All Blacks were suddenly in a world of trouble — a situation no one had seen coming. The week before, the All Blacks had comfortably defeated Scotland 31–16. The Scots, despite having won a Six Nations Grand Slam earlier in 1990, weren't able to cope with the speed and cohesion of the All Blacks in Dunedin. It had been another dynamic performance from the home side, stretching their unbeaten run to 13 games.

'We had beaten then comfortably enough in Dunedin and we believed we had a lot of room for improvement,' says Grant Fox, who was at No. 10 for the All Blacks in the series against Scotland. 'We went in [to the Eden Park test] with a game plan and it rained, and for 40 minutes we didn't really alter it and our skills weren't very good either. I'm not saying the plan was wrong — we didn't execute well.'

At 18–9 down, All Blacks captain Wayne Shelford, universally known as 'Buck', knew the game was in danger of slipping away. Shelford, who had led the side since late 1987 and was yet to suffer a defeat, gathered his team around him during a stoppage and let it be known what he wanted. As Fox recalls: 'I think Buck gave me a little bit of leeway for a while but then it was, "Hey, get it in front of us and get it down there." It was a pretty simple message and we ground out a win from applying field position pressure.'

Fox kicked the winning penalty with three minutes to go, further enhancing the growing belief that the world champion All Blacks had become unbeatable. The All Blacks, since winning the 1987 World Cup, had grown into a ruthless machine. The engine was new generation, next level, and Wales, Australia, Argentina, France, Ireland and Scotland had all experienced that for themselves. It looked amazing, but those who had lifted the bonnet and peeked under the hood could see there was a potentially significant fault.

This was an era of provincial power struggle. Canterbury had built a great team in the early 1980s, and after winning the Ranfurly Shield in 1982 went on to record 25 successful defences. That run ended in 1985 when, in front of 50,000 fans at the old Lancaster Park in Christchurch, Auckland took the Shield with a 28–23 victory in a game many still see as the most compelling provincial contest in New Zealand history.

Two provinces, with a long and intense rivalry, were battling for supremacy throughout the 1980s. Both Auckland and Canterbury were laden with men who had played test football. Both wanted more representation in the team and both felt their respective coaches should be rewarded with All Blacks positions. 'Grizz' Wyllie, a Canterbury legend, had been appointed head coach after the 1987 World Cup. That decision had not been universally accepted as a strong lobby had been pushing for Auckland coach John Hart to be given the All Blacks job. Wyllie and Hart had been assistant coaches to Brian Lochore at the 1987 World Cup, and when Hart missed out to Wyllie, tension escalated. Auckland dominated provincial rugby in a previously unknown way, making 62 successful defences of the Ranfurly Shield, so, despite the All Blacks being undefeated in Wyllie's three years in charge, there remained a constant narrative suggesting Hart's promotion to the top role was imminent.

Essentially, throughout the mid-to-late 1980s and early 1990s, the great Canterbury and Auckland sides were vying for control of the All Blacks and it made life difficult, and occasionally impossible, for Shelford as captain. He had played for Auckland between 1982 and 1985, but was committed throughout his All Blacks captaincy to the newly formed North Harbour union. The whole business of provincial 'dick measuring' was of little interest to him as All Blacks captain. By the time the national team was picked and assembled, he felt none of that was relevant: that, by then, everyone was simply an All Black … not an Auckland All Black or a Canterbury All Black … just an All Black.

'Canterbury and Auckland were playing different types of rugby in that period,' says Shelford. 'Canterbury were playing good forward stuff, good backs stuff but quite restrictive and yet expansive when they felt they needed to be. Auckland, when they went on that great Shield run in the later 1980s, created this open running style because they had such talented players and that went into the All Blacks as well with Grizz as the coach. But I think they [Auckland players] got a bit carried away with themselves in the end and they moved away from the All Blacks game plan at that time. They were trying to do the Auckland game plan and the two didn't fit.

'As captain you had to be mindful of that as we were heavily weighted with Cantabrians and Aucklanders and there is always that love–hate relationship even though we are in the All Blacks. It was still there — you would still hear "Let's play like we do in Auckland" and all that sort of shit and I would just say, "Let's play like the All Blacks" which is a bit of both. We need to get the job done up front and we play hard.'

As his tenure developed, the division within the team grew. The provincial rivalry that should have been laid at the All Blacks' door and forgotten about when players came into camp, increasingly wasn't, and the team didn't always unite as it should. That there were provincial cliques apparent off the field wasn't particularly new or damaging. The All Blacks were by no means the only international team in the world where players gravitated, socially, towards those they knew from their club or provincial football. What was concerning, however, was that the All Blacks' performance was occasionally damaged by the provincial battle for supremacy.

The first sign of this manifesting as a problem came in the second of a three-test series against the Wallabies in 1988. The All Blacks had won the first in Sydney 32–7, but at Ballymore two weeks later, they were disjointed. They were being beaten up by the Wallabies pack, and Shelford, perhaps not fully cognisant of why, could see that the tight five were confused about what was expected of them. There were three Aucklanders, a Cantabrian and Wellingtonian Murray Pierce in the tight five. Whatever was going on in their heads throughout the first half, Shelford knew it had to stop. 'I had to say to the forwards to pick their bloody game up or we would be sucking the hind tit. I took the two locks aside and gave them a bloody barrel-full. And all of a sudden we started winning ball, getting on the front foot and we drew the test. If we'd had another five minutes we probably would have won. But our forwards weren't there that day. Especially our tight forwards so I gave them a rev-up and a shake-up. That was my job as captain.'

Two years later, when the problem of confusion, or perhaps dissension, within the ranks arose against Scotland, Shelford was more aware of its root cause. He could sense that a moment like this had been coming — that it was increasingly difficult to contain the Auckland influence pervading all areas of the team. At 18–9 down, though, against a Scotland team that had to be taken seriously, Shelford knew the All Blacks would lose if they didn't get back to being the All Blacks.

'I talked to Foxy and I said just do what we do,' says Shelford. 'Play our game plan, don't do anything else. Play our game plan. We were chasing the game and our backs were trying to play this Auckland game plan and it wasn't working. JK [All Blacks wing

Sir John Kirwan] and all the boys, Foxy ... they wanted to this expansive game and I said no. We had to get back to what we all knew, which was All Blacks rugby. Just stick to what the coaches tell you. I am the mouth of the coach on the field so just get on with it. If you are in the shit and you are sticking to your plan and it is not working, then you change it. But we hadn't been sticking to our game plan. We clawed our way out in the end.'

There will forever be differing views on this, but arguably the second test against Scotland was Shelford's finest moment as captain. The All Blacks were in danger of losing until he intervened and forced everyone to return to the correct game plan. That's captaincy — having the force of personality and wherewithal to change the probable outcome of the game. Shelford's intervention stretched the unbeaten streak to 14 tests, but his reward for imposing himself — for doing his job — was to lose the All Blacks captaincy.

'I thought I had played about as well as I could, considering,' he says. 'When your forward pack is struggling the No. 8 is never in the game. Especially when the ball is being kicked all over the place, but I thought I played pretty well. I had to tell a few people to pull their heads in and we won the game so that was captaincy ... changing the course of the game. The decision was Grizz's. He dropped me, and my wife still hates him for that. He told me on the phone before the next test series. He used a weak excuse. He said, "You looked like you were carrying a knee injury or a calf injury" or something like that. But he was under so much pressure and I was going on 34 and I had had a good run so I thought, *Right, I am out of here*, and I moved on.'

* * *

vhat was an unhappy, unsuccessful and deeply
d Cup campaign in 1991, Sean Fitzpatrick
ealand almost certain his All Blacks days were
over. ... g to focus on his building trade again — give the
rugby away, or at least not bother to play seriously any more.

The World Cup had been such a miserable tournament
because the provincial divide that had split the team in the mid-
to-late 1980s wasn't fixed when Shelford was dropped as captain. If
anything, it only became worse when Aucklander Gary Whetton
took over and another Aucklander, Zinzan Brooke, replaced
Shelford at No. 8. In what can only be considered a moment of
madness — a triumph of disastrous logic — the New Zealand
Rugby Union decided in 1991 to bring Hart into the All Blacks
as co-coach to Wyllie. Both men were good coaches in their own
right and Hart was proving especially capable given what he had
built with Auckland. But to stick them together was like trying to
make an edible dish with banana and fish.

The two were never going to work well together — they
were different characters, different people and held different
rugby philosophies. Hart had earned the right to do the job, but
the smart thing would have been to have let Wyllie take the All
Blacks to the World Cup on his own in 1991 and then let Hart
take over on his own in 1992. Instead, they were stuck together
in an unhappy marriage that ended in acrimonious divorce when
both men were ditched after the tournament and Laurie Mains,
the coach of Otago, was given the All Blacks job in 1992.

So, as much as Fitzpatrick was sure he wanted to bring his test career to an end, he was just as certain that the new coach would feel the same way. The Auckland cabal that had dominated the All Blacks were shown up at the World Cup for being too old, arrogant and almost complacent about their right to be in the All Blacks.

A sobering moment had hit this home to Fitzpatrick. He and his wife were in Australia after the World Cup and when he opened the paper one morning, there was his arch-rival, Wallabies hooker Phil Kearns, beaming back at him from the back page. 'I used to eat him up for breakfast and spit him out,' says Fitzpatrick. 'He was like a little puppy. In 1990 he was getting better; by 1991 he was a much better player than me. I remember seeing him on the back page of the *Sydney Morning Herald* and he was holding the America's Cup in one hand and had the Rugby World Cup in the other and the headline said, "The world's best hooker now becomes the world's best sailor" as he'd done something on Sydney Harbour. And I looked at it and I said to [wife] Bronny, "*I'm* the best hooker in the world" and I literally thought I still was. And she said to me, "No, darling. You are a fat bastard."'

The culture of entitlement couldn't be condoned any longer in the All Blacks and Fitzpatrick was sure there would be a major cleanout of personnel and that it would include him. Which is why he was genuinely surprised to answer a phone call in early 1992 and hear the voice of Mains at the other end.

'I was 27 years old and I wanted to start building houses again — that was my job — and amazingly I got a phone call from Laurie asking me if I wanted to be an All Black again,' says Fitzpatrick. 'When he asked me, I thought, *Well, maybe he wants me to be*, and so I said, "Yes, I think I would like to be, Laurie."

And with that he said, "Well, you're probably not going to be." He said I was arrogant and the thing that hurt me the most of all was that he said, "You've lost respect for the All Blacks jersey." I thought, *Jesus!* I mean, that really hurt, and he said, "If you can show me in the next five to six weeks I might give you a chance to be in the All Blacks trials." I got as fit as I've ever been because I decided that I wanted to be an All Black again. When it came to the trial, Laurie got rid of almost everyone, and they mostly happened to be Aucklanders. But he threw me an olive branch and said, "You're not in my Probables team, but I'll make you captain of the Possibles." Literally, there was no one else.'

Captaincy, of any team, hadn't been on Fitzpatrick's radar. Being an All Black was always enough for him and he'd never forgotten that his first cap came in 1986 when the country's established test stars were banned from playing due to their rebel tour of South Africa. And even then, Fitzpatrick hadn't initially been picked to play against France. He was promoted from the bench on the eve of the game when Bruce Hemara popped a rib. It had never been easy for Fitzpatrick. After he had shown he was good enough to play test football, he was still behind Hika Reid and Andy Dalton once they became available again. His thoughts had never strayed far from playing well enough to hold his place.

When he was made captain of the Possibles, he didn't think too hard about whether that had any deeper, more significant meaning. Whetton, to no one's surprise, was one of the many Auckland casualties of the Mains regime and wasn't offered a trial. But while that left the captain's job vacant, no one actually saw it that way.

'Mike Brewer was always going to be the captain,' says Fitzpatrick. 'But about 60 minutes into the game Mike blew his calf muscle and with that he walked off and he said, "Jesus, I'm gone for good, this is major." And as soon as he said that I said to myself, "Shit, I wonder who's going to be captain now?" And that was literally it. We went to the changing room and I did not want to be captain — that wasn't on my list of things to do. They deliberated for more than two hours because they named the team there and then at the after-match, and I was named as captain. I subsequently found out from Earle Kirton, who was one of the other selectors and a coach, that the major concern about me being captain of the All Blacks was that Laurie didn't want me.'

To a certain extent, Mains' reluctance to appoint Fitzpatrick was understandable. Mains wanted to dilute the Auckland influence. The last seven or so years had established that the team in 1992 needed a new beginning: a less politically charged dynamic and more unified base from which to operate. Appointing an Aucklander as captain, particularly one with strong links to the previous regime, didn't feel like it was the fresh start the All Blacks needed.

There was also the fact that six weeks prior to the trial, Mains didn't have Fitzpatrick in his plans at all — he was throwing him a bone with the Possibles selection but that was perhaps more out of respect for what the All Blacks hooker had been rather than what the coach thought he still was.

And, while Auckland were still the country's dominant side and Canterbury not so far behind, both Otago and Waikato were greatly improved and contained new, exciting test prospects. Everything pointed towards change and a decommissioning of the Auckland power base as far as Mains was concerned and that's why he found it so hard to make peace with the idea of Fitzpatrick as captain.

But as hard as it was for Mains to coach a side with a captain he didn't want, it was harder for Fitzpatrick to be captain in that scenario. To not have the endorsement of the head coach left him isolated and uncertain. He had also inherited a relatively new team as a result of the post-World Cup cleanout. He didn't know many of them and the question of whether they respected him was especially hard to answer.

Every All Blacks captain knows that their job is a perennial quest to gain and then maintain the respect of their peers, and there was Fitzpatrick, coming into the job via the back door as it were and not with the head coach entirely convinced he was making the right call.

Then there was the whole anti-Auckland sentiment. It was still there despite the cleanout and Fitzpatrick detected that there were others in the squad who felt they should have been captain and spent much of 1992 and 1993 never quite on board. What didn't help, he says, was a running media narrative out of Auckland that Mains was the wrong choice as head coach. 'The Auckland mafia was against him which didn't make it easy for me,' says Fitzpatrick. 'A lot of my mates were the ones that were slagging him off. There was a billboard in Auckland as you drove along the motorway and we drove past it quite a few times, and it had: "What the All Blacks need is a coach, not a lorry." That was driven by some agency in Auckland.'

Like Shelford before him, Fitzpatrick discovered that being captain of the All Blacks in the late amateur era was a little like being head of a European monarchy in the Middle Ages. There was this sense that friends were really enemies and enemies potentially friends — that there were hidden knives everywhere, waiting to be stabbed into the captain's back. There were secret agendas, alliances being formed with mutual interests promoted and protected, and the captain often felt he couldn't trust anyone — not even long-term provincial team-mates. It was an era of distrust and mistrust, a constant battle of survival and unchecked personal ambition. Fitzpatrick could never stop worrying that there were silent resisters everywhere — players who gave the impression they backed him, but were working against him all the time.

Much like Shelford, Fitzpatrick could never be sure everyone was with him, and self-interest was arguably the All Blacks' greatest enemy in his first two years of captaincy. He had to captain the team with one eye roaming the ranks for troublemakers — for resisters to his regime — and as is so often the case, the results alluded to the fraught nature of his early tenure.

The All Blacks lost their first test under Fitzpatrick to the World XV and then lost the series to Australia, surrendering the Bledisloe Cup in the process. It was only when the All Blacks toured South Africa later in the year that the team began to unify and that Fitzpatrick's relationship with Mains improved.

'In 1992 and 1993 there were players in the All Blacks who thought they should have been the All Blacks captain and I won't say who, but it was a case of me having to deal with that which made me very open to letting people lead. A lot of people don't do that — especially in business — because they're scared they're going to lose their job. That never was a factor with me. I think that winning that game in South Africa was a turning point. I think Mike Brewer might have become available and I just assumed that he'd come back and he'd be captain. I can remember Laurie just sort of sitting down and he said, "No, I want you to continue as captain," which was sort of a vote of confidence.

'I started to gain a bit of confidence — a number of the players that I hadn't really rated, you know, Jamie Joseph, Arran Pene, those guys had real leadership qualities that really shone through. A lot of those guys really stepped up.'

'In 1992 and 1993 there were players in the All Blacks who thought they should have been the All Blacks captain and I won't say who, but it was a case of me having to deal with that which made me very open to letting people lead. A lot of people don't do that — especially in business — because they're scared they're going to lose their job. That never was a factor with me.'

— SEAN FITZPATRICK

* * *

Australia, in the end, walloped the All Blacks at Eden Park in early September 1986. They won 22–9 but the gulf was bigger than the scoreline suggests. The Wallabies scored the only two tries of the game, looked fitter, more cohesive, and came up with more creative rugby. But not at the expense of any of their graft, discipline or defensive grunt. Their victory secured them the Bledisloe Cup and a place in history. They had won a series in New Zealand — the most coveted prize in rugby.

That defeat should have been an awakening for the All Blacks: a game in which they made some significant realisations about the set-up of their team and management. They didn't though. There was only a superficial reaction to that series defeat, which was to drop David Kirk as captain. Kirk, first capped in 1985, was the obvious and perhaps only real choice to be made captain for the first test in 1986. That opening game against France and indeed the test that followed against Australia were problematic selection-wise as all the players who had toured South Africa with the rebel Cavaliers in April and May were banned from representing the All Blacks. Other than Kirk and John Kirwan, who had both declined invitations, the unsanctioned Cavaliers were basically the All Blacks by another name.

It was an unprecedented and regrettable situation that the All Blacks were going to have to play France with 11 new caps in the starting side. The so-called 'Baby Blacks' would be sent into battle while the men who saw themselves as the rightful incumbents would be nursing their wrath at having been disciplined for playing in South Africa. Once the Cavaliers were banned, it created two distinct All Blacks teams and obvious difficulties. How would the new players feel about being called up when they knew it was circumstance rather than their ability that had earned them selection? And what would happen once the Cavaliers became available again? Would they all be slotted straight back in? And of particular interest would be the captaincy.

'Brian Lochore [coach] rang me before the team was announced,' says Kirk. 'I thought I was the most likely person to captain the team given I was the captain of Auckland which was the leading province at the time, and there were so many players not available.

I had been in and around the All Blacks quite a bit, and as a halfback you are pretty influential in the team regardless of whether you are the captain or not because you are making a lot of calls.

'I didn't feel interim at all and that was one of the things Brian wanted to impress upon me and the team. It didn't matter the circumstances in which you were selected to represent your country. You were an All Black and you were expected to play like an All Black and represent the country like an All Black. There were no excuses. I thought it was absolutely the right approach to take. We were told by one of the great All Blacks players, captains and coaches that we should feel absolutely as much an All Black and as worthy an All Black as any other selected. That was quite correct. We were the best players available to be selected. So I guess in that context my captaincy was the same. I was selected on merit and I had to do the job the best I possibly could.'

The Baby Blacks beat France and then came within a point of winning the first test against the Wallabies in Wellington. Given the circumstances, it wasn't a bad return and Kirk deserved considerable credit for the way he saw past the politics of the situation and focused his captaincy on the practical rather than the emotional. To his mind, the requirements of the job had not changed as a result of the Cavaliers situation or indeed the creeping professionalisation of the game.

'Players were definitely going offshore to earn money in Italy and France. That was well known and they had been doing that for a while. But it was sort of out of sight out of mind. It wasn't really part of the conversation in New Zealand during that time. The players came back and no one was particularly interested. No one asked them how much they got paid or anything like that.

'There was, though, a rising engagement with sponsors. There was a requirement to go to functions and support the sponsors in some way or another. There were some TV ads, I think, but that was just taken as part of the gig. I don't recall that as captain I had to do much more than recognise sponsors in speeches and thanking them. Which was natural and normal and I don't recall it being intrusive.

'I think in every match that you are captain you have the same responsibilities and the same need to speak to players individually and to the team as a whole. Generally, it was about manner of play and what we were trying to achieve. Working out how we were going to play the game was important. It was all about playing the game at pace. Tap kicking at penalty. Getting the ball away quickly from scrums, quick ruck ball as opposed to holding the ball off the ground — all of that had to be understood clearly by everyone. A lot of the captaincy role was about reinforcing what the coach and team had agreed was the best way to play to win the match.

'And then there was just a natural enthusiasm and encouragement and energy that needs to come from the captain, and that was reasonably natural for me to be praising people and giving them confidence while also focusing on the grind, the hard work and the need to execute your positional requirements well.'

The hard part, as it transpired, was not living without the Cavaliers. It was learning to live with them again, and as much as Kirk had performed heroics in guiding the most inexperienced All Blacks side in history, his efforts were not appreciated or respected by the returning Cavaliers. The loss to the Wallabies at Eden Park, which came after a fortuitous second-test win in Dunedin, was symptomatic of something other than the Wallabies' obvious qualities. As well as the visitors had played, their victory owed something to the division within the All Blacks. They were not a happy or unified team in that third test.

'That was a very good Wallabies team and they outplayed us and deserved to win,' says Kirk. 'That had not been a happy team, though, once the Cavaliers came back in. They were not particularly accepting of my leadership. Particularly in the forwards — where there was a circling of the wagons. I think they were all feeling quite stressed because they hadn't expected to be banned for two tests and their careers to be on the line. They had expected that New Zealanders would admire them for finding a way to complete the tour. But as history shows, it didn't work out that way. Matches weren't televised and your average New Zealander thought making trips to South Africa for money was not a good idea.

'They were feeling under pressure and thought they had to rely on each other. They were a tight group and that largely included the exclusion of me. There was division in the team and definitely I was excluded. They were not open to me, listening to me or seeing me as their captain. The result was that I didn't feel like I could lead that group and that group didn't want me as their leader. I am not sure they would have wanted anyone who wasn't a Cavalier at that point. That was the nature of the captaincy in that period.

'It is not unusual for captains to be changed after a lost series, particularly given the circumstances in which I became the captain. I heard about it on the radio and I was pissed off. No one gives up on the All Blacks captaincy. I have never given up on anything. I knew I wasn't doing anything wrong and that I could captain the team successfully. I accept there was a special circumstance but I found it disappointing.'

There was Kirk battling politics and internal division within the All Blacks in 1986 — a scenario that was familiar to Fitzpatrick almost a decade later. The late amateur era was not one in which the thin-skinned or politically naive could survive in

'I think in every match that you are captain you have the same responsibilities and the same need to speak to players individually and to the team as a whole ... A lot of the captaincy role was about reinforcing what the coach and team had agreed was the best way to play to win the match. And then there was just a natural enthusiasm and encouragement and energy that needs to come from the captain, and that was reasonably natural for me to be praising people and giving them confidence while also focusing on the grind, the hard work and the need to execute your positional requirements well.'

— DAVID KIRK

the captaincy. The nature of test football didn't necessarily change much in that period. The players were fitter and better skilled as they trained more with their provinces. The rugby was faster and more fluid, but still governed largely by basic game plans as the old rules of only being allowed to assemble on the Wednesday before a test remained.

The All Blacks captain was still, really, nothing more than the chief orchestrator, albeit with slightly more front-of-house responsibilities at the increasing number of sponsor functions. If Kirk, Fitzpatrick or Shelford had sat down with the likes of Andy Leslie, Graham Mourie and Ian Kirkpatrick they would have discovered that the job looked much the same in 1972 as it did in 1994. Except for the major difference, that the last decade of the amateur era was subject to internecine politics that gave captaincy a *Game of Thrones* vibe that was neither enjoyable nor particularly helpful in regard to leading the team. Strangely, though, despite the fractious nature of that last decade, the All Blacks won 81 per cent of their tests between 1986 and 1993, while their winning ratio in the more settled period between 1972 and 1985 was 74 per cent.

Division had the strangely positive effect of accentuating how much responsibility the various captains of that period would delegate to others. Kirk, Shelford and Fitzpatrick all saw the value in empowering those around them. That was true of Leslie, Mourie and Kirkpatrick, too, but Kirk and Fitzpatrick in particular saw that they were respectively in higher need of wider support given the ructions. Both were confident enough in their own positions to see that letting other people have influence beyond the level they may have been offered in other regimes was not something to be feared — it was good leadership.

In the case of Kirk, the New Zealand Rugby Union came to realise that. After the All Blacks won one and lost one against France in late 1986, it dawned on the national body that dropping Kirk as captain had not done anything to heal the wounds caused by the Cavaliers tour. He wasn't the problem. The players who had rejected his captaincy were the problem. Most of the Cavaliers were dropped in 1987, and when the initial choice of captain,

Andy Dalton, was ruled out of the World Cup because of injury, Kirk found himself back at the helm.

'The Cavaliers tour was obviously disastrous for NZR at the time both from an international PR sense and because people were put off rugby,' says Kirk. 'They were really disenchanted with rugby between 1985 and 1986. The NZR to its credit dumped Colin Meads and Tiny Hill as selectors of the All Blacks team. Meads and Hill were rooted in the old style. In came John Hart and Alex Wyllie, who had had nothing to do with the Cavaliers tour — in fact they had been opposed to it and were bitterly disappointed that their players had run off without spending more time talking to them about it.

'There was a big change of the guard. Murray Mexted, Andy Haden, Mark Shaw, Gary Knight and John Ashworth … that was the end of that group of players. They were all Cavaliers. The squad of players chosen in 1987 had 16 Aucklanders in it so it was a natural squad for me to lead. I felt comfortable with them and most importantly they felt comfortable with me.'

CHAPTER THREE

SHARING THE LOAD

IT TOOK THE television match official (TMO) a full five minutes to decide that Richie McCaw had scored in the corner. The All Blacks captain had managed to fend off three South African defenders and somehow touch the ball down before he was bundled into touch. Dan Carter missed the conversion, so the score with two minutes remaining in Soweto was 22-all. Plenty of teams would have settled for a draw in the Republic against a good Springboks team. But not this All Blacks side. They were unbeaten in 2010 and hadn't lost since South Africa had beaten them in Hamilton in September 2009. That was 13 tests and 11 months ago. A draw was not going to bring satisfaction and no one in the All Blacks team that day needed to be told that.

Nor did anyone look at the clock and lack belief that it could be done. The All Blacks didn't lose conviction even when South Africa won the kick-off and were attacking in the last minute. The Boks were slow getting to a tackle ball in the middle of the field and the All Blacks counter-rucked them off it. They moved the ball left, Ma'a Nonu broke the tackle of John Smit and sped down the field before throwing a perfect pass to Israel Dagg, who scored to win the game.

The All Blacks scored 12 points in the final four minutes and yet, as miraculous as this was, it largely felt almost inevitable to the senior players. The victory hadn't happened by chance, and while it was the captain who sparked the comeback by scoring the first of the two tries, it was by no means his influence alone that turned the game.

By 2010 the All Blacks didn't just have a captain — they had a leadership team. McCaw had a coach-appointed group with whom he worked. This was the new way of the All Blacks — the captain wasn't the lone figure he sometimes was in the amateur and early professional period. The game had become too detailed and complex, and so consuming in terms of time and commitment, that it was impossible for the captain to reach the entire squad. And that was the other thing — rugby had ceased to be a 15-man game. It was now a 22-man game on match days and a 30-man — sometimes more — operation the rest of the time. Injuries were inevitable and regular and so there was constant chopping and changing of personnel. With extended coaching and management teams that could sometimes involve as many as 15 staff, the captain had to have help.

The set-up became almost akin to that of government — the captain was the prime minister and the leadership group the cabinet. Decisions weren't made in isolation or without deep consideration and it became a committee-based process where information was fed in, analysed, dissected and action plans formed.

To some extent, maybe the All Blacks had always been like this. Andy Leslie had the likes of Ian Kirkpatrick and Bryan

Williams advising him. Graham Mourie had strong leaders such as Andy Dalton, Andy Haden and Stu Wilson to help him. And throughout the late amateur period there was an expectation that senior players would lead areas of the team. But what was different in 2010 was the scale and overt, non-assumed nature of the leadership group. It became an official, recognised body with specific powers and responsibilities. And unlike previous eras, players didn't drift into the leadership group on account of seniority. This was an appointed group — by the coaches — and membership became something to which young players could aspire.

Those final minutes in Soweto weren't quite as random as they appeared. The All Blacks hadn't got lucky at the end. Those 12 points were reward for effective planning and collective leadership. Several times during Super Rugby in 2010 the All Blacks leadership had jumped on planes after they had played and met to discuss the season ahead. They wanted a new level of detail in their game. They wanted to examine how they would react under pressure; think about how they would communicate and who would say what. They wanted to have a collective certainty, or at least as much as they could, about how they would play and create pressure and how they would respond to it.

McCaw led the discussions and he held the ultimate authority, but this was collaborative decision-making and planning on a level the All Blacks had previously never seen. Specifically, that game in Soweto had been talked about and targeted for months. The All Blacks had lost twice in South Africa the year before — as well as the defeat in Hamilton — and winning in the Republic was a major goal in 2010. 'Richie was an unbelievable captain but he was not always going to touch everyone and inspire everyone and that is why a lot of guys around him were key,' says Mils Muliaina, who was part of the leadership group in 2010. 'He was never going to motivate someone like Jerry Collins with what he said and given the difference in their upbringings. But he had Keven Mealamu, who could, and there were leaders in the group who all touched different guys. That's what Richie was so good at. He would send the right messages to the right guys and then they would go off and send the right messages to the other young guys and everyone ended up on the same page. There was a lot of emphasis on making sure everyone knew what the captain needed.

'We got to the stage where we were one leadership group and we started talking about game plans. I can remember in 2009 South Africa had given us a few hidings so in 2010 we sat down as a leadership group and decided how we were going to win this game in Soweto. We went away from all our strengths and decided to target their strengths which at the time were their lineout, their ball carriers. We stripped it right back to target individuals and try to put them off their game.

'We sat there and we said, "Right, we will target Victor Matfield. What doesn't he like?" And we went through it all — targeting specific areas of the game and specific individuals. And that's why we won like that. We had so much trust and confidence in what we were doing. A lot of that understanding came from the losses we had endured together and also from the meetings we had. That's probably why Richie was so good because he trusted the guys around him.'

* * *

Sean Fitzpatrick was on the All Blacks' team bus making its way to Ellis Park to play the 1995 World Cup final when he decided he was going to retire. Win or lose, Fitzpatrick was going to bow out. He was 32 and it would be the right time to leave it all behind. No one really knew what rugby's future looked like and Fitzpatrick wasn't sure whether, after four years as captain and 10 years an All Black, he wanted to be part of the brave new professional world.

When the All Blacks lost that epic encounter in South Africa, he was emotionally broken. The loss had pierced his soul and he couldn't imagine, in the days after the 15–12 defeat, finding the mental energy to pick himself up and stick the black jersey on again.

'I can remember driving to that game in '95 and I said, "Whatever happens, this is it. Win or lose, I'm going to retire." We lost. It wrecked my pride. But I was having a beer with a mate, a good mate, and he said, "Fitzy, you have to come back here next year and be the first team to win a series against South Africa." No one had ever done it, and the South Africans, for me, they were the greatest side to play against.'

He kept thinking about that for the remainder of 1995 and the prospect of playing South Africa in 1996 was enough to keep him on the park. He led the All Blacks to a Bledisloe Cup series win a month after the World Cup and then to a drawn series in France at the end of the year. Laurie Mains, having been coach since 1992, stood down and that paved the way for John Hart, in December 1995, to finally be elevated to the job he had coveted.

'My wife and I were building another house and I can still remember I was up a ladder when Harty turned up unannounced,' says Fitzpatrick. 'He came in and said, "Do you still want to be an All Black?" And I thought straight back to Laurie, and I said, "I'm not sure." And he said, "If you play, you will be my captain. I need you to commit." And I did and it was probably the best decision I ever made.'

In theory, test rugby was vastly different in 1996 in comparison with 1995. The big difference was time. The players were paid in 1996 — enough to give up all other work if they wanted to — and therefore they could train more, plan more and analyse more. The old assembly rules were scrapped so preparation for a test match could begin earlier.

Some players quickly adapted to this changed world, largely because they didn't allow the word professionalism to scare them and also because many of them had effectively been professional in every sense prior to actually being paid. 'The money side of it, it didn't really change things much,' says Fitzpatrick. 'We went from earning nothing to earning $300,000 a year. And I can always remember Harty saying to us, "Right, you guys are all earning $45,000 a year. Put the other money away, keep working. So most of us actually kept working and doing what we were doing.'

Fitzpatrick's view that life didn't change much was a reflection of the standards to which he had long held himself and his team accountable. The great Auckland teams of the 1980s and 1990s were professional in every sense other than being paid. The players, many of whom ended up in the All Blacks, brought self-discipline and self-reliance into the environment. And for most of them it was relatively easy to do so because they operated in the real world — they had jobs and responsibilities, and basics such as timekeeping, being well presented, problem-solving and decision-making came naturally. They were good men for Fitzpatrick to have around as they were self-reliant, independent and knew their role in driving a higher standard of performance.

That professional mind-set was critical from Hart's point of view as he came into the job with a clear vision of how an All Blacks team should be set up in the professional era. He could see that the public and media scrutiny would intensify, that the off-field demands made of the players, and in particular the captain, would increase and that the All Blacks would morph, to some degree, into a corporate entity. Standards would be vital on and off the field and Hart knew that Fitzpatrick was the only man in the country who could lead the All Blacks into the professional age.

'I'd done a lot of reading on professionalism and I'd done a lot of research into American football, basketball, trying to get an understanding of what is professionalism,' says Hart. 'The first thing I decided to do was bring together a squad of 45 people who I thought could be All Blacks and gave them what was in fact a one-day conference on professionalism. I brought people from all around the place to speak. People like Paul Holmes to talk about the media and what they would be like; an American footballer — a Kiwi playing over there — because I recognised that there was a huge shift going on. All of a sudden, these guys had to realise that they were in the public eye, they had to respect that they had to work with media and they had to work with sponsors, that they had contractual requirements and relationships with them now which they had never had.

'I was really lucky — I had a great skipper. Sean had grown with me through the Auckland team, and the most professional team I ever coached was the Auckland team in the '80s and we had a tracksuit and a pair of boots and they had to give the tracksuit back at the end of the year. Sean understood the challenge and the change. He understood what professionalism meant. He led by example and he talked by example and he understood sponsors, he understood media and he understood what he had to do.

'He had a hard year in 1995 and for him it was almost a decision of retiring. He was thinking about that and I went to him and said I need you to be part of this rebirth of the game and so we had a really good understanding from the start. He knew what

'I was really lucky — I had a great skipper ... Sean [Fitzpatrick] understood the challenge and the change. He understood what professionalism meant. He led by example and he talked by example and he understood sponsors, he understood media and he understood what he had to do.'

— JOHN HART

I was about and what we needed to do. He was probably the best captain I ever had because he was not only a fantastic player and dominated his position absolutely, but on and off the field, he was beyond reproach.

'He was also a great captain because he had a great lieutenant in Zinzan Brooke. Zinzan was the tactician, the genius, and so Fitzy's role on the field was not so much tactical. His role was leadership, man management, motivational and dealing with the referee. Zinny was a freak in terms of his skill level and that balance became very important. That helped us in 1996 and 1997 to get on a roll on and off the field.'

* * *

The All Blacks were never comfortable, never convincing, but at 14–9 ahead in Sydney with three minutes to go, they were the favourites to win the third Bledisloe Cup clash of 1998. The visitors had taken an 11–0 lead into half-time and had set themselves up to break what was a four-game losing streak. It was a tough, tough time for the All Blacks. After beating a weak and demoralised England twice in June, they had then collapsed, losing to Australia twice and South Africa twice, putting themselves under almost unprecedented pressure to avoid a record fifth consecutive defeat.

They were a team under media siege. They were fielding criticism from all corners and they couldn't catch a break. The All Blacks had been 23–5 ahead in their previous test in Durban and somehow lost 24–23, the final try by Springboks hooker James Dalton one that would never have been given had there been, as there is today, a TMO.

They had to hang on for three more minutes in Sydney and the rot could be stopped. But when No. 8 Xavier Rush spilled a high ball, he handed possession to Australia. The Wallabies, smelling blood, drove through their forwards to reach the All Blacks' 22 and then halfback George Gregan broke left, only to switch the ball to the charging Matt Burke returning on the angle and the Wallabies fullback scored. It was all over. The All Blacks had done the unthinkable and lost five tests in a row and captain Taine Randell was crushed. 'It really came crashing down on me after the last game. Up until then, losing hurt but we always knew we had a game next week and we had a chance to make it up. I don't think at any time did I ever think we weren't going to beat the opposition. Seriously, we'd just lost four in a row, we're definitely going to win this fifth game.

'There was never any lack of confidence, maybe that was the problem. We always had confidence that we were going to win, that we were always better than the opposition. At that point, though, it was shit, we've lost five in a row, we can't make it up.'

The All Blacks had lost just one test in 1996 and none in 1997 and then fell off the cliff in 1998. No one had seen their collapse coming. The squad was inundated with talent. In the back three there was Christian Cullen, Jeff Wilson and Jonah Lomu. The playmaking duo of Justin Marshall and Andrew Mehrtens were in their prime and there were seasoned warhorses up front in Ian Jones, Robin Brooke, Craig Dowd and Olo Brown. Randell himself was a significant talent having featured regularly in the loose trio in 1997. There was no shortage of ability, but there was a shortage of leadership and a lack of maturity and worldliness about the All Blacks in 1998.

Fitzpatrick had been forced to retire due to a chronic knee injury, Zinzan Brooke had joined Harlequins in London and veteran centre Frank Bunce had gone to France. The brilliant Michael Jones was still around, but age and injury had taken their toll and he was no longer in the sort of form to command regular selection.

Losing Fitzpatrick, Brooke, Bunce and Jones robbed the All Blacks of almost 250 test caps. But that wasn't the full extent of what was lost. Fitzpatrick had been a brilliant captain. He instilled calm, drove standards at training, effortlessly managed referees and sponsors, and ensured test preparation flowed without hitch or drama. His partnership with Brooke brought the All Blacks good decision-making on the field. Those two were a step ahead of their opponents, always aware of strengths and weaknesses and constantly communicating about how they could be exploited. It was a powerful combination and that particular axis had been instrumental in the All Blacks' success for the last three years. Those two, Jones and Bunce also brought life experience to the table, a factor that was not fully recognised at the time, but was hugely important in gluing the All Blacks together.

Those men who had served mostly in the amateur period came with ingrained qualities gained through having real-world experience. All Blacks teams of the amateur period had the pioneering spirit within them long after the pioneering spirit was active in daily life. Those teams of yesteryear took pride that they could think their way through a problem.

This wasn't the case with the emerging generation of All Blacks such as Randell, Reuben Thorne, Anton Oliver, Wilson, Cullen, Carlos Spencer, Marshall and Mehrtens. This group hadn't been exposed to the real world. They came through school, and in some cases university, and in others early apprenticeships and then graduated to professional rugby. The rugby system back then did little to develop them as people or demand that they extend themselves intellectually or practically. It was a system that catered for their needs: told them where to be and when. It was a system that protected them from the mundane chores of life that, however tedious, breed self-reliance and appreciation of discipline.

More importantly, the system fostered a lack of accountability and a mild sense of entitlement — perhaps an inevitability in a high-performance environment where the goal is to leave the athlete as free as possible to achieve their best performances. Professional rugby was a bubble, shielding players from responsibilities that shape the wider populace.

Rugby's new entrants were not equipped to be leaders in 1998, but the All Blacks had to have a captain. When it came down to it, Hart felt he had just one option and it was 23-year-old Randell, who had 12 caps and one full season of test football behind him. 'You have to remember that in 1997 I had just graduated at university,' says Randell. 'I was still flatting in 1998 and had a brand-new [All Blacks-sponsored] Ford Fairmont. All my mates were driving around in dunger cars and would be in flat egg fights. No problem for them, they were driving shit wagons, but when it's my turn a few eggs came in destroying the paint.

'Harty had been through the Auckland era where he had a core group of experienced players, all the way through. I think it would have been the first time for him that all of a sudden you've got to play young kids. So, I mean, for example, the front-row guys, your gnarliest guys, were Anton Oliver, who I was older than. Kees Meeuws, I was older than. Carl Hoeft, I was way older than. Norm Maxwell was the youngest, so the tight five, where you want your most experience, they were 23 and younger and they were the best in the country. Reuben Thorne … I was older than him. Dylan Mika was the same age, so where we wanted the most experience, we didn't have it. We didn't know what we didn't know, though.

'And that was just circumstances — Fitzy and those guys had gone. I don't think Harty had been through such a cleanout of experience, and what I think New Zealand Rugby learned from that is that it's not about one person or one coach. Yes, you have these iconic Richie McCaws, but in successful teams there are a whole lot below them.'

It was a tough time for the All Blacks. The game was growing in popularity. Media coverage was accelerating as the internet took a fledgling hold and sponsors were digging their hooks deeper into the team. Sports science was infiltrating and the ability to analyse opponents was improving, and the days of gathering up on a Wednesday night for a test were long gone as were the days of the long tour. So while the All Blacks were together as much as they were in the amateur era, it didn't come with the same opportunities to get to know one another. Everything was hurried, done under pressure, and it would be prepare for one game and then immediately reset to prepare for the next. Many of the players of that period were swept along by the frantic nature of it all, unsure how to make a leadership contribution, and worse, unaware that they were even expected to. It took 12 years for the All Blacks to reconfigure their rugby development system to generate well-equipped leaders who arrived in the national team with the necessary skills and understanding to effectively support the captain.

Randell was the first captain to be exposed to this imbalanced world where the demands of his role far outweighed his ability to fulfil them and that of his senior players to support him. Oliver and Thorne, who succeeded him, would suffer the same fate of not necessarily being well enough equipped individually to captain the All Blacks and certainly not well enough supported by their senior players. It's easy enough to see, given that things didn't really get better until late 2010, that they were the lost generation.

* * *

There was no way All Blacks coach Steve Hansen was going to allow history to repeat in 2016. He'd seen how a lack of leadership had derailed the All Blacks in 1998 and didn't want a repeat 18 years later when the situation was remarkably similar. After the 2015 World Cup, captain Richie McCaw retired. He had been the skipper since 2006, captained the team more than 100 times and was widely recognised as the greatest player and leader in rugby history.

Dan Carter — the man many would see as the best No. 10 to have ever played and the man who kicked and directed the All Blacks to victory in the 2015 World Cup — also retired. Keven Mealamu, Tony Woodcock, Conrad Smith and Ma'a Nonu retired, too, and the All Blacks lost more than 800 test caps and six men who had been enormous personalities and leaders for more than a decade. It was a giant hole — considerably bigger than the one created when Fitzpatrick, Brooke and Bunce left in 1998.

Hansen, though, had a number of distinct advantages. Unlike Hart, who didn't have much, if any, notice that his three veterans would be leaving, Hansen had known for the better part of three years that there would be a post-2015 cleanout. McCaw didn't confirm 2015 would be his last season until after the World Cup, but everyone knew it was. Hansen had time to prepare in a way Hart never did. Also, Hansen had the benefit of a system that was cognisant of the weaknesses exposed in 1998. By 2016, rugby was doing what (or maybe all) it could to plug real-life experience into young men who didn't have any real-life experience.

Provincial academy programmes insisted that members had to be studying or working towards some other qualification. Super Rugby clubs had personal development managers who were there to ensure that players were creating opportunities for themselves away from rugby. And the All Blacks spent inordinate amounts of their preparation focused on leadership. They saw it as a skill that could be developed, much like their passing and catching.

The leadership group concept which was working so well by 2010 continued to evolve. The group became bigger and contained not just those who were there on account of their seniority. In 2013 Sam Cane was elevated to the group. He was 21 and had only played a few tests because he was the understudy to McCaw. But he was seen as a potential future captain and with McCaw certain to hang up his boots in 2015 it made sense to try to fast-track Cane's leadership skills. That was the same reason Beauden Barrett, 22, was elevated to the leadership group. He, like Cane, was going to be a key player in 2016 and most likely at first-five, so it seemed logical to be growing his understanding of test football.

And, naturally, as part of this grooming mentality, the All Blacks had a succession plan with the captaincy. Hansen didn't like the idea of being forced, as Hart was, to thrust responsibility on a young pair of shoulders that were not ready to support the weight of captaincy. So, on a beautiful winter's day in Rome, 2012, Kieran Read was named as All Blacks captain for the test against Italy at Stadio Olimpico.

The then 27-year-old No. 8, who had been an All Black since 2008, was the obvious choice to groom as McCaw's successor. He was a world-class player. He was assured of his position in the team, had been an age-grade captain, and also had led Canterbury to the provincial title when he was just 22. He had a maturity and authority that stood out among his peers. During the next three years, Read was given ample exposure to the captaincy. He led the team in June 2013 when McCaw was on sabbatical and then five more times when the regular skipper was either injured or deliberately stood down to give Read the experience. It meant that when McCaw retired, Read had captained the All Blacks in nine tests and therefore had reasonable knowledge and experience of the role when he was awarded it permanently in February 2016.

The All Blacks lost close to 1000 caps after the 2015 World Cup and yet managed to begin the 2016 season with a captain and leadership group who were, in comparison with their equivalents of 1998, miles ahead in terms of their readiness to handle the responsibility of test football. Not only had the leaders been groomed to be ready, Hansen afforded them time off during the 2016 Super Rugby season to help build specific game understanding and get a handle on what their new roles would entail. The leadership group would meet several times before the first test series against Wales in June, while a wider squad of players would also be given time off Super Rugby to attend All Blacks training camps to advance their knowledge of what the national team was trying to achieve.

'We've spent a month working with the leadership because that's the area where we really want to up the ante in,' Hansen said when he unveiled his first squad of the year. 'We have known for quite some time that six of the guys were going to be leaving, with 1000 test matches between them. We've planned for that. They had that sense of belief, and that's the thing that Reado when he comes in as skipper will have to exude — that self-confidence under pressure.'

The difference between 1998 and 2016 can best be seen in the respective results. In 1998 the All Blacks won two and lost five. In 2016 the All Blacks won 13 of 14 tests, which saw them average 45 points per test and produce some of the best attacking rugby of the professional age. And the results were indicative of how the role of the captain had changed since those early professional years.

Read came into the job having been preparing to do so for almost four years. Unlike the old amateur or early professional period, nothing was assumed. The captain wasn't expected to work things out on his own, use his Kiwi intuition to fix things. This latter era has seen nothing left to chance. Leaders are identified and built. At both Super Rugby and international level there are mental skills coaches working with players, driving them into thinking more deeply about their preparation, communication and motivation. Leadership is recognised as a skill that has to be worked on rather than something that simply develops organically over time.

The test preparation period has fallen into a deeply ingrained routine for the All Blacks. They assemble on a Sunday and are addressed as a whole by the coach. They have a light session on Monday and a video review of their previous test. There is a full-on training on Tuesday when the team is named internally. They have a day off on Wednesday, skills or conditioning on Thursday morning followed by a collective session later in the afternoon, and a captain's run on Friday. In between those sessions there are endless meetings. There are leadership group meetings; units such as the midfield and loose trio will get together once or twice a week and map out the specifics of their roles. There are team meetings. Backs meetings, forwards meetings and one-on-one meetings with the coaches. There will be opposition analysis sessions and personal performance reviews and there are daily media requirements where at least two players will be required. And typically on a Friday morning there will be some kind of commercial obligation to fulfil on behalf of the sponsors.

It can be overwhelming. The complexity of the game plan is incredible in comparison with where it was in 1998 and the volume of people involved has almost doubled given the number of specialist coaches attached to the team and the fact the All Blacks pick between 30 and 32 players for most tests.

For the captain, specifically, in many respects the job remains the same — he is still the chief orchestrator and co-ordinator. The external demands of the team have grown but that burden is shared collectively now. The captain does his share of media and commercial work, but it's not extensive or obviously more than anyone else's.

What has had the greatest impact on determining the captain's role is the relative strength of his wider leadership team. A captain with experience and genuine leaders around him can focus more on his own role as a player and trust the information he's receiving on the field from his lieutenants. A captain who doesn't have that strength and experience around him will be stretched too thinly during the build-up helping others and inevitably his performance will be compromised. Without trust and confidence in his leaders, he'll no doubt make too many decisions on the field without appropriate guidance or good intelligence and compromise the performance of the team. The biggest change in the captain's role in the late professional era is the amount of time they spend managing the leadership group. That's almost the captain's key responsibility — to ensure that the advisory council is doing what it should.

'The big shift in the game that I have seen from amateur to professional, is that leadership is no longer the domain of an individual,' says Hart. 'And it did used to be. It was perceived like that and now shared leadership is the key to success of winning teams. Leadership goes right across the board. They don't have to be captains but they lead in their own way and I think that is something Steve Hansen has done fantastically well. He built that leadership team so they had that capability of thinking on and off the field and that wasn't as evident in the amateur game. The amateur game you didn't really have that. You relied on the captain a lot, maybe too much. It was something I saw that we had to change and I started to try to bring a leadership group together.

'The big shift in the game that I have seen from amateur to professional, is that leadership is no longer the domain of an individual. And it did used to be. It was perceived like that and now shared leadership is the key to success of winning teams. Leadership goes right across the board. They don't have to be captains but they lead in their own way ... The amateur game you didn't really have that. You relied on the captain a lot, maybe too much.'

— JOHN HART

'But it took time because a lot of them weren't tuned to it. It's not what they wanted to do. Look at Jeff Wilson. Jeff was one of the greatest players I ever coached, but in a leadership role, then, no, he was an individual. Josh Kronfeld, individual. Don't want to be leaders, don't want that responsibility. I look at Jeff now and I am in admiration of how he has grown as an individual and what he is doing with his life and the way he presents. But that's maturity.

'The whole leadership thing has grown and the requirements of it have grown and I think there is now a real understanding that the demands on the players and the management are so great that it's got to be shared. You've got to have a lot of people involved and not just one or two. And that I think is the key to success.'

CHAPTER FOUR

TOUGH LOVE

THE LOBBY OF the Royal Garden Hotel is bustling as always. There are minor celebrities hoping to be recognised as they wait to check in. There are the usual demanding non-celebrity guests who have the sort of income that makes them think they can bark at staff, and there is also, pacing around and looking a little lost and out of place, Hika Elliot. The latter has been called to London for the All Blacks' last test of 2012. He was in England with the New Zealand Maori team and on his way home when he was asked to change his plans and meet up with the All Blacks who needed him as a replacement for Andrew Hore.

Elliot is all nervous energy when he sees the All Blacks' bus pull up outside the hotel, but as the players file through the lobby, they greet him with hugs, high-fives and the sort of bonhomie that takes the edge off his nervousness. Until captain Richie McCaw enters the hotel. He sees Elliot and barely registers he's there. The skipper thrusts a hand out, has it shaken, but doesn't make eye contact, doesn't break stride and those watching couldn't be sure he even acknowledged his new team-mate.

What they can be sure about is that McCaw obviously doesn't want Elliot there. He's not a fan, doesn't much like him or rate him, but the team needs a specialist hooker at short notice and so Elliot will have to do. He's been with the All Blacks before, winning a few caps in 2010, but failed to convince on the field and certainly failed off it where his behaviour at times was unacceptably bad. A few days later when McCaw is asked how the new boy is settling in, he shrugs, puffs his cheeks and after a bit of non-committal rambling says that the system usually weeds out those who aren't up to it and they don't last in the All Blacks.

It's an illuminating exchange without the skipper meaning it to be. It illustrates that the All Blacks, deep into the professional age, still believe in a tough-love mentality. There's a hierarchy within the team and those at the bottom have to earn the right to be respected. They have to fend for themselves, and only once they have paid their dues, played a handful of tests, are they actually embraced by those long-serving players.

This is how things had been in the All Blacks since year dot. Richard Loe can remember his first experience as an All Black. He was called up to join the squad on a tour of France in 1986 and picked to play against the French Barbarians. Loe was 26 and carving out a reputation as a hard man in the provincial game, a tough operator in the front row who'd happily stick his fingers in someone's eye. None of that carried any weight once he joined the All Blacks. 'We got to the hotel,' says Loe, 'and Cowboy [senior player Mark Shaw] says, "You're with me." We went up to the room and I put my bags down and he said, "Milk, no sugar" and then lay on his bed. He said bugger all to me after that until we were on our way to the game and he said, "Hey pal, don't be a oncer."'

This was the life of a new All Black — to be either ignored by the established players or treated like the hired help. The culture was not naturally inclusive. It was a tough place for new arrivals regardless of their age, experience or standing in the game. New All Blacks had everything to prove and no one was going to help them do that. And this was as true of the All Blacks in 2012 as it was in 1992 and 1972 and all points in between.

In 2003 when Mils Muliaina was first picked in the All Blacks he was stunned to find that the environment was not supportive or embracing of new arrivals. He was selected after a brilliant campaign with the champion Blues where his work at fullback and centre alluded to his potential to be a long-term, great All Black. He was brought into the squad with other new and exciting talent such as Dan Carter, Joe Rokocoko and Ma'a Nonu, but rather than have someone greet him at the door sort of thing, with a welcoming smile and cup of tea, he found he was mostly ignored and got the distinct vibe he should keep his head down and keep quiet.

'There were cliques everywhere,' he says. 'If you weren't a Canterbury man you just kept your head down. It was massively like that. It had that element of yesteryear when you think about it. You look after yourself, think about number one and do your own job. It wasn't about being accountable to your mates. It was about you doing your thing and making sure you were on the field and starting. They talk about it now, guys coming in and embracing their differences. But we couldn't do it back then. It was you go over there with your mates and we'll go over there with our mates.'

The world's greatest rugby team operated much like a boarding school riddled with institutional bullying. Throughout history, there have been different reactions to the system. Some have loved it, found that the fear factor has brought the best out of them. Some players have embraced the struggle and found rejection and isolation a powerful motivator. Plenty of good people, though, have not enjoyed the environment. They weren't motivated by the sense of not being wanted, of having players whom they admired and respected treat them with disdain and indifference.

It could be lonely and intimidating, and over the years some All Blacks have been genuinely fearful of their team-mates. It was an exercise in survival for new entrants until they could find a way to gain respect. There were cliques, usually along provincial lines. There were tensions due to competitive pressure for places in the team and an overriding sense that it was best to look after number one at all times.

And there was a back seat on the bus which strangely for grown men was a real thing. The team bus has long been an essential part of the All Blacks' psychology. It is arguably where All Blacks of all eras have spent the bulk of their time. No matter how the build-up to a test week has changed, it has still required the All Blacks to travel to and from training, to and from games, and to and from almost anywhere. The bus has, therefore, developed symbolism and much of the All Blacks' folklore is built around the fabled back seat.

The symbolism is easy enough to follow: the longer someone was an All Black, the further down the bus they would sit. The ultimate goal was to reach the back seat, because those who sat there became the guardians and enforcers of various aspects of the team's off-field traditions and expectations. The back seat was the unofficial wider leadership group, left to run matters off the field as they saw fit with the captain almost entirely detached from the process. He would be at the front with the coach, mostly oblivious to whatever was going on, rarely feeling he needed to be made aware of the particulars.

It was a system that distanced the captain from the team, which had both negative and positive connotations. The upside was that the captain was exonerated from having to manage and monitor off-field behaviour and didn't have to be a social handbrake, trying to determine when things had crossed from having fun to getting out of hand. He had what presidents like to call plausible deniability — the luxury of saying, if things really had become unacceptable, that it had nothing to do with him. That space was important as it let the players organically find their hierarchy and natural order, and if the back seat was doing its job, operating sensibly and relatively sensitively, then it could iron out plenty of creases.

Andy Dalton, who would captain the All Blacks in 17 tests, insists that when he first toured with the side in 1978, he was summoned from his seat somewhere near the front of the bus. 'I was made to stand in front of the back seat of the bus and Bryan Williams said, "What are you going to do on this tour to help us?" So I explained and then he asked, "What does it mean to you to be an All Black?" I told them I wanted to be in the team that won the series and if I could be part of the team then great and if I wasn't then I would do everything I could to help the team be successful. That had a huge impact on me. It showed me just how big my responsibility was.'

The downside, though, was that the captain was never aware of which individuals may have been struggling in the environment and, a little like *Lord of the Flies*, there were periods when the back seat became a little too powerful. It also became a separate and significant aspiration for some players: they coveted a place on that back seat more than they should, and throughout the 1980s and 1990s it wasn't uncommon for fist fights to break out as some players literally tried to storm the back of the bus and stage a coup d'état.

When Sean Fitzpatrick became captain in 1992, the back seat was arguably at the peak of its powers and had become a destructive rather than regulatory force. 'I wanted to change it because I didn't like it,' he says. 'During my time [pre-captaincy] I was always scared: scared of talking, afraid of the back seat almost, which I felt had got worse. And, for a while, even though I wasn't in the back seat, I became one of those, in that clique. Andrew Mehrtens came into the team and he was a breath of fresh air. You know that was 1995 that he became an All Black and he really changed my attitude towards that and [helped me] realise that the young kids needed to have a say. We became very open and everyone was allowed to contribute. Whereas if you have a dominant back seat, that doesn't happen, and sometimes you have the wrong type of people on the back seat, if they've got different agendas. I think that really helped me because it meant I was across everything and I was delegating. Richard Loe was always a big figure in the team so I'd make sure, because you know he could be a bit heavy-handed at times, that that wasn't happening.'

* * *

Every captain of the last 50 years would like to think that they ran an inclusive environment that empowered everyone to contribute and be at their best. And to some degree, there would be truth in that. But only to some degree, as the prevailing culture of the All Blacks — from the earliest teams through to 2015 — has carried an element of tough love. Regardless of who has been captain, it has never been easy for new or young players to come into the team and feel that they have the right to speak. The right to be airing their views or saying what they think will and won't work.

Even Sonny Bill Williams, who was picked by the All Blacks in 2010 after a relatively short but highly successful and high-profile career with the NRL, found out the hard way that reputations earned elsewhere didn't translate to respect within the All Blacks. Williams was fast-tracked into the team after half a season with Canterbury and many established All Blacks leaders didn't like that he arrived with a heavy media following. He cut a lonely and isolated figure in those early years — a man who had everything except the thing he desperately wanted — which was acceptance and belonging. 'When you come with a big profile, it was really tough,' Williams would say in 2019 of that period. 'At times I probably didn't help myself because I was shy and quiet instead of making myself a bit more vulnerable. But that was the era of the old-school guy — to shut up and get on with it.'

For most of the All Blacks' history the captain has been removed from the internal off-field mechanisms of the team. He's been up the front of the bus, his back literally turned on the shenanigans that may be happening behind him. In the early professional years, the culture of paying dues and having to earn respect was softened but not eradicated. Fitzpatrick's last two years in charge saw the process of change begin: saw barriers start to come down and a greater awareness spread across the team about inclusivity and acceptance, but it was a slow process.

Clearly Mils Muliaina didn't feel that the side captained by Reuben Thorne in 2002 and 2003 had evolved greatly in regard to inclusivity, and even throughout Richie McCaw's long period of captaincy between 2006 and 2015, there was still a lingering sense that the new men were best to keep their heads down and stay quiet.

McCaw emerged through a school of hard knocks. When he came into the great Canterbury team of the early 2000s, he was competing for a place against a handful of established All Blacks such as Todd Blackadder, Thorne and Scott Robertson. McCaw was 19 and desperate to prove himself and win acceptance from the senior players. His coach at that time was Steve Hansen, who can recall that McCaw was so eager at training, stealing so much possession from the established players, that it reached the stage where the youngster's well-being was endangered. 'Toddy, Reuben and Razor came to me at one point and said, "Look, if he comes into another ruck and pinches another ball we are going to snot him,"' recalled Hansen on the eve of McCaw captaining the All Blacks for the 100th time. 'I said, "If you snot him, I will be snotting the lot of you, so leave him alone. He's only a baby, just look after him and get there quicker than he is." I had to go to him [McCaw] quietly and say, "Let them win a couple, you are starting to piss them off."'

It was a story illustrative of the age and explains partly why McCaw, having had to earn respect the hard way, retained an element of that thinking within his own captaincy. He was, largely, a product of his environment, and as someone who had responded well to a culture of having to prove himself, didn't see any danger in maintaining it, albeit in a less pronounced way.

By 2008, two years into McCaw's tenure, the experience for new All Blacks was vastly different. The new men were presented with a manual when they arrived — a sort of quick guide to the All Blacks. It told them everything they needed to know and senior players were encouraged to reach out to new boys and welcome them. Aaron Smith, who came into the team in 2012, says that an encounter with veteran hooker Keven Mealamu had a massively positive impact. 'I can remember my first day as an All Black. He came in and sat next to me at lunch and said, "I don't want you to feel like this team is a burden, I just want you to express yourself and be yourself." I still remember that.'

As much as life changed and eased for new players, McCaw himself remained a little aloof and distanced. It wasn't so much deliberate or calculated, more a consequence of his natural shyness and phenomenal drive to win. It was also amplified by his standing in the game, and his reputation created a barrier. Julian Savea, who was considered by Hansen to be a better player than the great Jonah Lomu, was so in awe of his captain when he first became an All Black that he once hid when he saw McCaw coming his way. Other players, too, say they were nervous around McCaw for no other reason than that his greatness as a player humbled them. 'He was a little bit removed,' says Ali Williams, the former lock forward who won 78 caps between 2002 and 2012 and remains a close personal friend of McCaw. 'I think that was one of my biggest roles within the team — to create the connection between the leadership and Richie mainly, the coaches and the players. I was great friends with the newest guy, I was best friends with the captain, and so I was the guy that was put in that position.

'I think the scary thing with him was he wasn't there to make friends. He was there to fucking win. He was that narrow. He was so driven. At the World Cup in 2011 he sits behind me on the bus. I turned around and I said, "Look, talk to me when you want to talk to me", because I could see, we all knew he was so focused. He spoke to me six weeks later, roughly before the semi-final. He was that focused. Fucking driven and I respected that and he respected that but he also needed balance.'

* * *

The Wallabies, having posted a record victory the week before in Perth, are confident, more so than usual, that they are going to finally break their Eden Park hoodoo. They haven't won in Auckland since 1986, but 17 August 2019 has a ring to it. Many in Australia feel it will be the date the Wallabies make history and regain the Bledisloe Cup for the first time since 2002 and bring the All Blacks' 25-year unbeaten stretch at Eden Park to an end.

Almost half an hour of the game has gone and the Wallabies, 3–0 down, are moving the ball right in what is their sixth phase of attack. There's space to run, or at least it looks like there is, when veteran fullback Kurtley Beale comes into the line. But it was a well-laid trap as he's tackled, almost exactly as the ball arrives, by All Blacks wing George Bridge. The ball spills loose and is picked up by All Blacks first-five Richie Mo'unga, who speeds away to score under the posts. Barely a minute later, an aimless hoof by the Wallabies is picked up by Beauden Barrett, who runs left, passing to Bridge, who runs a stunning angle that sees him ease past the flailing Wallabies' defence and then feed the ball to the supporting Aaron Smith, who scores. It's a three-minute blast in which the game turns the way of the All Blacks and it's all down to the 24-year-old Bridge, who is playing just his fourth test.

The killer blow is struck with 15 minutes to go when the 22-year-old Jordie Barrett threads a grubber kick through the defence. Sevu Reece, who is also 22 and playing his second test, somehow manages to fly-hack it at full speed over the head of the onrushing Wallabies fullback Reece Hodge and then sprint after it and touch down for an astonishing individual try. The All Blacks, under all sorts of pressure to bounce back from their catastrophe in Perth, win 36–0, and as much as the victory is a triumph for the character of the players, it's a triumph of selection, too.

The selectors played what many considered a high-risk hand by dropping the experienced and established Owen Franks, Ben Smith and Rieko Ioane from the starting line-up. The All Blacks were desperate to win and they left 250 test caps out of their starting team and the decision to include Bridge and Reece drew particular attention. Bridge had won his first cap in November 2018 when he was part of an extended squad that travelled to Japan, while Reece had only come into the All Blacks frame in July after a stunning Super Rugby campaign. What made his inclusion more dramatic was that he didn't have a contract when the season kicked off and was only involved after the Crusaders needed a late medical replacement for Israel Dagg.

Bridge and Reece were part of a backline that included the 24-year-old Mo'unga at first-five, who had only been in the team since 2018. At centre was the 24-year-old centre Jack Goodhue, who'd made his test debut in the same game as Mo'unga, and it became apparent at the World Cup that the profile of the 2019 team differed greatly to that of the 2015 side. The team that had won in England had 1200-plus test caps between them. There were five players who each had played more than 100 tests and it included 13 previous World Cup winners, two men who were playing their fourth tournament and two who were at their third.

In 2019 there were 13 players who were playing at their first World Cup, five of whom had only become All Blacks in 2018 and another, Reece, who had joined the team just a few months earlier. The average age of the backline was 25 compared with 29 in 2015. There had been a significant departure from previous years where the older and more experienced athletes were seen as the men to throw into tight situations and big tournaments. The All Blacks had opted to pick young, inexperienced players for the simple reason they felt they were best equipped to deliver the right result — and that signified the dramatic change in culture that had been driven by Kieran Read since he arrived as captain in 2016.

'I guess I came in at the end of that era where as a young player you didn't talk, sat quietly and earned your respect on the field which I don't think is a bad thing,' Read said when the All Blacks were in the Japanese spa town of Beppu, preparing to play Canada in their second World Cup pool game. 'And certainly that was the way — until you did what you needed to do on the field, then you got the respect of the senior guys and perhaps got a wee conversation with them.

'For some guys it works. I was capable of doing it. I was a quiet guy back then so I wouldn't have said anything anyway. I know exactly what they [new players] are feeling because I had all the same feelings when I came into a side with Dan Carter, Reuben Thorne and Richie McCaw. Having the confidence to go out there and play comes from having trust in these young guys and talking to them. It is about having a conversation with them to find out about them. I can't expect them to initiate that. Any chance you get, be it over lunch or dinner, to sit next to them and maybe find out one thing about them, you take it.

'And then you can tell them to back themselves, "You are here for a reason, go play", and then they truly believe it. That for me has become crucial. When new guys come in, if you can have a conversation with them, then on the field where they may need to say something to you, they will be more inclined to tell you something you need to know rather than not.'

Read came into the job having already made the decision to not soften the tough-love culture but to eradicate it. He knew that, like him, others had found the need to prove themselves under an element of duress motivating. He suspected, however, that others had found the environment intimidating to the point of crushing and he felt it was counter-productive to pick talented youngsters and then not support them to deliver what they had been put in the team to do.

He couldn't see the logic or value of starving new recruits of confidence and making them struggle to fit in. He wasn't convinced that was best for the team and he liked the idea of young players being secure enough to speak their minds the moment they arrived. The old ways had worked — he wasn't dismissive of the concept of paying dues, but he didn't feel that the concept would get the best out of Generation Y and Millennials. He had this vision of creating an egalitarian team where those with one cap were treated just the same as those with 100.

Read recognised that Generation Y operate on a different emotional plane with different expectations, and hence he asked his senior players to bend the culture of the team to include and empower everyone regardless of time served in the jersey. He wanted a genuinely inclusive team and his captaincy defined by his ability to bring down the barriers that were preventing the All Blacks from harnessing the true power of their diversity.

'The guys coming through now have grown up with iPads and iPhones and all that, social media, which is different to when I grew up,' said Read. 'Consciously, in recent times I have come to realise this generation are potentially more emotionally charged and fluctuate more than perhaps me and guys older than me because we never really had those opportunities to be that way when we were growing up. But the key thing for me is that because of my upbringing it didn't matter where you were from or what your background was. I played with lots of different guys and it was just team-mates. So you adjusted to that and I could hang with whomever in the team.'

Throughout Read's captaincy there was a media desire to paint him as a McCaw disciple — as a similar character and captain. But it was never like that. Read served his leadership apprenticeship under McCaw, and while he adopted some of his mentor's attributes such as the will to win, he was a totally different person and captained the team with an inclusivity that never interested his predecessor. Where McCaw was slightly aloof and removed, Read was gregarious and connected. McCaw, for all his brilliance as a player and on-field leadership, never had the common touch. Read was much more of a social chameleon — as capable of busting dance moves with Ardie Savea as he was of talking dairy farming with Sam Whitelock, and he constantly impressed upon his leadership group the need to embrace the next generation.

It was a continuous process changing the minds and attitudes of those longer-serving players who had graduated from the school of hard knocks, but it was obvious that by the time the World Cup came around, there was universal buy-in to Read's egalitarian vision. 'Most of the kids are pretty good but you get some who have come out of First XV which is televised and they are big rock stars,' said long-serving hooker Dane Coles in Perth before the first Bledisloe Cup test of 2019. 'When they come into the professional environment they want it straight away. I had to wait three years playing off the bench behind [Andrew] Hore. Some of these young guys are impatient and have to understand their time will come. Just put the work in and your time will come but it is a generational thing.

'The hard conversations are sometimes what they need. A few words from an older player can help them see what is going on. But you have to encourage them too and tell them when they are playing well because things have changed and there is a lot more getting around the young fellas, having a yarn with them when they arrive. We are more inclusive now and it doesn't matter if you have played one test or 100, we are treated all the same. But I still think there is a little bit of room for the old-school mentality.'

Sam Cane, who, like Coles, had first been picked in 2012, was another who had come to see the value and importance of Read's plan. If he was unsure at first, he lost his reticence and by August 2019 he was welcoming the next generation. 'It is the evolution of high-performance environments,' he says. 'Eight years ago when I came in you wouldn't speak much for the first couple of years, but if you went back 10 years again it would be worse. I think the leaders set the tone and the leaders of that time had transitioned through that era so they had that little bit of old-school mentality about them of having to earn your stripes which I still think there is a little bit of a place for.

'The hard conversations are sometimes what they need. A few words from an older player can help them see what is going on. But you have to encourage them too and tell them when they are playing well because things have changed. ... We are more inclusive now and it doesn't matter if you have played one test or 100, we are treated all the same. But I still think there is a little bit of room for the old-school mentality.'

— DANE COLES

'It [the All Blacks] is an environment now where you are encouraged to come in and be yourself and if you have something to say then it is valued straight off the bat. I remember my first training and I was terrified about dropping the ball because I was unknown and unproven and I was probably doubting myself because I didn't have the self-confidence to know whether I should be there. So, now, I definitely make a conscious effort to not take things too seriously. Away from the rugby I try to be myself and in my down time let my guard down to let them [younger players] know they can take the piss out of me and I can do the same.'

Read didn't win a World Cup as captain but he did succeed in bringing down the last barriers to ensure that All Blacks never again had to fear their team-mates more than they did their opposition.

CHAPTER FIVE

HAPPY HOUR

TIME WAS RUNNING out for the All Blacks in the first test of their Grand Slam quest in 1978. They were desperate to become the first New Zealand side to beat all four Home Unions and yet here they were in Dublin, in the first of the four tests, locked at 6-all against the Irish. Four days earlier, they had famously lost 12–0 to Munster and so not only was it looking like the All Blacks' Grand Slam quest would fail at the first hurdle, they were also in danger of seeing the whole tour hit a major obstacle.

But if there was rising panic in the ranks, it didn't show. If captain Graham Mourie was feeling the pressure, he hid it well. Mourie stayed calm and controlled. He stayed focused and alert and he exuded a conviction that eased the nerves of those around him. And with clear heads and belief, the All Blacks manufactured a winning try from a lineout close to the Irish line. The ball was tapped to halfback Dave Loveridge, who came back towards the touchline and fed to hooker Andy Dalton, who crashed over to win the game 10–6.

There has been conjecture over the years as to whether it was a planned move, but that essentially fails to see the bigger picture. Planned move or not, the winning try was testament to the cohesion, resilience and confidence within the squad. The All Blacks won that game not because of what they had perfected on the training field, but because of how they were conducting themselves off it. They were a team comfortable in each other's company because Mourie had arrived in the UK determined to ensure that everyone had a good time. The senior players — the back seat of the bus — were connected with each other and with Mourie and they instilled a culture that allowed players to enjoy their rugby, but to also enjoy the times when they weren't playing rugby.

This was an age when alcohol was a huge part of the wider game and indeed the All Blacks. The booze flowed in most rugby environments and the All Blacks were no exception. They, like most other teams, had drinking rituals. They had institutionalised traditions such as so-called kangaroo court sessions where players were accused and found guilty of all sorts of good-humoured misdemeanours and asked to drink as punishment. It was always intended to be good-natured and ice-breaking: alcohol was a lubricant in the All Blacks' working parts, often the preferred means to bring players closer together and facilitate friendships.

On a long tour when the All Blacks would play midweek games and then tests a few days later, the drinking sessions could pile up and progressively become more outrageous. Worse still, was that the alcohol was often used as a weapon or a tool by which senior players could exert their control. It was a means to victimise some players, force them to drink themselves into an advanced state of inebriation and then humiliate them. It was a means by which senior players could stigmatise others — equate someone's inability to handle their alcohol with some kind of failing in masculinity. Strangely, this excessive alcohol use and enforced culture of bullying others to drink too much was condoned by All Blacks management as it was deemed to be a legitimate means of preserving and maintaining tradition. Mourie, though, wasn't prepared to let the side's ambition be sacrificed on the altar of excess, and while he was happy to let players enjoy themselves on the 1978 tour and allow traditions and rituals to be observed, he was also conscious that enforced booze sessions could be divisive and potentially fraught for some players.

The winning try in Dublin, then, was possible because the squad was united without players harbouring discontent about being forced to drink if they didn't want to. There was respect for the individual which made the All Blacks stronger and more cohesive, and so often in test football, it is these hidden, hard-to-detect differences that are the separation points between two teams. The All Blacks needed something miraculous late in the game and they could conjure it because they believed in each other and they believed in their captain.

'The aim was that everybody had a good time,' says Mourie of that 1978 tour. 'You weren't there to stop people enjoying themselves but just to provide an environment where everybody could enjoy themselves. It wasn't that you banned drinking, but you'd make sure there was milk and soft drink available at team sessions and nobody had to carry Grizz Wyllie's whisky bottle around and drink every time he drank. I guess my role was to make sure everybody enjoyed their time and Beegee [Bryan Williams] was a very good influence in that regard. I guess what

I would say about that try in Ireland was the attitude of that team was if you've got confidence and keep playing until the last minutes ... things can happen. There was no panic. If you're confident that what you're doing is the right thing, keep playing and keep applying as much pressure on yourself to be as good as you can until the end of the game and not doubt yourselves. That was really what that Irish try was about, I guess.'

The Grand Slam quest of 1978 did not end at Lansdowne Road the way it did in 1973 and perhaps it is by comparing these two respective tests that the impact of alcohol and strong leadership around it can be best understood. Mourie had a strong and supportive leadership group in 1978 that helped him enforce a more inclusive and less divisive culture around alcohol.

On the 1972–73 tour the All Blacks led 10–3 in Dublin only to concede seven points in the final quarter and blow the Grand Slam. It was a game they should have won, but they lost concentration and didn't have the clinical edge they needed. In 1978 the All Blacks had the composure and awareness to win; in 1973 they didn't, and Bryan Williams, who was an integral member of both teams, is certain that the heavy drinking and general lack of support for captain Ian Kirkpatrick on the earlier tour was a significant influence on the respective results.

'In those days there was a bit of a drinking and partying culture,' says Williams. 'The captain obviously wasn't in the back seat and so this group was meant to set protocols unofficially. I found myself in the back seat in 1972 two years after I made my debut and on that tour to the UK we became known as the black hat brigade. Tane Norton, Grizz and Alan Sutherland had these Stetsons and Sid Going and I had these black berets. Unfortunately, the British media decided it had a sinister undertone to it. It was just a bit of fun initially, but once the media started getting into us, we thought we would carry on with it. We were getting under their skin a bit.

'With that sort of culture you are always going to get a bit of indiscipline with guys who don't know when to call it quits. Back in those days we had one coach, one captain and one manager so a lot fell back on the captain's shoulders, so I did for feel for him. I don't think we were well managed as a team and some of the senior guys on that tour went overboard. There is no doubt about it. There was some silly things happening on and off the field. There were some senior guys who should have been getting alongside Kirky and helping him out. But they didn't. They were the ringleaders and troublemakers.

'I must say as one who had been part of Kirky's era I really felt for him. In retrospect I'm glad we didn't achieve a Grand Slam as it would have been an injustice to the teams that had gone before. I was away for four and a half months and I came home and said to myself I am never going to be part of a team that behaves like that again. That was a real conscious awakening for me that I was going to try to set the tone alongside others in regard to behaviour and what is expected of an All Black.

'From then the All Blacks culture improved a great deal. J.J. Stewart arrived as coach and the new broom had swept things clear. People like Grizz, Sid Going and Alan Sutherland were gone. The new coach decided they were potentially trouble and decided to start afresh to the extent that when we had our Grand Slam in 1978 our behaviour was impeccable and we were well led by Graham Mourie.'

* * *

When Springboks centre Marius Joubert coasted in for his third try at Ellis Park in 2004, he turned a bad test for the All Blacks into a particularly bad test. His hat-trick meant the Boks had won 40–26 and had totally outclassed an All Blacks side that was fractured, sluggish and individualistic. They were weak at set piece, ineffective at the breakdown, and their defence was erratic and reactive. The story in Johannesburg was largely similar to how it had been the week before in Sydney where the All Blacks had lost 23–18, failing to score a try or look threatening on attack.

It had been a disappointing but illuminating two weeks for the All Blacks coaching team which had taken over earlier that year. Prior to the test in Sydney, the All Blacks were undefeated in 2004. The team, captained by Tana Umaga, had appeared mostly united and self-reliant when they had played in New Zealand. Umaga, who had taken over from Reuben Thorne, was naturally quiet but enormously respected. He was a world-class midfielder with more than 50 test caps and had a natural empathy and compassion that made him a popular figure with his peers.

But he didn't have a great deal of support in leading the team. That particular squad lacked strong, experienced, mature figures who were capable of getting alongside the skipper and helping out. That became clearer to the coaches once they had hit the road and saw how many players in the squad were insular and unworldly. It was perhaps a cruel generalisation to brand them a PlayStation squad, but it was apparent when the All Blacks were in Sydney that too many players were wedded to their hotel rooms and lacked a breadth to their individual horizons. What became yet more obvious when they were in South Africa was that players didn't think about the collective good of the All Blacks, they only thought about themselves.

Watching the game develop at Ellis Park, the coaches could see that individuals were trying to protect their contracts. There was no collective mentality of sacrificing for others and Umaga struck a lonely figure trying to unite a group that had no sense of team. The coaching group left the stadium knowing that things had to change when they got home. A few hours later they had to totally reassess the scale of change they would have to implement as, however bad the All Blacks had been at Ellis Park, they plunged to new depths when the booze began to flow after the game.

As it was the last game of the Tri Nations, the players had planned to hold a 'court' session. The fact the All Blacks had finished last in the competition after suffering two successive defeats had not deterred the enthusiasm to crack open the beers. Tradition was tradition, after all, and what ensued was an epic drinking session that ended in total carnage. An afternoon kick-off had meant the All Blacks were back at their hotel in the early evening and by 8 pm there were players lying face down among the manicured bushes of the well-kept gardens. Those who were there say several All Blacks had to be placed in the recovery position such was their comatose state, and that for those capable, much of the later evening was spent carrying virtually unconscious players to their rooms.

'We got a hiding,' recalls Mils Muliaina, who had played at fullback in that test. 'The culture wasn't that great. There was a lot of selfishness. There were guys thinking about themselves and with the way we played ... the whole week was crap. And then what happened later … you would never see that again and it should have never got to that. Some of those guys who were a bit selfish had a chip on their shoulder about other things. I can remember putting guys to bed. I was carrying them out of this five-star hotel. We played at three o'clock in the afternoon so it wasn't like we were pulling them out at midnight. It was a next-level court session and I had never seen anything like it before or after.'

It was shocking to everyone that the All Blacks, the world's greatest rugby team, were blind drunk and rolling around in their own vomit only hours after a heavy loss. The players weren't shocked, though, as monumental drinking sessions were very much the norm even in the professional age. Muliaina can remember making his debut for Auckland as a 19-year-old and being handed a beer before he even made it to the shower after the game. He reckons he was drunk before he was fully dressed and yet no one saw this as wrong. Heavy drinking was all part of the package in the 2000s just as it had been in the 1970s, 1980s and 1990s.

Anton Oliver lifted the lid on that when he published his biography in 2006. He'd been captain of the All Blacks in 2001, a position he'd enjoyed until there was a sudden coaching change later in the year which saw John Mitchell replace Wayne Smith. Under Mitchell, Oliver felt the drinking went to a new level of bad — condoned and encouraged and used entirely as a means to degrade and compromise those who were obviously not seasoned alcohol users.

He made specific reference in his book to a court session in Edinburgh after the All Blacks had beaten Scotland 37–12.

'He [manager Andrew Martin] was asked to consume a lot of beer, rapidly, and was soon in serious difficulty. I hated what was happening. Unbeknown to me, Martin had been sick, vomiting the night before, and suffering from diarrhoea as well. Everyone was being asked to drink far too much. Lots of boys were off their faces. Halfway through the court session I stopped drinking altogether, I was so disgusted by what was happening. I remember talking to Tana Umaga and him saying he was disgusted too. We had several young men in the team and I thought, *We are teaching them that this is what it is to be an All Black — to drink lots of booze.*

'I refer a lot to the drinking that went on in the All Blacks. It is because it was such a large part of life on tour. This is something that characterised the All Black scene for years, something that, in my later years, I and others, including Doc John Mayhew and [former manager] Andrew Martin, were concerned about. Unless you were able to duck it on religious grounds, it was hard to avoid and to be honest, nobody wanted to avoid it. Excessive drinking was accepted, but in time this attitude had to change.'

Smith, ditched as head coach in 2001 before he could implement the cultural change around drinking that he was hoping to, was back as an assistant to Graham Henry in 2004 and threatened to quit that night in Johannesburg unless there was a radical shift in attitudes towards alcohol. As someone who had played for the All Blacks in the 1980s and then held coaching roles between 1999 and 2001 before returning in 2004, Smith knew that change would only be achieved if there was buy-in from everyone.

The coaches had to demand things be different and the players had to drive it, as without that unity of purpose the old ways would find a way to continue. He also knew that the captain had to have stronger leaders around him — men to help him impose higher standards and stamp out the institutional drinking element. If Umaga was a lone voice, he'd be overpowered by the players as this, essentially, was why the excessive drinking culture had lasted as long as it had.

* * *

'Everyone was being asked to drink far too much. Lots of boys were off their faces. Halfway through the court session I stopped drinking altogether, I was so disgusted by what was happening. I remember talking to Tana Umaga and him saying he was disgusted too. We had several young men in the team and I thought, *We are teaching them that this is what it is to be an All Black — to drink lots of booze.'*

— ANTON OLIVER

Throughout the last 50 years, All Blacks captains were left compromised by the drinking culture. Standards were mostly, exclusively, set by the back seat and the captain simply had to trust that they would adopt a degree of responsibility and sensitivity in regard to applying peer pressure on others to drink. As Grant Fox recalls it: 'When it came to drinking, it was more the back seat who ran that and the manager, too, had a lot of influence. You only know what you know and it was institutionalised because we didn't know any different. That was okay then. The drinking on the bus after games, the kangaroo court sessions … they were all normal. The captain didn't sit at the back of the bus. He was up the front. Away from the playing and training the back seat was much more influential. If [manager] John Sturgeon didn't think it was right he would say so and he would tell the back seat and maybe the captain although I never saw that.'

And this was the issue — the captain was not the decision-maker when it came to drinking. He was left in a difficult position of wanting everyone to relax and enjoy themselves, but to also remember they were All Blacks with a set of values to uphold. He also wanted to be one of the boys, show he was a good sport, and yet he had to be careful when others overstepped the mark not to come across as a killjoy. It could get awkward as the ritual drinking sessions were not his gig to run or influence.

Mostly it was the back seat who would set the tone and run the session, but in 2001 Oliver says Mitchell and his assistant coach Robbie Deans were heavily involved in encouraging and promoting organised drinking. When the full might of the All Blacks machinery was determined to drink, what could the captain do to stop or regulate it?

'That was a tricky one because I was a guy who did like to let my hair down when I could,' says Reuben Thorne, who took over the captaincy from Oliver in 2002. 'As the captain it's a tricky one. I look at players now and they're so much better educated around alcohol than they were when I started. You know back when I first started, we were taking those first steps out of an amateur game and so the drinking culture was completely different and it evolved reasonably quickly and became a lot better. For a captain, you've got to put some real thought into that and how you manage yourself around the others. If I look back, I would probably do it differently, but yeah, I would get involved and have fun with the boys. I thought that was a big part of it, the social side and the camaraderie that you built within the group. I would stay with the boys and have a good time but make sure you don't do anything stupid.'

For his successors, Umaga and McCaw, the situation around booze became easier to handle. When the All Blacks returned from South Africa in 2004 they did indeed instigate the radical changes they promised. A leadership group was selected and empowered to take greater control of the team. The captain and this group would have more say in how the team ran on and off the field and the relationship with the coaches would become more collaborative and collegiate rather than dictatorial and prescriptive. The decision was made to no longer condone institutional drinking sessions and accept a greater degree of personal and collective responsibility around alcohol. Drinking wasn't banned, but drinking to excess, as a means to celebrate or humiliate others, was. The leadership group was asked to set sensible protocols around drinking and for players to understand the impact it had on athletic performance and the public image of the All Blacks.

Players would still go out and drink but they were more conscious about how much and how often. And no one was made to do it if they didn't want to. It alleviated the sense of difficulty some captains had felt over the years about not knowing their role in proceedings. It became easier for Umaga and McCaw, who had both entered the professional game when binge drinking was prevalent, to have a few drinks with the team on occasions when it was deemed acceptable and then make their excuses and leave.

'The captain potentially set the tone,' says Ali Williams about nights the leadership group had designated were okay to enjoy with alcohol. 'If they got excited, it was okay to get excited. I think that's the part that Richie found hard, because deep down inside he is just a lad too. But his desire to win and make this team better was overpowering. Some nights I'd have to rip him out to try and get a beer you know, it was just that hard. Tana was the same, he didn't drink a lot. Reuben was more of a settled type of guy, not really energetic or excitable. But the captain sets your tone initially and then you go out.

'And I think that's the hard part for the captain because if the players know the captain is on a different channel for that night then they steer away from him. So you could feel isolated as a captain. The day after, those of us who had been out would tell our stories and jokes, all that sort of shit, but the captain wasn't really tied into it. You know, Dan [Carter], myself, Horey [Andrew Hore] … we'd have a little story and if Richie hadn't come out he wouldn't connect to the story. But more often than not I'd make one up about him and make him feel like he was living life vicariously through our nonsense.'

CHAPTER SIX

GREAT EXPECTATIONS

THE ALL BLACKS are huddled under their posts half an hour into the first Bledisloe Cup test of 2008. Things aren't going well in Sydney. Wallabies wing Peter Hynes has just scored to push Australia 17–5 ahead. The game is salvageable for New Zealand but unlikely given the way they are playing. Unlikely because they don't have their captain Richie McCaw on the field. He's injured and his absence is hurting the All Blacks. They lost their previous test in Dunedin without him — succumbing to a late Springboks try that was partly the cause of South African brilliance but made possible because of New Zealand's lack of sensible decision-making and leadership. And they are missing him even more in Sydney where the Wallabies are slick and cohesive and the All Blacks disjointed and inaccurate — unsure what they are trying to do and seemingly rudderless.

Rodney So'oialo is the captain, but he's out of ideas and short of influence. It feels like the team is on the edge of an implosion — the pressure about to crush them. The All Blacks rarely lose two tests in a row. It hasn't happened since 2004, and to intensify

92

things, this particular test is the first time the All Blacks have met the Wallabies since Robbie Deans was appointed coach. Deans and Graham Henry had gone head to head for the All Blacks job in late 2007 — the latter being reappointed, leaving Deans to jump on a plane to Australia minutes after he'd been rejected by his home country and sign a four-year contract to coach the Wallabies.

The tension could hardly be greater. The expectation couldn't be higher. And the All Blacks, without McCaw, are sinking fast. A random fan in the crowd is thinking the same thing, as, somehow, he managed to leap over the security barrier undetected and burrow into the All Blacks' huddle and offer them his wisdom. 'This guy somehow makes it into the huddle and started abusing us,' recalls lock Ali Williams. 'He was like, "Fuck sake boys, let's get this fucking sorted." It was unbelievable. No one saw it, no security guards saw him walk in. He was wearing an All Blacks shirt so we didn't notice at first. And what we do normally is get in a huddle, listen and then get on with it. So after a minute we suddenly say, "Who the fuck is this guy?" Anyway, it was quite a funny thing.'

It wasn't so funny by full-time when the All Blacks had lost 34–19 in a performance that had few, if any, highlights. The pressure cranked. The storyline for the media was too easy: Henry had won the job ahead of Deans and that looked like the wrong choice.

The players felt like they had let the jersey down. No one had stood up. Countless errors were made, compounded by poor decisions. The leaders had gone missing and their sense of disappointment was palpable. So too was the rising tide of anxiety that in seven days they would be playing the Wallabies again in Auckland and potentially facing a third straight defeat. Strangely, it was Deans who cast an entirely different light on what lay ahead when he predicted the return game at Eden Park would be different for one highly specific reason: he expected McCaw to play.

The All Blacks' grip on the social and economic landscape was suddenly precarious, meaning the second Bledisloe Cup test of 2008 would have an enormous bearing on the future of the game in New Zealand. If the All Blacks lost a third straight test the immediate future of Henry and his coaching team would be in peril, a handful of senior playing careers would most likely end and the popularity of the game itself would be challenged. The decision to reappoint Henry after the All Blacks' failure at the 2007 World Cup was not universally approved, and in Christchurch, where Deans was held in considerable esteem, there was anger.

Plenty of fans, maybe half the country, wanted Henry out and one more defeat was going to tip some over the edge. Compounding matters was the economic backdrop. The Global Financial Crisis had pushed petrol prices close to $2 a litre and disposable income in most households was drying up. The second test was a huge game and most of the All Blacks squad had never experienced pressure or expectation like it.

When the All Blacks announced their team, McCaw was indeed in it. The skipper had damaged his knee six weeks earlier playing against England and hadn't played since. A lay-off of that length would usually see a player, even a test player, make his way back into action either off the bench or via a lower level of rugby. Not McCaw. This moment was made for him. He was the only man in the country who had the ability to miss six weeks of football and come straight back into a test match.

He was the best player on the park. He transformed the performance of the All Blacks. Awful in Sydney, superb in Auckland, and it was all down to one man. The All Blacks won 39–10 and McCaw was at the heart of everything they did. The team was in a hole and McCaw dug them out of it. He tackled the Wallabies into submission. He outplayed George Smith at the breakdown and he was almost glued to the ball. When the final whistle blew, Fox Sports Australia commentator Greg Clark said: 'What a turnaround by the All Blacks. A famous victory this week for the All Blacks. Lost by 15 in Sydney, seven days later in Auckland, 39 points to 10 and they are on top of the Tri Nations after being written off by a lot of people in their own country.' 'Yeah what a difference McCaw makes,' offered Clark's co-commentator Phil Kearns. 'A brilliant performance by him tonight.' Even more succinct was Deans, who said: 'He is hugely influential, not only on the game but on people around him. He is the most obvious point of difference between when the All Blacks have thrived and when they haven't.'

Williams agrees with that assessment. He can remember the impact McCaw made when he returned to training ahead of that second Bledisloe Cup test in 2008. 'The interesting part of when Richie comes back from injury, is he actually trains. When, normally, some guys can potentially be nervous about their injury and maybe don't train all week or whatever, he turned up on Monday and trained full-on all week. You look at him fucking go and I think that inspires and I wouldn't underestimate that. I wouldn't underestimate that at all. It's stupid not to say there are influential people in the world. And he is one of them, especially around that team because you feel more comfortable when he's there.'

* * *

Expectation is a curious thing when it comes to the All Blacks because it is always there. Sometimes, as was the case in August 2008, it's intense, relentless and all-consuming. And other times, it eases off to just being intense and relentless. There's never any escaping it. There's never been an All Blacks side that has taken the field with the knowledge they are not expected to win. Plenty of times they have been the underdog, the weaker team, and yet that has never changed anyone's expectation in regard to victory. New Zealand's rugby public are unforgiving and ridiculously unrealistic, but it's been this way for as long as anyone can remember and is not going to change.

Success has bred the expectation of success, and constantly winning for the last century hasn't seen the All Blacks rewarded with any leeway to lose a few tests without fear of recrimination. Constantly winning hasn't banked them any goodwill with the public. What it has done is intensify expectation and burdened each generation with a legacy to uphold and enhance and it's hard to know whether the All Blacks are in a virtuous or vicious cycle.

The All Blacks have won 79 per cent of all their tests. It's an incredible record and no other sports team has a success rate remotely close. In the professional era the success ratio is 84 per cent. In the twenty-first century it rises to 86 per cent, and in the last decade the All Blacks have won 89 per cent of their tests.

The statistics are confronting and, for some, overwhelming. There has been no shortage of good players who have come into the All Blacks and been overawed by the pressure and the constant need to succeed. Not everyone has relished the scrutiny and intensity of expectation. Some have found it too demanding being expected to win every test. Defeats tend to result in appallingly long media dissections and overanalysis. A defeat has to mean something more — allude to some deeper failing than the opposition having their day.

Former All Blacks coach Steve Hansen reckoned that the intensity of expectation effectively created three different types of All Black. There were those like Dan Carter, McCaw and Kieran Read who were so good, so assured and confident that they immediately found their feet and made an impact. There were those such as Ben Smith who were full of self-doubt to begin with, battled away and over time started to believe they belonged there. And then there were those gifted enough to be great All Blacks but lacked the mental resilience to cope. Into that category went the supremely talented Isaia Toeava, who could do incredible things playing for the Blues but not when he played for the All Blacks.

And, broadly, there have been two distinct philosophies applied to deal with expectation. In the amateur era, the All Blacks were driven by a fear of losing. They knew they were expected to win but reversed their thinking to be motivated to avoid defeat. 'If there was any constant driving force it was the fact that we had the fear of losing,' Ian MacRae, who had been part of the great All Blacks side in the late 1960s that won a record 17 tests in a row, told reporters in 2014. 'I don't mean fear, it was just so important for us not to lose because that's what everyone expected.'

Attitudes didn't change much, if at all, over the years, as Alan Whetton, who played in the 1987 All Blacks World Cup team, said in 2008: 'You can talk about winning, but I always talk about the fear of losing. It's not a nice feeling. It's not about winning. It's about not losing. The losses were very unfortunate. The loss far outweighs any form of winning. You suffer a loss and boy, I tell you, we're at a funeral. The beer tastes flat. The jokes are hollow. We can go out and get pissed and lose it in alcohol, but it only lasts a night. It's a reality the next day that stays with you — all week when you're on a tour. If it's a huge game it stays with you for the rest of your life. If that isn't motivation enough, I don't know what is. Once you have suffered a major loss, it's some place you don't want to go.'

Fear drove All Blacks teams in the amateur era. They lived off it, found motivation in it and it dominated much of their thinking. Much of the communication in that era conveyed a negative, threatening tone. Some captains and coaches came at their team with a 'we need to perform or else' approach. 'It was an era of stirring team talks,' says Bryan Williams, who played under multiple captains between 1970 and 1978. 'Coaches in particular but captains, too, were the guys who did the talking and everyone else listened. I was more of a sensitive soul so didn't like being told off. I liked my captains to be rational and well thought out. There were plenty of clichéd talks. Many of them used to do it and I used to wonder whether they couldn't come up with something a bit more constructive.'

The fear of losing began to lessen in the professional era. It was, says Grant Fox, inevitable that attitudes would change. 'The fear of losing has always been part of the All Blacks' psyche. I think that was never going to survive when the game went professional. They play more tests than we did and they have a level of rugby just below test rugby. For us to get up mentally, we only had to do it so infrequently, whereas for these guys the hardest thing about playing is the mental approach. The more they play, the harder it is going to be. There is no doubt. So they started to take the process away from the emotional fear of losing. You can't keep playing on that. It happens so often that it is too hard to play it. It is about process. Winning is a by-product of the process.'

'The loss far outweighs any form of winning. You suffer a loss and boy, I tell you, we're at a funeral. The beer tastes flat. The jokes are hollow ... It's a reality ... that stays with you — all week when you're on a tour. If it's a huge game it stays with you for the rest of your life.'

— ALAN WHETTON

It may seem almost moot to detail the different mental approaches, but the prevailing mind-sets had an impact on the way the various teams in the two eras were captained. In the modern era, the captains rarely give the fire-and-brimstone speeches so prevalent in the amateur era. Communication is rarely emotional or motivational, only practical and task-related. Captains don't drive fear and a sense of dread about the consequences of losing — instead, almost conversely, captains of the professional era have had to relentlessly encourage their players to be bold enough to chase victory and to trust their natural skills, cohesion and planning to get the job done.

On the eve of the 2015 World Cup, All Blacks coach Steve Hansen revealed in a TVNZ interview: 'For a long time I think the All Blacks were driven by a fear of losing. Over time I think we've changed that to really not fear losing, because when you fear something you stop taking risks, and if you don't take risks you don't get the big rewards. I think winning the World Cup in 2011 took a big monkey off a lot of people's backs … not only the players but the whole country.'

* * *

There's something about Richie McCaw's demeanour that makes it clear he's in full business mode. He's clipped without being rude or deliberately obtuse. He smiles a few times, but it's more forced than genuine and more for the sake of appearances than anything

'For a long time I think the All Blacks were driven by a fear of losing. Over time I think we've changed that to really not fear losing, because when you fear something you stop taking risks, and if you don't take risks you don't get the big rewards. I think winning the World Cup in 2011 took a big monkey off a lot of people's backs … not only the players but the whole country.'
— STEVE HANSEN

else. He'd rather not be addressing the media three days out from the 2015 World Cup final, but he knows he has to. It's another task. A box that has to be ticked. Another job he has to do as captain. And it's obvious he doesn't want the session to drag a second past the allocated 15 minutes. Not this week. Not when the All Blacks are less than 72 hours away from playing the Wallabies in the World Cup final. Not when the All Blacks are maybe less than 72 hours away from making history and becoming the first team to win consecutive World Cups.

As he's still giving the last part of his answer to the last question, he stands to leave. There's maybe more than 200 journalists at the All Blacks' base, which is at Pennyhill south-west of London, and McCaw doesn't want to engage with any of them as he makes his way out of the temporary marquee erected for media events at the five-star resort.

But he's foiled. Standing at the back of the room are Newstalk ZB hosts Mike Hosking and his wife Kate Hawkesby. They have recently arrived in London and, like most celebrity media, are afflicted by a chronic, misguided sense of entitlement. As McCaw approaches, he senses that they haven't read his mood. He can see that Hawkesby, with All Blacks media manager Jo Malcolm, is coming at him with a camera. McCaw's back stiffens. Never has the expression 'a face like thunder' rung more true. He wants to keep walking but knows there will be an unpleasant scene if he does. Malcolm has already called for his attention and he can't pretend he didn't hear. So he stops and listens to the request and with a smile even more forced than any he managed during the press conference, he poses for a photo with Hawkesby. He's clearly raging that he's been duped into this and as soon as the flash has gone off, he's on his way at military pace.

Part of his annoyance, and only part, was that McCaw had a respectful and strong relationship with the established rugby media. He fulfilled his mandatory requirements with an openness and good humour and was available to a select few for longer sit-down interviews as long as they didn't ask too often. In return, the established rugby media let him live his life without probing him about his love interests or anything not related to the game. It probably wouldn't be true to say McCaw liked or necessarily enjoyed the media requirement of his role, but he understood the importance of it and some of the finer mechanics.

He proved that in Paris in 2013 when a scheduled All Blacks media day was effectively hijacked by jersey sponsor adidas. Rather than have the usual interviews at the team hotel, adidas had built a pub that they were hoping to promote and persuaded the All Blacks to conduct interviews there. But the venue hadn't been finished and media were kept outside in the freezing November rain for more than two hours. When McCaw and Kieran Read arrived, they were mobbed by French journalists and the whole circus was shut down after four minutes. The New Zealand media contingent were angry and then 24 hours later apoplectic. It turned out that McCaw and Read had been driven to the adidas pub with a reporter from French paper *L'Équipe* in the vehicle, with enough time and access to produce a 4000-word epic feature.

New Zealand media companies spend millions sending reporters around the world to cover the All Blacks, and to see a French paper afforded such incredible access to the captain created obvious disgruntlement. McCaw, to his eternal credit, didn't need this to be spelt out, which is why, a day later, he's striding across the lobby of the All Blacks' swanky Parisian hotel to make an unsolicited apology. The whole business of the reporter in the car was sprung on him and he had no idea it was going to happen. He didn't feel good seeing New Zealand media being marginalised and he would be having words with the relevant people to ensure it didn't happen again. He knew the financial investment media companies in New Zealand were making and the role the beat writers played in promoting the sport and the national team. So the Hawkesby incident, he knew, would have annoyed the regular rugby media who would have seen it in a similar light to the adidas debacle where an undeserving party was given favourable treatment.

But the real source of his annoyance was having to do something he didn't want to do — and while it may have only taken 30 seconds or so, it was a most unwelcome distraction at a time when McCaw had zero tolerance for unwelcome distractions. The style in which they did it may have varied, but captains in the last 50 years have been unified in the way they have taken control in times of increased pressure and expectation. The shutters come down and they have no interest in having to do things that are not on their list of planned events. Their focus becomes yet more intense and they are gripped by one thought, one goal and one ferocious desire to get the job done.

Life in the All Blacks is always tense and demanding but there are some games, some occasions, some moments in time that stand out as exceptional even in an environment where victory is always expected. The mood will be different once the squad has assembled. The players filter off the bus at training without saying a word. There are fewer laughs to be heard when they are warming up. There is no idle banter between drills. And the captain, through his words, deeds and actions, has a greater presence: a greater sense of being the team's figurehead. The best captains have been at their best in the most difficult times. An intensification of pressure has brought them more prominently to the helm. Back an All Blacks side into a corner and it is the captain who will lead the fight out of it.

In 1976 the All Blacks faced a four-test tour in South Africa which, then, was deemed the toughest challenge in the world game. The All Blacks had never won a series in the Republic and they knew they would face numerous obstacles in their quest to make history. There was, obviously, an excellent Springboks side to conquer but so too would there be home-town referees, rabid crowds and provincial sides with the singular goal of taking scalps ... literally.

For Andy Leslie, appointed captain in 1974 on his debut, the tour was his moment to come of age. 'South Africa at that stage was our World Cup so there was an expectation, there was a pressure which was different to anything else. Every game you were being set up to be knocked off, under huge pressure, and there wasn't the neutral referee situation then that there is now. The management group was Noel Stanley, J.J. Stewart and basically myself, and what we had to deal with, now you have 15 people doing what those three people used to do. So the pressure was on and I think the spotlight was on.'

The All Blacks came agonisingly close to a series win in 1976. Most observers who watched the tour unfold say the All Blacks would most likely have won had there been neutral referees. Leslie's reaction at the end of the second test, which the All Blacks won to make the series one-all, best illustrates the pressure he was under and the level of effort he produced. 'I vomited,' he says. 'It was a release from the pressure. I think we all felt the same.

We were never in a position to be able to say, "Shit, we've won that" with 10 minutes to go. No, you never relaxed until the final whistle. You are completely involved. I can remember after the last test when we'd lost, how sad and disappointed our dressing room was. It was pretty quiet and it wasn't so different after that second test which we won. We were happy, but I'll tell you what, we used to sit exhausted and there wasn't that much elation. Everyone was more sort of relieved, to be honest.'

In the professional age it has been easier to pick the influence of the captain on those occasions when expectation has been greatest. A typical test week since the introduction of leadership groups and collaborative relationships with management has seen the coaches drive much of the strategy and tone earlier in the week with the players and captain taking increasing control closer to game day. But if the team is under pressure, in desperate need of a win, or the occasion is bigger than normal, the captain will take greater control earlier in the week. They will have a little bit more to say. The tone in which they say it may change.

Communication will be blunt but effective and there was a priceless example of this in 2012 when the All Blacks, for the first time, had to travel from Argentina to South Africa to play their final Rugby Championship match. The squad was tired and jet-lagged when they trained on the Thursday before the test against the Boks in Soweto. Balls were being dropped. Mistakes were being made. There was no zip or hunger and so McCaw stopped the session to launch a stinging verbal onslaught.

The All Blacks had a Grand Slam in their sights if they could win, which would also put them in touching distance of the world record for consecutive victories. It was a huge game as far as he was concerned. He made it clear that he didn't particularly care that everyone was tired and sore because the Boks were waiting for them on Saturday and they certainly wouldn't be sympathetic about the physical and mental state of the All Blacks. His language would have embarrassed his mother, but he got his point across, and the next 20 minutes saw a rise in standards and the All Blacks won 32–16 a few days later.

The bigger the game, the more McCaw would demand and give of himself, and the more he would ask of others. Expectation was not his enemy, which was true also of Tana Umaga before him. In 2005, a few weeks before the Lions series, Umaga was happy to chat after the Hurricanes had been knocked out of Super Rugby. He leant against the wall in the tunnel leading to the home-side changing room and explained that he'd been eagerly awaiting the series as it was the big occasions that he enjoyed the most. The New Zealand public, he said, held expectations that were relentlessly hard to meet, but he never wanted that to change, for it was an essential part of the All Blacks' success.

And when that expectation heightened, his captaincy sharpened. Ali Williams can remember when the All Blacks were under pressure in 2004 having scraped a last-minute win against the Boks in Christchurch. 'Tana was a very calm, cool captain and didn't really talk a lot. But there was one time, around an off-field incident, that a different voice came out. He didn't come at me first, he came at himself and I think that's the mark of an amazing person as captain, when they say, "I'm gonna tell you where I fucked up, what I did wrong, how I did it and what I want to do differently. And I'm going to tell you how you fucked up."'

Kieran Read learned the same art of knowing when to change his demeanour and impose himself more forcefully in the team's preparation. It wasn't something that initially came naturally to him at the start of his tenure. In 2016 the All Blacks weren't under real pressure until they lost to Ireland in Chicago in early November and had to play them again two weeks later in Dublin. Expectation was high for the rematch, and while the All Blacks won 21–9, it was an ill-disciplined and frantic performance. The All Blacks had responded to defeat with brutality and they regretted that they hadn't trusted their full array of skills to subdue the Irish. The way they responded to that loss in Chicago was a sign perhaps that in Read's first year as captain, he didn't have the same ability as McCaw and Umaga to impose himself; to flick the switch and change the tone.

'It is your values, your behaviour. How you communicate. How you use your words,' explains Grant Fox about the art of captaincy under pressure. 'I didn't see a lot of McCaw directly close up even though I was around. The bits I saw, Richie wasn't a man of many words. He didn't need to be for a start. The really important thing for captains is respect not friendship. You don't have to be liked, but you have to be respected and trusted. I know Richie was a guy who didn't worry about being liked. Trusted and respected … that would have been important to him but he earned that. Just being the man he was created that naturally. Reado, to a point, early in his captaincy, probably still wanted to be friends. And that's okay but it makes it harder to have those inconvenient conversations or give those very direct, blunt messages.'

By 2019, there's no doubt Read had created the distance he needed to demand more of others and take greater control at difficult times. After the All Blacks fell to a record defeat in the first Bledisloe Cup test of the year in Perth, they were in a world of heavy external criticism. They had drawn with the Boks before the loss in Perth and there was good reason to wonder not only whether they were going to lose the Bledisloe Cup, but also whether their whole World Cup campaign was imploding. Much like the situation in 2008, the All Blacks had seven days to turn things around at Eden Park, and much like what happened 11 years previously, it was the captain who was the inspiration in a spirited and emphatic recovery.

The All Blacks won the return match 36–0 and Read led the way with 14 huge tackles, eight damaging ball carries and a destructive showing in the lineout. He also, according to All Blacks coach Steve Hansen, had taken control of the team's preparation earlier in the week and held everyone, including himself, accountable to deliver a higher quality of performance. 'There have been a lot of things said in the media and a lot of things spoken about within the team, and that creates the pressure to have to step up,' said Hansen. 'The guy that led from the front was one of the guys who copped a lot of criticism. I'm extremely proud of how [Read] led the week and how he played tonight. Everyone externally was starting to get a bit shaky, starting to question whether the coaches still had it, the players still had it. I thought Reado was massive. He answered a lot of questions for a lot of people externally. He leads from the front and he's starting to get more and more demanding, which I like. That's important that he demands, and has expectations. He's a smart captain.'

CHAPTER SEVEN

EXORCISING THE DEMONS

THE SPECIFICS AND the demands of the job have changed over the years, but every All Blacks captain of the last 50 years will have been plagued by insecurities and self-doubt at some stage in their respective careers. It's unimaginable that anyone could take the job on and never once question their right to do so.

The job comes with a scrutiny that puts it alongside the prime minister in terms of profile and public expectation. There is nowhere to hide, and while leadership roles in any sports team or major corporation carry additional responsibilities, the All Blacks captaincy is next level in that regard. The legacy has to be upheld. The history has to be acknowledged and enhanced, and probably it is the most intimidating sports team in the world to be part of. The players are connected as much by fear as they are driven by their hunger for success and it takes a strong, confident and assured personality to captain a team where failure is never tolerated.

Captaincy of the All Blacks can be lonely. The players room in pairs but not the captain — he's a single occupant wherever the team stays. The external expectation is relentless, and as Grant Fox, who enjoyed a long test career before becoming a selector in 2012, says: 'I know the internal workings of an All Blacks set-up. Guys place much more pressure on themselves than the public do. Much more.'

For the captain, the pressure can be enough to break them at times. It comes from outside the camp and very much from within, and keeping the inevitable mental demons at bay is a constant demand of the role. And while it's a gross simplification, it's not a gross exaggeration to suggest that those captains who were best able to believe in themselves and project that inner confidence are the men who enjoyed the most success.

Heavy is the head that wears the crown is a phrase to which every All Blacks captain can relate. Some, such as Taine Randell, felt nothing but stress and inadequacy throughout their tenure. Others, such as Sean Fitzpatrick, had to battle to find captaincy enjoyable. He didn't want it in 1992, knew he wasn't the preferred choice of his coach and took, he says, three, maybe even four years to build the confidence he needed to effectively do the role. Graham Mourie, another anointed at a relatively young age, was not instantly comfortable at having to address his peers and command them in battle. 'My psychology was that I found it difficult to be a captain initially and certainly was pretty surprised when it happened,' he says. 'I remember having a bit of a chat with B.J. Lochore about 10 years ago and we both felt that we were happy just to be in the team and that the captaincy … we could do it, I guess. I was a relatively quiet kid, noisy with my mates, but I came from a rural farming background. I remember the first time I had to give a team talk, the night before a game, I thought,

Shit, what the hell am I going to say? But because of that I probably did things a little differently to some of the other captains that I'd served under and tended to steer more towards facilitation and bringing people out of their shells and getting other people to contribute. I guess I didn't feel there was any sort of template that I felt I could follow from my previous experience.'

As much as the job is about inspiring others, it is about convincing self. Being captain of the All Blacks is about finding the mental strength to accept the honour and believe it is deserved.

* * *

Taine Randell can't recall specifically when it was that the enormity of the job he had been asked to do hit him. He doesn't even think there was one specific moment when he registered within himself that he was operating outside his comfort zone. It was more that he had a voice constantly in his head, questioning his worthiness and readiness to lead an All Blacks side that included heavyweight performers such as Olo Brown, Craig Dowd, Ian Jones, Robin Brooke and Michael Jones.

That he was plagued throughout his captaincy with feelings of self-doubt and uncertainty was not necessarily surprising. He was only 23, and by his own admission, not ready to captain the All Blacks. He'd toured South Africa in 1996, but didn't win his first test cap until 1997, and while he had been captain of Otago and the Highlanders, he didn't think that one season of test football qualified him to lead the best rugby side in the world.

All Blacks coach John Hart wasn't convinced Randell was ready either, but he had no other option by June 1998. Sean Fitzpatrick had retired, Zinzan Brooke was offshore and Michael Jones was battling injury. It was a twist of fate Hart couldn't possibly have predicted and he came to see Randell as his only option.

'I was 23 and had one full year of test rugby,' says Randell. 'It was always intimidating. You're sort of like, "Fuck it's Michael Jones, fuck it's Robin Brooke." That was not the most comfortable time. It was a real transition team — we'd lost a lot of legends. Zinzan Brooke, Fitzpatrick, Frank Bunce and others were coming near the end of their careers. This coincided with some pretty good opposition. The Wallabies had come into a peak period with some legendary players and the Springboks were strong, too.'

The doubting voice in Randell's head was never silenced in 1998. After beating a weak England team twice, the All Blacks endured a five-test losing streak. They just couldn't win. They didn't have the mental edge required to hang tough through 80 minutes. They didn't have the composure or certainty they needed in those critical moments and Randell's captaincy increasingly came under the media spotlight.

He did his best to battle through his doubts and keep telling himself he was the right man to captain the All Blacks. 'I guess just blind ambition, I think, got me through,' he says. 'I said to myself, "Fuck it, I'm in this job, it is awesome, I'm just going to do it." I had blind, youthful enthusiasm and I guess confidence. At that age you're bulletproof, you do whatever you want — "Oh yeah, do this, go to Otago University, yeah sweet, sweet, play for the All Blacks, yeah awesome, captain yeah" — you take it in your stride. Being a babe in the woods was quite a good thing because if I realised then what I know now, I would have realised how woefully unprepared I was. But I guess with youth and positivity you crack on.'

Randell was able to paper over the cracks until the end of the season. After each Tri Nations loss he could pick himself up and tell the team that they had another test coming in which they could make amends. Despite the mounting defeats, confidence didn't drain out of the team. They knew they had enough talent to win. They knew they weren't being horribly outclassed by either Australia or South Africa, and with a bit of luck, a bit of mental fortitude and a bit of smart decision-making when it mattered, the win would come.

But it didn't — and when there were no more games left in 1998, Randell was consumed by the sense he wasn't the right man to lead the team. The bubble burst, his exuberance and bravado were no longer capable of masking his true feelings, and he knew that if he wasn't sure about himself, then it was highly probable that he didn't have the universal respect or support of his team-mates and they wouldn't be sure about him either.

The World Cup was looming and Randell couldn't see that the All Blacks would win it if he was at the helm. So he flew to Auckland in late 1998 and told Hart how he was feeling. 'He didn't want the job in '99,' says Hart. 'But I had no option. That was a terrible situation. I took him for a walk and he said, "I don't really want to be captain." And I said, "Well, mate, somehow we've got to work this through and make you successful and we're going to bring in some support for you or whatever." But we never really managed to do that. It was a very young team. Or the older guys weren't leaders. And they're not all leaders. I mean you've seen the All Blacks side now, there are some that are not leaders, they just do their job but they've got no other contribution to make. And it's not something that's born into everyone by any means —

it's born into a few and then those few can grow it, and by growing it they expand and help others to grow too.'

Captain and coach reached an agreement that they would give things more time before reaching a definitive decision. Hart also connected Randell with former NZR board member Kevin Roberts, who was the global head of Saatchi & Saatchi. 'When I saw Kevin, mentally I was all over the place and he was fantastic from a strategic point of view,' says Randell. 'He gave a lot of outside context: "This is the sort of person you are and you've got to do this." And I actually thought, *Okay, that makes sense*. He understood the role of an All Blacks captain better than I did even though I'd just had a season playing it. And it was clear to me, and to him as well probably, that I wasn't ready to be All Blacks captain.

'I was worried about talking to John Hart, who is this corporate titan and he spoke a lot flasher than us simpletons from the provinces. So that was intimidating. We had a woman, Jane Dent, who was fantastic with the media, but was just so intimidating. She would tell me this is what you've got to say and I was like, *Fuck, I can barely string two words together*. You had all this sort of stuff and so with Kevin he said you're just not ready for it. My first season with the All Blacks [1997] was awesome. There were all these great players to learn from. But going into 1999, I was not ready to be All Blacks captain.'

As the 1999 Super Rugby season played out, Randell began to change his mind. He led a Highlanders team that surprised everyone by making the final. He also felt that he was playing better than he had in 1998, and the combination of good form and winning more bolstered his confidence. He started to believe in himself and, by June, when the first tests were to be played, he convinced himself he was the right man to captain the All Blacks and carried on in the role until the team famously crashed out of the 1999 World Cup in one of the greatest upsets of all time.

The All Blacks' 43–31 World Cup semi-final loss to France served as proof that Randell never quite managed to eradicate the self-doubt that had gripped him on day one in the job. That loss also brought the resignation of Hart, and when new coach Wayne Smith arrived, he appointed Todd Blackadder as his captain, but continued to pick Randell in his back row. That Randell was dropped as captain but still deemed good enough to play test football confirmed his standing in history as the All Blacks' greatest victim of circumstance. Captaincy was forced upon him when he was not equipped to cope with the responsibilities that came with it.

Like so many captains before him, he didn't ask for the job, but once it was bestowed upon him, he tried, the best he could, to fulfil his obligations. But the statistics reveal the truth about his readiness. The All Blacks won 57 per cent of the tests in which Randell was in charge. In the 29 other tests in which he played when he wasn't the captain, his win ratio was 81 per cent.

'I wasn't surprised, not surprised in the least that Wayne Smith came in and said I was going to be in the team and I wasn't going to be captain,' says Randell. 'I wasn't relieved but my main thing was to be an All Black. When I was a little kid, I wanted to play for the All Blacks. The captaincy, that never really figured when I was doing my daydreaming. That was never part of it, just being in the All Blacks was.'

* * *

New Zealand's media never lacked for creativity when it came to finding new and cruel ways to describe the performances of Reuben Thorne when he was All Blacks captain between 2002 and 2003. His crime, it seemed, was that he wasn't a towering personality or a set-the-world-on-fire sort of player. His brand was built on stoicism and stability. He was all about honest toil, consistency and level-headedness — factors that were critical in the mechanics of test football, but not sexy or easy for a quick-fix media to appreciate.

Thorne had been an All Black since 1999. His solid defence and low error rate in the No. 6 jersey appealed first to John Hart, then Wayne Smith. John Mitchell, when he was appointed head coach in late 2001, wanted a solid, reliable figure as his captain and he could see no better man for the job than Thorne. The All Blacks, he reasoned, needed a quietly demanding figure whose command would be built on his effort, his calmness, and his constant ability to be in the right places doing the right things. Thorne, to some extent, was a throwback to the yesteryears of provincial hard men being awarded the captaincy on account of the respect in which they were held by their peers.

When Thorne led the Crusaders to the Super Rugby title in 2002, without losing a game, it effectively secured his promotion to the captaincy and was why, despite never coveting the job, he wasn't surprised to find Mitchell and assistant Robbie Deans sitting in his lounge a week before the test season kicked off. 'They said that they had seen that I'd done a good job with the Crusaders and asked if I could be the All Blacks captain,' says

Thorne. 'They came and said, "Look, we want you to do it, you do a good job" — that was basically it. You don't really have the option to turn it down unless you have really strong feelings why you shouldn't. And obviously it is a great honour and something to make you really proud to be asked to do that — so yeah, it was pretty cool really.

'I was good friends with some of the guys who had been captains before me like Todd Blackadder so you're aware of the extra spotlight that goes on that position. Even though I was aware of it, I probably didn't comprehend quite how much would be involved. I was nervous because I'm not someone who seeks the spotlight or enjoys squirming in front of the TV cameras. But I love the All Blacks, I love the game of rugby, I love giving my best to it, and when a coach comes to me and asks me to do something, then my natural response is I'll do this and I'll give it my best shot.'

Thorne's attitude won him the respect of the coaches and also his team-mates, who admired his pragmatic, non-emotional responses to on- and off-field situations. It also helped that throughout 2002 there were several tests when the All Blacks starting XV included 14 of his Crusaders team-mates. His peers also appreciated that with the dynamic Richie McCaw at openside flanker and Scott Robertson's athleticism at No. 8, the All Blacks needed a steady workhorse at blindside to provide the right balance in the loose trio.

But while Thorne was admired and respected internally, externally the picture was different. His natural quietness and awkwardness in front of the media was interpreted as a lack of charisma and his no-frills football was seen as a lack of ability.

There were other blindside flankers within New Zealand and around the world who brought high-impact defence to the role and there were some who were devastating ball carriers. Thorne was neither of those things, so the media had what they saw as an easy target as Thorne didn't meet their expectations of what they wanted from an All Blacks captain.

Throughout 2002 and 2003 his work was heavily critiqued and he faced strong personal attacks on several occasions. When the All Blacks lost to England in 2003, Thorne was savaged. At one stage England had been reduced to 13 men, having seen two forwards yellow-carded. But the All Blacks couldn't budge the visitors' six-man scrum and in a five-minute spell camped on England's line with a two-man advantage, they couldn't score any points. They lost the test 15–13 and Thorne was branded Captain Invisible. Other media outlets liked to slyly refer to him as a non-playing captain, and in addition to the derogatory headlines and monikers there were endless opinion pieces devoted to detailing his perceived weaknesses. He was the captain the media didn't want and in his two years at the helm he had a powerful enemy opposed to his captaincy.

'Yeah, well it does,' he says to the question of whether it affected his confidence. 'New Zealand's a small place, so the media can be very powerful because it's got such a broad reach. If they put an opinion piece out there that is negative, then the public tend to believe that's right or there's something behind it, so it is tough, because you say you don't read it, but everybody sees it and you hear it and you know it because, as I say, it's a small place.

'So at times I'd feel it, but I thought, *I've got the backing of my team, I've got the backing of the coaches*, and I felt privileged to be able to do what I was doing. I felt at the time I had good support from my team-mates and they all backed me because the people on the field know what you do. The coaches were the same. They said, "Look, keep playing well, we're happy with what you're doing." Those are the opinions that matter to me, so that helped. But there were times when it was annoying. It was frustrating, hard for my family to deal with it. But I thought, *There's not much I can do about it*, so I just got on and focused on playing.

'I don't recall any moments when I froze or thought, *I shouldn't be here*. I thought, *I know what I'm doing. I'm good at what I'm doing, these boys are backing me* — that outweighed the negative side of it.'

Like Randell before him, Thorne's tenure ended with World Cup defeat in 2003 which also saw Mitchell lose his job to Graham Henry. The new broom wasn't a fan of Thorne and made that clear long before he picked his first squad of 2004. It was

'I don't recall any moments when I froze or thought, *I shouldn't be here*. I thought, *I know what I'm doing. I'm good at what I'm doing, these boys are backing me* — that outweighed the negative side of it.'

— REUBEN THORNE

well flagged that Thorne wouldn't be included. Henry wanted a higher-impact No. 6. He wanted a dynamic ball carrier and high-impact defender — attributes he didn't feel Thorne possessed.

Interestingly, though, Henry had a change of heart about Thorne two years after not picking him. He recalled the former captain in 2006, believing then that the All Blacks needed his stoicism and stability. Thorne came back into the squad and it was during this second stint between 2006 and 2007 that he was better able to appreciate how much the media had a poisoned perception of him.

'We used to have these really full-on reviews,' he says. 'Richie was the captain and our own analysis team would go through and award points for your performance. Basically, every action on the field was measured so you'd have a score that reflected the work, the effort and the impact that you'd had on the game. We played the Springboks in Christchurch and the next day all the stats came out for our performances — really in-depth stuff done by the coaches. I got 269 and Richie, who always pretty much got the top score, got 270. So there was one point difference between us, and in the media, I think because of preconceived perceptions, they did the newspaper scores and you know it was ... Reuben Thorne, workmanlike, 6/10; Richie McCaw, outstanding, 9/10.

'It was ingrained and hard to change those perceptions no matter how well you played. I think a lot of them were preconceived and it was hard to break that. You would have had to do something amazing to change those perceptions. I think because of the type of player that I was — I wasn't flash or flamboyant or scoring tries — it was hard to shake that perception.

'People in New Zealand expect or want their captain to be something a little more than that. They want them to be the star, they want that person to be a larger-than-life sort of character or an amazing athlete that's going to score tries and dominate people week in week out, and for me it was really hard to shake that off.'

* * *

In the aftermath of the All Blacks' 2007 World Cup failure, Richie McCaw was consumed with doubt about whether he should carry on as captain. It was alien territory for someone whose career hadn't experienced so much as a blip up until then. McCaw was the golden child of New Zealand rugby. Capped when he was just 20 in 2001, he'd quickly become a national treasure. He was the player everyone else wished they could be and the influence he wielded was phenomenal.

When Tana Umaga retired in 2005, McCaw was the only choice to take over. He was a world-class player. He had the respect of his team-mates and opponents. He was brave and dynamic. He was high-impact and influential. He was intelligent, approachable, humble and grounded. He was articulate, conscious of the history that came with the jersey and committed in a way that, probably, no other All Black ever has been. He relished responsibility, and while he was naturally quiet and a little reserved socially, he was driven by this need to constantly improve and demand a similar attitude from his peers.

When he took over the captaincy in 2006, the All Blacks lost just one test that year and finished the season as unbackable favourites to win the 2007 World Cup. In McCaw, the All Blacks had the charismatic, iconic captain required to win a World Cup. Or so everyone thought. And they also had a wider leadership group and management model that set them apart. There were experienced players packed around McCaw and an awareness among management that leadership was a skill that had to be actively developed and practised.

The All Blacks had built mental resilience and leadership strategies to make them better decision-makers and better able to cope with the pressure of test football. The psychological fault line that had been exposed as running through the team at previous World Cups had been fixed. Or so they thought.

And this was why McCaw was so down after the All Blacks were shockingly dumped out of the World Cup quarter-final by France. The coaches and leaders had spent four years building towards 2007. They had lost just five tests in the cycle prior to the World Cup. They had identified their weaknesses in leadership and thought they had fixed them. They thought they had the mental resilience to back up their obvious talent — and to find out, on the biggest stage of all, that it was all an illusion, was a crushing blow for McCaw.

His captaincy had failed to deliver the result the All Blacks wanted and he wasn't spared in the official review of the failure commissioned by his own employer. New Zealand Rugby paid for an independent report to be conducted into the 2007 campaign and it concluded: 'We consider that on-field leadership and decision making was a factor in the loss in the quarter-final. Arguably, the team and its leadership group has only occasionally been tested to the same degree over the last four years. The trend, as witnessed in Melbourne earlier in 2007, was for the leaders to revert to type and let McCaw make the calls. ... [T]he leadership model failed to deliver what was its most important objective — decisions which give the best chance of winning the game. The team failed to ensure that the right decisions were taken at critical moments.'

It was a damning appraisal of McCaw's captaincy and also the leadership group around him and it was no surprise the captain lost his confidence. The acknowledgement by the independent report that there was a lack of support from his leadership group may have brought to the front of his mind some thoughts that had previously been lurking somewhere near the back.

Throughout the latter part of 2006 and through much of 2007 there were some close to the team who insisted there was not universal support for McCaw. At that time, the Hurricanes and Crusaders were great rivals — played each other in the 2006 Super Rugby final — and between them provided the bulk of the All Blacks squad. There was a suggestion that many of the Hurricanes players wanted a Hurricane to replace Umaga as captain and weren't sold on McCaw. Such rumours often find oxygen and circulate without substance — but the fact the skipper was left isolated on the field during that World Cup quarter-final hints at the possibility of a divide.

There was also an incident in April 2006 when the Crusaders played the Hurricanes in Wellington. McCaw was at the bottom of a ruck when he felt a pair of hands grip him by the throat and squeeze. He was strangled for 24 seconds and almost passed out, leaving one Crusader who spoke to the *New Zealand Herald* to brand it 'the most despicable thing I have ever seen on a rugby pitch'. In that same game, loose forward Jerry Collins, the man believed to be the Hurricanes' preferred choice as All Blacks captain, bounced the ball off McCaw's head after the referee had blown his whistle. It was a pointed act — done for no other reason than to let McCaw know he was being targeted. Come the 2006 Super Rugby final, even through the thick fog, it was obvious Ma'a Nonu was harbouring a vendetta of some kind and the Hurricanes' treatment of McCaw was so overtly aggressive that it prompted media to ask whether the All Blacks skipper knew of any reason why he was being singled out. 'I dunno mate' was all he could manage before saying there was nothing too serious about it all. And maybe there wasn't, but in 2008 Collins was told by the All Blacks coaches he wasn't going to be picked and was then given permission to quit his contract a year early.

Whether it was ever a big deal, something that undermined his confidence, McCaw's bigger worry was his readiness to do the job. The tough questions he had to ask were about himself and not others. 'I questioned whether I was good enough to do it or the right person to do it,' he revealed almost seven years later ahead of his 100th test as captain. 'You can either man up and

'You can either man up and get on with it or drift away and remember that experience as one you couldn't handle. Being the person I am, as soon as I thought like that I thought, *There's no way I'd want to do that*. I don't think you'd carry on doing it if you didn't want it. You've got to want to put yourself under the pressure that comes with it otherwise you wouldn't last.'

—RICHIE McCAW

get on with it or drift away and remember that experience as one you couldn't handle. Being the person I am, as soon as I thought like that I thought, *There's no way I'd want to do that*. I don't think you'd carry on doing it if you didn't want it. You've got to want to put yourself under the pressure that comes with it otherwise you wouldn't last. I remember one day I got over it and got on with it.'

CHAPTER EIGHT

BEST IN SHOW

CAPTAINCY OF THE All Blacks is a never-ending quest to win respect and trust. A captain can only command those around him if they believe in him; if his team-mates are convinced by his worthiness. They have to trust that the captain is capable of doing himself what he asks of others. They need to see him lead by example. The team is glued together by the collective confidence held in the skipper, and respect doesn't automatically come with the position.

The captain can't be an effective captain simply because he's been asked to do the role. Respect has to be earned and everyone ever asked to lead the All Blacks has faced that moment, where they have sat alone, asking themselves exactly how they intend to go about winning the confidence of their team-mates.

The job has so many facets that a captain can self-style his role almost any way he chooses. He can pick an area in which to specialise and build his reputation as an orator, as a media manipulator, as a confidant, as a protector of values. There is no map to success when it comes to being the All Blacks captain; no one way to get the job done. In theory, there are limitless ways in which to build the respect needed to be an effective captain and yet, as true as that is, there is really only one route to follow. Form is everything when it comes to being the All Blacks captain — get that bit right, be the best player, and respect, confidence and trust will always be there.

* * *

It was odd bordering on ridiculous that the day before the 2007 World Cup quarter-final against France, All Blacks captain Richie McCaw signed a contract extension through to 2009. He wanted his housekeeping to be out of the way long before the tournament started, but for reasons beyond his control, negotiations dragged on until October and he ended up signing a deal out of frustration. That the captain was tidying up contractual business less than 24 hours before the game was symptomatic of the distractions and confusion that had consumed the squad. It had been a weird year and certainly an odd World Cup campaign. McCaw, along with 21 other All Blacks, had been asked to miss the first seven weeks of Super Rugby. The coaching team had become paranoid about physical burnout ahead of the tournament and hit upon this plan to give the bulk of their squad an extended pre-season in which they could condition. It was an idea that was good in theory but the practical implementation of which was disastrous, and McCaw only played half a season of Super Rugby and battled along with the other late entrants to integrate so late in the piece.

When the All Blacks coaches continued to rest and rotate their players ahead of the tournament, it meant that McCaw still hadn't found anything close to his best form. The disjointed nature of it all had prevented him from building his rhythm. He wasn't quite reading the game the way he normally did. He was half a metre off where he usually would be because his anticipation wasn't quite as sharp as a result of his lack of game time.

Once the All Blacks arrived in France, there was a sense of the world being against them. Before they played Portugal in Lyon, a World Rugby official approached team management and asked if the All Blacks could take it easy in the scrums. The governing body was worried about the Portuguese being injured and so while every other serious contender was knocking lumps out of one another, the All Blacks were being asked, just minutes before a test, to take it easy. A week later in Scotland and Dan Carter had a poor day goal-kicking in Edinburgh. But it turned out he had been given the wrong balls with which to practise before the game. And why were the All Blacks even in Scotland? Because the Scots had voted for France to be hosts and a 'home' glamour clash against New Zealand was their reward. It was surreal to be in Edinburgh and yet all the ground announcements being in French first, English second.

Just as weird was that the All Blacks' quarter-final against France was played in Cardiff and the build-up was dominated by a subplot about uniform. The French had 'darkened' their traditional jersey so that it was almost black. New Zealand Rugby chief executive Chris Moller felt this was deliberate, done with the goal of forcing the All Blacks out of their traditional jersey in Cardiff. It might have seemed a little petty, but the French lived off symbolism and would see it as an early victory if New Zealand weren't wearing black. It would, seen through the eyes of the French, make the All Blacks less intimidating if they were wearing their alternative jersey, and it felt like another attempt to destabilise the favourites.

Moller expected World Rugby to back him and to agree that the only way to avoid a colour clash in the quarter-final was to ask the French to play in their alternative white shirt and New Zealand in black. They didn't and then they added to the sense that unseen forces were conspiring against the All Blacks when they appointed the 28-year-old Wayne Barnes, with barely two years' experience, as referee. The hosts versus the favourites — the biggest clash of the four quarter-finals — and the game is awarded to the youngest and most inexperienced referee ...?

The performance against France was riddled with flaws and illustrated that the All Blacks lacked a collective focus and understanding of just how intense the occasion was going to be. They looked like a team that had taken a knife to a gunfight. The decision-making collapsed in the second half. France, after taking a 20–18 lead, had no intention of doing anything other than defending it, giving the All Blacks 13 minutes to score three points. Four million New Zealanders screamed to set up for a drop goal, but it never happened.

There were endless periods of pick and drive by the All Blacks forwards — a procession of one-off runners flopping maybe six inches further forward before precious seconds were eaten up digging the ball out to repeat the whole process. It was frantic, unstructured, panic-ridden rugby and it alluded to McCaw's lack of influence at openside and command of those around him. In stark contrast was his opposite number, Thierry Dusautoir, who made a stupid number of tackles and was the man of the match.

The media reacted to that defeat by going on a five-month witch hunt, while New Zealand Rugby commissioned an independent review which was effectively a witch hunt by another name. McCaw's reaction was considerably more productive. He asked himself whether he still wanted to play test rugby and the answer was an emphatic yes. He asked himself whether he still wanted to be captain and the answer, after a bit of time, was an emphatic yes. Once he decided that, he revisited the contract he signed on the eve of the quarter-final and extended it through to 2011. He knew he wanted to stay for the long haul and try to earn redemption in 2011. And then he asked himself what he could do to become a better captain.

It was a question that had twisted others into knots. But not McCaw. He fixed on one idea that was simple and achievable. He decided that captaincy began with being the best player. He would lead through the quality of his performances. McCaw had been World Rugby Player of the Year in 2006 and the All Blacks had lost just one game; but in 2007 he never hit those same individual heights and New Zealand crashed out of the World Cup early. There was a connection to be made between form and influence.

There were multiple aspects to the job and it was easy to get bogged down in micro-analysis, fret about the small stuff and make a complicated list of areas in which he had to improve. But he decided against all that, reasoning that if he played well, got that bit right, then the detail would fall into place. It was that simple and it was also stunningly effective as the All Blacks won every test in 2008 in which McCaw was the captain.

Clarity of purpose transformed McCaw in 2008. It seemed almost impossible that he could find room to improve given that in 2006 All Blacks coach Graham Henry boldly stated after the Bledisloe Cup victory in Brisbane that he didn't believe anyone could play better than McCaw did that night. But after the All Blacks had beaten the Boks 19–0 in Cape Town, Henry revised his statement. He reckoned McCaw had done the impossible and had played better than he had in Australia two years earlier. That performance in Cape Town came after McCaw had single-handedly transformed the All Blacks from bumbling in Sydney without him to brilliant at Eden Park with him. When the All Blacks secured the Bledisloe Cup in Brisbane, it was again McCaw who was man of the match. And that was the story in Dublin and Cardiff as the All Blacks tried to secure a Grand Slam.

By late November 2008 the findings of the independent review into the World Cup failure felt like they belonged to another era entirely. McCaw was a different sort of captain after the World Cup. He had this incredible influence through the way he played. He made himself the central figure of every test and by doing so he made better decisions as captain. He was more confident and decisive about what he wanted tactically. He was willing to demand more of those around him. He was more willing to engage with referees — not bug them or berate them, but communicate respectfully and build rapport with them. And his leadership group supported him more, said more on the field and helped him develop a wider scope of vision about how various tests were evolving. Maybe most importantly, McCaw's stunning form inspired other senior players such as Dan Carter, Mils Muliaina, Keven Mealamu and Ali Williams to a higher level of performance.

Focusing on his performance transformed McCaw in 2008, and ahead of the final test of the year against England he was happy to say: 'I feel like I'm better now than I was 12 to 18 months ago. Experience definitely makes you stronger, you learn to trust your gut instincts a lot more and be a lot more confident in yourself. It also helps that when you try a few things and they come off, you grow in confidence. But the first thing you have to do as captain is perform. It depends on the type of leadership you are after, but I believe that if you are performing to a high standard then the other stuff, the peripheral stuff, will all follow.

'So if you get into situations and you believe in what you are trying to do, you don't panic, you stay composed. It's not as if you panicked before, it's just you know what works and you get a better feel for what is going on. It's the little things, the subtle things that can make the difference. I have asked myself why it is that I keep playing the game. And it's because I love training all week to test myself against the best. I love the competition and the best part of being captain is that you see how your influence can help other guys perform.'

McCaw would never say he had cracked the captaincy code but he kind of had. He was World Rugby Player of the Year in 2009 and 2010 — and in 2011, with a broken foot, he still managed to play at an extraordinary level. He was shortlisted again in 2012 and probably would have been in 2013 and 2014 but for the fact it seemed the judging panel felt it was important to acknowledge other players. And in his last season, McCaw was as influential and brilliant as he was in 2008, and surely it couldn't be a coincidence that the best captain in the All Blacks' history was also universally recognised as the best player in All Blacks history.

* * *

McCaw was by no means the first All Blacks captain to hit on the idea that effective captaincy was built on form. It became the central theme of Sean Fitzpatrick's captaincy — the mantra to which he clung after a rocky start. Captaincy initially felt like a poisoned chalice for Fitzpatrick when he was appointed in 1992. He knew that coach Laurie Mains had been reluctant to give him the job and he knew that he was not universally popular as there were some who saw him as the unwanted remnants of an Auckland contingent that had been allowed to dominate the All Blacks.

'I have asked myself why it is that I keep playing the game. And it's because I love training all week to test myself against the best. I love the competition and the best part of being captain is that you see how your influence can help other guys perform.'

—RICHIE McCAW

His discomfort intensified after his first test in charge. It was the All Blacks' centenary year and they celebrated by playing a three-test series against a World XV. The first test in Christchurch saw the World XV win 28–14 and Fitzpatrick's confidence drop. He was in a job he didn't want, with a new coach he didn't know and who obviously didn't rate him, and he was trying to unite what was a much-changed All Blacks side which contained a handful of players who, as time would show, weren't up to test football.

'I didn't enjoy it,' says Fitzpatrick. 'It was our centenary year and we played the World XV in the first test match. We were playing against all of these great players and I looked at the All

Blacks and Laurie [Mains] had literally cleaned the house out. Laurie had gone, "Right, we're on a mission here, we need to get rid of some people that may have been good All Blacks but I don't care, they're not good people." I had Grant Fox there and I had John Kirwan and I banked on them. I said, "Look, please tell me how I'm going. Tell me if I am saying too much, or not enough or talking rubbish." I wasn't a great speaker, I'd never really done any preparation in terms of game plan, hadn't really spent too much time with the older guys or the younger guys, and you know, I just kept with my guys to be honest.

'After that first test which we lost, I remember being in Wellington in my room, by myself which I didn't like, and I remember [manager] John Sturgeon knocking on my door. Sturge came in and sat down and he had a cup of tea, and he said, "Fitzy, are you enjoying yourself?" and I said, "Sturge, I am bloody hating it." And he said, "Do you know what you have to do? You need to be the best player on the field, forget about everything else and that will look after itself, just get out there and lead from the front." That was probably the best advice I got from anyone.'

That advice didn't necessarily transform Fitzpatrick but it gave him a focal point to which he would return throughout his captaincy. When he or the team were under pressure, he'd simply remind himself that the best way to deal with it was to produce a compelling personal performance. It's what he did in 1993 when the All Blacks were under siege following a terrible second test against the British & Irish Lions. The All Blacks had edged the first thanks to a dubious penalty, but in Wellington they were destroyed at the lineout by the Lions' giant lock Martin Bayfield. It was a horror show and the 20–7 defeat meant the series was up for grabs in Auckland, and Fitzpatrick, who was singled out by the media for an especially poor performance at Athletic Park, knew he had to lead the team's response. He did that by fixing the lineout and turning an area of weakness in the second test into an area of strength by the third. There was a more dynamic effort by the pack in the loose and Fitzpatrick even managed to score a try himself. It was an emphatic response by the All Blacks and Fitzpatrick led it with his own performance.

* * *

It's not normal for this particular group of teenage boys to be so quiet and attentive. But the situation is not normal. The Rosehill College First XV is being addressed by their most famous old boy — Kieran James Read. It's late May 2017 and Read, who was appointed All Blacks captain in 2016, has just re-signed with New Zealand Rugby for another two years. He wanted to be at his alma mater for the announcement as he's decided, albeit given his test commitments it is a token gesture, to commit his provincial contract to his native Counties Manukau. As interesting and poetic as it is that having grown up in Pukekohe he's decided to nominally finish his career there, the media's real interest is in the state of his broken thumb and whether it will heal in time for him to play the first test against the touring British & Irish Lions.

Read had broken his thumb in late April. It was going to be tight whether his bone would heal in time to lead the All Blacks in that first test at Eden Park. He wasn't going to be passed fit in time to play any rugby before that first test, so he would have to take on the Lions having not played any rugby for seven weeks.

There was an understandable nervousness around the country about that prospect. Read had been late starting the Super Rugby season due to surgery on his wrist and so had only played six games in 2017. That was far from the ideal preparation to play a series that was easily going to be the biggest rugby event in New Zealand since

'Sturge came in and sat down and he had a cup of tea, and he said, "Fitzy, are you enjoying yourself?" and I said, "Sturge, I am bloody hating it." And he said, "Do you know what you have to do? You need to be the best player on the field, forget about everything else and that will look after itself, just get out there and lead from the front." That was probably the best advice I got from anyone.'

—SEAN FITZPATRICK

the 2011 World Cup. The Lions would be bringing 20,000 to 35,000 fans with them and arguably one of the best squads they had ever assembled. They would be coached by a Kiwi, Warren Gatland, and the pressure would be huge for both teams.

Eden Park was a sea of red jerseys come that first test on 24 June. It might as well have been a home game for the Lions and all the pressure, all the weight of expectation was sitting with the All Blacks. They were the world champions. They were the number one-ranked team. They were the home side. The nation was anxious for victory. And in the All Blacks No. 8 shirt was Read, whose bone had healed in time.

But there were doubts about his ability to deliver given his lack of game time. Would he manage even 50 minutes before his lungs were heaving and legs too jellied to support him? Would he be able to inspire those around him if he was toiling to live with the pace and intensity? The All Blacks needed leadership and certainty in such a major test and it had to come from their captain. A nation expected.

Read delivered. The pressure brought the best out of him and he gave the most inspiring performance of his tenure. He was on hand to carry hard into the Lions and there were more than a few tackles that damaged some of their trickier ball runners. His most influential moment, though, came after 54 minutes when the All Blacks had a scrum penalty advantage but somehow Read flipped the ball to Aaron Smith to create a try for Rieko Ioane. That was the killer blow and it capped a brilliant performance by the captain.

As Patrick McKendry of the *New Zealand Herald* put it: 'Kieran Read, the All Blacks skipper who hadn't played any rugby in six weeks, will look back on this pulsating test against the Lions and perhaps believe that this was where he stamped his mark as a leader in every sense. The 31-year-old, playing in his 98th test in his second year as captain, was astonishing at Eden Park tonight in what was probably his greatest test since he played the majority of the 2015 World Cup final against the Wallabies at Twickenham with a sprained ankle.

'With the ball, he carried and carried. Without it, he tackled himself to a standstill, broken thumb be damned. Ask Owen Farrell, the Lions No. 10 who was driven back into the turf by Read in the second half and wasn't in a hurry to get up again.'

This was a seminal moment in Read's captaincy. It established that he had that priceless gift of being able to lift his own performance on the biggest occasions and use his form to inspire others. That first test against the Lions was the exact point in time at which Read fully emerged from the shadow of McCaw. After that game, Read was more secure and certain about his right to lead the team, and it became apparent that while he was respected by his peers before that game, there was increased admiration after it.

Pick any point in All Blacks history and it is likely to prove true that if the captain played well, the team played well. The better a captain plays, the more commanding he becomes and everything else seems to click into place. Form is a captain's best weapon in the quest to win the respect and trust of his peers. When the All Blacks went through the late 1960s on a 17-test unbeaten stretch, captain Brian Lochore established himself as the best No. 8 in the world. When Buck Shelford was in his prime, smashing off the back of the scrum between 1987 and 1990, the All Blacks didn't lose a game.

The All Blacks hammered the Lions, won the Tri Nations and picked up a Grand Slam in 2005 — a year in which captain Tana Umaga provided a midfield masterclass. The All Blacks won their only test series in South Africa in 1996 and never has Fitzpatrick played better. As John Hart says of Fitzpatrick in that series and in particular the last test in Pretoria: 'When you see him on the ground, absolutely shattered like that, recognising what had just happened, it brings it all home. In those last 10 minutes he and Zinzan Brooke were just colossal because that Springboks team threw everything at us in that corner for five or six minutes and those guys kept standing up. Sean's leadership in that situation was graphic to me. I could see it happening on the field, his talk, by what he was doing, he was crashing into the game, and to see him on the ground afterwards, he was stuffed. He was done and there was a fantastic moment because he delivered the dream by, I think, leading by example at the crucial time and the hardest of times.'

And then of course there was McCaw, whose captaincy became so assured when he realised that he needn't worry about anything else other than being his world-class best. He led the All Blacks to two World Cups and a 90 per cent win rate. The micro-analysts will get caught up in the way he communicated, the things he said, the decisions he made and say all of these defined his leadership. But what really defined his captaincy was his brilliant form at openside flanker.

Conversely, it has proven equally the case that when a captain is struggling for form, the team tends to struggle with him. In 1998 Randell was mostly forced out of position at No. 8 and that, combined with the burden of captaincy, had an impact on his form. 'I know I'm not the first person that captaincy did affect my playing,' he says. 'I was worrying about everyone else doing their own jobs, and I wasn't worrying about my core role and that did affect my performance. I had made my mark in the All Blacks as a flanker, but what made it a wee bit harder is that we used to lack at No. 8 so I ended up playing 8 as the fill-in.'

When he settled into the No. 8 role in 1999 and played better as a result, he captained the side more effectively. The All Blacks came into the 1999 World Cup having endured a solitary defeat that year and Randell was a better captain on account of playing better.

In 2018 the All Blacks took on an air of vulnerability. They lost to the Boks in Wellington, then a few weeks later lost to Ireland. In between were titanic struggles against South Africa and England that were both won by a single point.

There was much made at the time that the core problem for the All Blacks was that they couldn't ignite their attack in the face of the rush defence employed by the South Africans, English and Irish. But maybe the bigger problem was that Read, who had undergone major back surgery in early 2018, was playing at about 95 per cent of capacity. He returned to play in July but the medics had warned it would take 18 months for him to recover fully — to rebuild the same power and agility he'd had before damaging a disc. Read wasn't at the top of his game in 2018 and that had a major influence on why the All Blacks were vulnerable.

When he was back at 100 per cent in 2019, the All Blacks were a different team. When he played near his best at Eden Park, thumping into Wallabies with his crunching defence, the All Blacks won 36–0. When he was using his deft handling skills to charge into the Boks and then offload out of the contact in the opening World Cup pool clash, the All Blacks won 23–13. And when he was the chief ball carrier against Ireland in the quarter-final and man of the match, the All Blacks were sensational, winning 46–14. But against England the following week, he barely trained due to a tight calf and then barely featured in a strangely meek and reactive performance by the All Blacks. They were dumped out of the tournament after losing 19–7, and on a night when they needed a heroic effort from their skipper, they didn't get one.

Captaincy is complex and multifaceted and yet it can just as easily be reduced to saying it's as simple as focusing on being the best player. For All Blacks captains of all eras it has rung true that if they play well, they will have captained well.

CHAPTER NINE

HARDEST OF HARD MEN

AS GRANT FOX readied himself to kick off in Dublin, no All Black needed the obvious to be stated that the Irish were a little fired up. Certainly, Buck Shelford, who was captain that day in November 1989, was acutely aware that Ireland were ready to play. The skipper had worked this out for himself when he was targeted by Ireland's captain, Willie Anderson, during the haka. Anderson, like some demented general of an army that were ready to die, persuaded his team-mates to link arms and then advance, in an arrow formation, at the All Blacks as they performed. It ended up with Anderson, literally, in Shelford's face and the two men touching noses at one point. Lansdowne Road had never seen anything like it. The All Blacks hadn't seen anything like it. The game was quite clearly going to explode into life.

Fox kicked off, the ball held in the wind and an All Blacks forward tapped it back. The Irish poured through, lock Donal Lenihan hacked on, and Shelford covering back dived on the ball to be met by the full force of the Irish pack. The referee blew for a scrum and as the bodies lifted, Shelford remained on the turf.

Shelford never remained on the turf. This was the man who, in the infamous 'Battle of Nantes' in 1986, had played on with a ripped scrotum. The French had laid into him at the bottom of a ruck and his testicle had partly unravelled down his leg. Folklore has it that he calmly asked to be stitched up on the side of the field and returned to play. He lost two teeth and still played on. It was a concussion later in the second half that forced him off and Shelford's toughness became legendary around the world.

So, when he stayed down in Dublin, his team-mates signalled anxiously for medical help. 'I thought I had broken my neck,' says Shelford. 'I got caught in a tackle and it crushed something in my neck. Dave Abercrombie was the physio and he got his fingers into me and he pushed and pushed until the muscle released the nerve and I was okay.'

Except Shelford wasn't really okay. He played on, even scored the try that pushed the All Blacks out to a 23–6 lead, but the damage he had received in the first minute was significant. The muscle on the top of his shoulder atrophied after that tackle — and has never grown again. His right shoulder is deformed, lacking definition. That he played on with significant nerve damage was more significant than his feat in France where his testicle had been ripped. He has endured a lifetime of discomfort as a result of playing on that day, but if he was given his time again, he wouldn't have done anything differently.

As Shelford lay in agony after that first collision, it brought to the front of his mind a conversation he'd had with team-mate Zinzan Brooke before the All Blacks had departed for Ireland. There were plenty within the Auckland-heavy All Blacks who wanted Brooke — the ultra-talented No. 8 in possession of a freakish skill-set and a popular figure within his provincial side — to be picked ahead of Shelford. The captain knew this and of course he knew of the provincial power struggle playing out between Auckland and Canterbury at that time.

If Brooke was given just a hint of a chance — a sniff of game time — Shelford couldn't be sure of the consequences. 'Before we went away on tour, Zinny asked if he could talk to me at the dinner we were having with our families,' says Shelford. 'I thought he wanted to talk to me about signing a contract to play league with Manly so we went down to my room. He said to me, "I have been told by John Hart that I am going to be the No. 8 in the test matches." And I said, "Zinny, if you are playing well enough and playing better than me then I will stand down." I thought, *We will see where this runs*. He was playing a different type of game to me and Grizz [Wyllie] liked my game rather than Zinny's game. Zinny was allowed to do what he wanted in the Auckland team, but Alex wanted a No. 8 who was going to carry the ball forward off the back of the scrum. A real tough footballer to get over the gain line, but he [Brooke] was all fancy stuff. I love Zinny, and he is a great footballer, but he didn't have a great tour at all. He was a great person off the field, but his football wasn't that great whether he was playing 6 or No. 8 and he didn't get that test spot.

'When he did finally get the No. 8 position for the World Cup in 1991 he didn't shine at all. And in 1992 Laurie Mains came in and he wanted a No. 8 who could take the ball forward, not fluff around the field. He was an old-school coach like Grizz. Harty had more flamboyant ideas. Everyone was picking that Harty would take over the All Blacks in 1992. But he didn't even get a look-in as an assistant coach. NZR said they didn't want either of them [Wyllie or Hart] because of the shit that had gone down, the power struggle. So it wasn't Zinny, but possibly the system, Harty, pushing their agenda through the players, trying to get Zinny in there in 1989 to change the game to play like Auckland.'

But overriding everything — the pain, the power struggle, the fear of giving Brooke a chance to steal the No. 8 jersey — was this overwhelming need to portray strength as captain. Playing through extreme pain was very much part of the gig in Shelford's view. This was an era when no one gave up their place in the team. He was also conscious of the challenge Ireland had made. Anderson had come after him during the haka, so how would it look if the All Blacks captain only managed 30 seconds on the field? An already hyped crowd would have gone ballistic seeing Shelford forced off that early and the psychological boost for Ireland would have been huge. He wasn't going to give them the satisfaction.

He held this sense that an All Blacks captain had to be tougher than that. He had to project an aura of invincibility and be prepared to haul himself through any physical pain. That was the job. The role demanded an element of bravery that bordered on madness. There were different rules when you were the All Blacks captain — a different threshold when it came to being hurt. Maybe the respective captains of the Wallabies or Springboks would surrender to a permanently damaged neck — but not the captain of the All Blacks.

'Today's era is quite different because you are playing with 23 players,' he says. 'In my day you weren't. You were playing the whole game and you didn't give it away for anything. You would play through anything. If we broke fingers, you would stay on the field. Tape the bastards up and get on with it. Six or seven stitches … you play on. Concussion … captains wouldn't let you go off the field. Jock [captain Hobbs] wouldn't let me go off in Nantes when I was concussed. Today Jock would not have done that and nor would I. It was just how leadership was back then.'

* * *

One of Edinburgh's lazy winds was whipping across the field at the Peffermill sports ground in November 2017. A lazy wind, as locals relish telling visitors, is one that doesn't bother to go round you. New Zealand's media contingent covering the All Blacks' end-of-year tour had been battling that wind for the better part of an hour. There was nowhere to escape from it, no shelter to be found anywhere, so it was a case of digging in and seeing out the time, waiting for the All Blacks to finally arrive and begin training.

'In my day you … were playing the whole game and you didn't give it away for anything. You would play through anything. If we broke fingers, you would stay on the field. Tape the bastards up and get on with it. Six or seven stitches … you play on. Concussion … captains wouldn't let you go off the field. … It was just how leadership was back then.'

—BUCK SHELFORD

The session had been delayed. The All Blacks had pushed things back an hour and the delay was intriguing. The All Blacks didn't normally change their routine. That's why, when the squad did finally emerge into the gloom of an Edinburgh day in which the sun had barely managed to lift itself much above the ramparts of the city's iconic castle, the media were furiously scanning to see if someone was missing or heavily strapped. Everyone, though, was present and correct.

Training finished without a drama, but then came the text that the team naming had been delayed by two hours. It would be at 6 pm not 4 pm. Again, this was unusual, and again this had the media working all sorts of theories as to why the All Blacks were continuing to change their plans ahead of playing Scotland. The team, when it was revealed, would likely explain all. But it didn't. There were no surprises in the selection. The big names were all there. There were no heavyweight omissions. The delay was unexplained.

The answer finally presented itself at the post-match press conference. The All Blacks had won 22–17 in a game that required them to dig deeper than they imagined they would have to. The Scots had them rattled in the final 10 minutes and the All Blacks, who had spent 20 minutes of the game a man down due to being shown two yellow cards, had emptied themselves to survive that final quarter. No one did more to protect the lead than captain Kieran Read. His ability to make telling tackles was crucial. He threw himself at everything and used all of his experience to stretch the legality of his performance.

It was an industrial effort by the captain — effective, heroic even — and as he sat in front of the media, it became obvious how much of a toll it had taken. Read was twisting in his chair. He couldn't get comfortable. His voice was shaky. He was distracted. He was exhausted and he was in agony. Read had played through the pain barrier. The delay in naming the team had been about

All Blacks captain Graham Mourie makes a break and is chased by England lock
Maurice Colclough at Twickenham in 1979. (PA Images Archive)

All Blacks halfback David Kirk makes it to the try-line against France in the 1987
World Cup final. It is the moment the captain knew his side was going to win the
tournament. (Bob Thomas/Bob Thomas Sports Photography)

All Blacks captain Sean Fitzpatrick celebrates after the second test match between South Africa Springboks and New Zealand which sealed the All Blacks test series victory in August 1996 in Pretoria. (David Rogers/Hulton Archive)

Justin Marshall never captained the All Blacks again after this game against England in November 1997 which ended in a 26-all draw and prevented New Zealand from posting the perfect season. (Clive Brunskill/Getty Images Sport)

James Dalton of South Africa scores the match-winning try during the Tri-Nations match against New Zealand in August 1998 in Durban. South Africa won the match 24–23. (David Rogers/Getty Images Sport)

Taine Randell was stunned when France bounced back in the second half to
beat the All Blacks 43–31 in the 1999 World Cup semi-final at Twickenham.
(David Rogers/Getty Images Sport)

The British and Irish Lions tour manager, Bill Beaumont (left), sits with All Blacks captain Tana Umaga at the reception held at the New Zealand Parliament Building in June 2005 in Wellington. (David Rogers/Getty Images Sport)

All Blacks captain Richie McCaw and his deputy, Kieran Read, work together during the captain's run at Ellis Park before playing South Africa in the 2013 Rugby Championship. (David Rogers/Getty Images Sport)

After finding themselves 19–0 down after as many minutes, many of the All Blacks playing against Ireland in Dublin in 2013 were looking at captain Richie McCaw for inspiration. (David Rogers/Getty Images Sport)

Richie McCaw punched the air in Dublin in 2013 after Aaron Cruden, at the second attempt, converted Ryan Crotty's try to give the All Blacks a 24–22 victory and the perfect season they were chasing. (Peter Muhly/AFP)

The 82,000-strong crowd in London greeted this game-winning try by All Blacks captain Richie McCaw in 2014 with a relentless and resounding chorus of booing and jeering. (EMPICS Sport/PA Images)

All Blacks' Kieran Read remonstrates with referee Romain Poite of France, after Poite awards a scrum rather than a penalty in the last minute during the third test match between the All Blacks and the British & Irish Lions in July 2017 in Auckland. (David Rogers/Getty Images Sport)

Kieran Read makes a critical break against the Wallabies in Dunedin in 2017. It led to a late try by Beauden Barrett to save the test and secure the Bledisloe Cup. (AFP Contributor/AFP)

Sam Cane poses for pictures on the family farm in May 2020, the day after he was announced as the new All Blacks captain. Cane had captained the All Blacks on three previous occasions. (Michael Bradley/Getty Images Sport)

him … a disc in his back had been troubling him for a few weeks and it had flared after the first test of the tour against France. No one was sure when he had arrived in Edinburgh whether it would settle enough for him to play. When he got through training and didn't react, he was named, but he was sore.

Really sore when he played at Murrayfield and yet no one would ever have known until he walked off and the adrenaline drained and, without it, he was left to feel the full impact of the damage. The disc was bulging to the point where it was pressing on his nerves and transferring down his leg. He would need major corrective surgery when he returned to New Zealand and the recovery time was going to be seven months, although the medics warned it would really take about 18 for him to fully recover.

He travelled with the squad to their final match of the tour in Cardiff and stood on the side of the training field at Sophia Gardens, barely able to stand. The injury had consumed him by that point — rendered him unable to even put his shoes on without help — and he couldn't possibly play. After the All Blacks had beaten Wales 33–18 without Read, coach Steve Hansen revealed that the skipper was in a bad way and had spent most of Thursday and Friday bedridden. To see Read so damaged in Cardiff was to realise how tough he had done it in Edinburgh and just how able he was to play through extraordinary pain.

He stayed on the field against Scotland because his young side needed him. They had suffered a horrendous year with injuries which had seen them lose veterans such as Owen Franks, Brodie Retallick, Dane Coles, Ben Smith and Jerome Kaino — all of whom were in the leadership group. The skipper had a massive role to play and he was going to play it — damaged back or not.

It was no longer an era when players never came off or protected their positions the way they had in the amateur period, but despite that, Read's mind-set as captain was no different to Shelford's — he was just as sure that the skipper was held to different standards.

* * *

Rugby is a hard game played by hard men and around the world there are stories of extreme valour: of players soldiering on with all sorts of injuries. But even in this world of hard men doing hard things, All Blacks captains have stood out as being among the hardest. They have seemingly felt compelled to push themselves more than others. It has never been spoken about publicly. All Blacks captains haven't said in the wake of extreme feats of human endurance why they felt they had to battle on. It certainly hasn't been forced upon them — no coach or manager has ever asked an All Blacks captain to endanger their health or well-being. And yet various All Blacks captains have felt this need to push themselves beyond the parameters of what most would consider feasible.

Shelford and Read held expectations that were neither formally set nor specifically passed on. They simply assumed it was their duty as captain to play on regardless. That same attitude was held by Sean Fitzpatrick and Richie McCaw. The former set a world record of playing 63 consecutive tests which was testament to his durability and capacity to absorb relentless punishment. Fitzpatrick is the first to agree that he pushed the boundaries as captain. He was quite brilliant at irritating the opposition — be it by flopping over the ball, lying on the wrong side of a ruck, or generally interfering with the supply of possession. He was also a notorious chatterbox, freely offering advice to opponents and, as Irish prop Nick Popplewell discovered, also to referees: 'They were so good at that. Referees always gave them any rub of the ball going and you had Fitzpatrick basically refereeing the match anyway. That's the way it was.'

As a result of the way he played, Fitzpatrick often came in for special physical treatment. He was regularly targeted, some opponents becoming overwhelmed with frustration. One of those was Springboks prop Johan le Roux in 1994, who bit Fitzpatrick's ear. It was an ugly incident that saw the All Blacks captain dripping in blood with part of his soft cartilage on the outer rim missing. The skipper didn't react much other than to inform referee Brian Stirling what had happened. After that, he calmly had it bandaged so he could continue.

There was no way a despicable act like that would remove the captain from the field. In 1997 Fitzpatrick was stamped in the face by André Venter. The Springboks flanker saw the All Blacks skipper at the back of a ruck and couldn't resist — smashing his boot down on Fitzpatrick's chin. It was another horrific incident that saw Venter red-carded and the All Blacks captain barely react.

Fitzpatrick's durability was legendary. He was the man who couldn't be hurt; couldn't ever be dented or persuaded to vacate his beloved No. 2 jersey. He saw that toughness as a big part of his leadership and it also shaped the careers of those unfortunate enough to be ranked behind him in the All Blacks. Warren Gatland famously never got to play a test when he was the All Blacks reserve hooker as Fitzpatrick was famously never injured nor ever came off the field. It was the same for Norm Hewitt — stuck on the bench for an eternity, because no matter how much punishment Fitzpatrick took, he would find a way to keep going. A combination of toughness, durability and sheer bloody wilfulness made Fitzpatrick the captain he was. It was another means for him to earn the respect he needed.

And then of course there was McCaw, who played through the 2011 World Cup with a broken bone in his foot and three years later got through two tests against England with broken ribs. The incredible thing about 2011 was the way he was able to hide the extent of the damage from his team-mates, coaches, the public and media. Everyone knew he had an injury problem as he was rested for the pool games against Japan and Canada. But no one had any inkling that the surgery he'd had earlier in the year had not been successful and his right foot was in fact in horrible shape.

He need painkillers and the medicinal power of adrenaline just to be able to get his boot on without writhing in agony. As he revealed in his biography: 'I can't walk properly most of the time and I've got to be careful to mask the worst effects of the injury, not just from the media but also from all the people constantly coming and going from the hotel. Not to mention the team and the coaches. I don't want people worrying about me; I want to give the impression I'm always going to play. I'm confident that even if I don't train at all, I can still go out and perform. I'm going to keep playing on it as long as I can stand up and do my job. … I've got to be optimistic. And sometimes, towards the end of the week, when the oral anti-inflams and Panadols and a lot of rest have done their work, I can almost convince myself it's just a soft-tissue injury. "Nah, I'll be fine," I keep telling anyone who'll listen, media, team-mates, coaches, myself. "Just can't train because it'll get a bit sore, but I'm ready to go. I'm good to go." And I am. I believe it.'

In 2014 he damaged his ribs in the second of three tests against England but played on. When he was examined after the game in Dunedin, the team doctor diagnosed it as bruising and McCaw played the following week in Hamilton. Whether his ribs were broken in Dunedin or not, no one can be sure, but after 80 minutes in Hamilton, they definitely were. But again, no one would ever have known how much pain McCaw was in or that he was even injured.

Precedent has most definitely been set when it comes to what the All Blacks captain must be able to endure. Shelford, Read, Fitzpatrick and McCaw all managed to play through extreme pain and have essentially made that a requirement of the job. It is now expected that the All Blacks captain will only leave the field or not be available for selection in extraordinary circumstances. Being tough wins respect and increases the authority of the skipper. The job is effectively about standing taller than the rest; about being seen as worthy; and in a hard game, the All Blacks captain has to be the hardest.

They need durability and a sense of invincibility, which bodes well for Sam Cane, who broke his neck in Pretoria in 2018 and was able to stand up and walk off the field. He returned to play seven months later and so has already proven his capacity to endure; his ability to withstand pain that would have broken others.

CHAPTER TEN

WORKING-CLASS MAN

IT'S NEARLY AN hour since the game finished and despite the fact that those involved have already showered, done their best to rehydrate and refuel, they are still dripping with sweat. It's no wonder. The temperature is 31 degrees in the early evening and there is no air conditioning in any of the function rooms at Apia Park, or if there is, it is doing little to offset the effects of the heat and near 100 per cent humidity.

Jerome Kaino, the fabled All Blacks hard man who was born in Samoa, is one of those players whose thermostat hasn't quite reset, and he is a mix of emotions as he talks to a media contingent that is struggling just as much with the heat, having only sat passively in it for the last two hours.

Kaino knows he has banked a legacy memory — been part of a historic test match which saw the All Blacks play in Samoa for the first time in history. He's elated that the game and the build-up brought so much to his country of birth and relieved that the All Blacks managed to claw their way to a 25–16 victory. A little bit of him, though, is disappointed: collectively the All

Blacks didn't gel, or play particularly well, and Kaino struggled to impose himself. He managed 62 minutes in the oppressive conditions, which was a fair effort. Except he knows that for much of those 62 minutes he was chasing the game, toiling to get where he should have been as his lungs were heaving and legs heavy as he tried to almost literally cut a path through air that felt as thick as soup.

The prevailing emotion he's feeling, however, is a sense of awe and bewilderment at what he witnessed from his captain. Richie McCaw went for the full 80 minutes and he covered his usual almost 10 kilometres. He ran and ran, virtually oblivious to the heat and humidity. He seemed immune to the conditions as he cleaned out rucks, chased defenders and popped up as if he had cloned himself. There were 29 players who battled to make any kind of impression in Apia and one who owned the contest. 'I watched him when I was on the bench after I came off,' said Kaino. 'That guy is amazing. I don't know how he does it and my respect for him is enormous. We were in awe of him.'

Kaino, if he was to be honest, did know how McCaw managed to produce such a performance in extreme conditions. Having come into the All Blacks as a 20-year-old in 2004 before winning his first cap in 2006, Kaino had spent the better part of a decade training and playing alongside his captain. They were both loose forwards, so much of their conditioning work had been similar; the coaches' expectations about their athleticism and physicality were similar, too, and while Kaino, having been a bit wild in his early twenties, became disciplined and committed to his training and developed into a world-class player, he knew he wasn't in the same league as McCaw.

The standards McCaw set were almost unreachable for everyone else. Partly because McCaw was blessed with a natural capacity to endure and push his physical boundaries. But mostly it was because, as captain, he was determined to set standards to which everyone else had to aspire. His philosophy that the captain had to be the best player worked back into his thinking that to be the best player, he had to train harder than everyone else. His status as the fittest in the squad had to be undisputed — morph into All Blacks folklore almost — so as new players would arrive in the team aware of the legend and already determined to meet expectations.

For McCaw, it wasn't about occasionally leading the way. It was about *always* leading the way. At the 2007 World Cup the All Blacks became obsessed about their fitness, and having held a training camp in Corsica en route, they still had another 10 days to kill in Marseilles before they played their first game. Their hotel, in the salubrious suburb of Palm Beach, was set into a cliff, providing unrestricted views of the Mediterranean, with a white-sand beach within an easy stroll. There was also an infinity swimming pool, so perhaps wary that such a luxurious setting could lull the players into holiday mode, the All Blacks coaches organised for the first few days of training to be tough but different.

The players were put on bikes and paddle boats and they were asked to run in what became, effectively, a modified triathlon. It was supposed to be fun as well as tough — a chance to bond the squad and bring them closer. There was no sign that McCaw saw it that way. His only goal was to push himself to breaking point and beat everyone else. Which he did. He was a man possessed on the bike leg, and when it came to running in the blazing heat of a late French summer, no one got near him.

This was the story of his captaincy: his work ethic admired and respected by a peer group that were inspired to match it, although mostly conscious they never could. As proof of sorts as to how ingrained in legend McCaw's work ethic became, four years later in the build-up to the 2011 World Cup, veteran lock Brad Thorn was the last forward still going as the squad completed the dreaded yo-yo test at Waitakere Stadium in Auckland. McCaw wasn't doing it as he was resting his famously broken foot, but Thorn wanted to beat him anyway. The yo-yo test is an aerobic challenge where participants run back and forth between two points, but the time they have to do it gets progressively shorter. As Thorn started to reach his limit, he yelled out in his gravelly voice, 'What's McCaw's record?'

When the All Blacks won the 2011 World Cup a month or so later, Thorn collapsed in a heap on the Eden Park turf. He was physically drained and emotionally broken from the effort and realisation of what had been achieved, and as the tears flowed, it was likely that at least one of them was dedicated to the memory of beating McCaw's record that day.

And just as likely is that McCaw felt equally proud because his desire to set the highest standards was not driven by any egotistical need. It was the captaincy that demanded he lead the way, but as much as his almost insane work ethic was about proving his worth to hold that particular office, it was also about inspiring others to reach greater heights. The wider All Blacks ethos throughout McCaw's time as captain was continual improvement. Rugby evolves and the All Blacks' opponents continually find ways to improve. Standing still means going backwards and so McCaw was attempting to sustain a virtuous cycle where his work ethic would earn the respect of his team-mates and their respect for him would instil in them a desire to be fitter, faster, stronger, leaner and more skilled. And in turn these qualities would enable the All Blacks to play better; to stay ahead of the chasing pack and play the sort of rugby to which they aspired.

'We never said … "I'm going to do this to work hard for Richie." No, it wasn't that,' says Ali Williams, who played at the 2003, 2007 and 2011 World Cups with McCaw. 'And I think that's the beauty of his captaincy and his leadership — it was about empowering people to do things for themselves, not because of him, or let him down, or let the coach down. We all collectively, I wouldn't say followed, but respected and honoured and admired. I would say we idolised the guy in such a unique way because of the mental shift he made. I'm not talking about doing the work physically, but the mental work to become even better. That was where the massive shift was.'

* * *

Wallabies coach Ewen McKenzie, as he often did, had left the coaching box to watch the last four minutes of the third Bledisloe Cup match of 2014 from the tunnel at Suncorp Stadium. Unbeknown to anyone but the Rugby Australia board, McKenzie had tendered his resignation earlier that day. An internal scandal had engulfed him, but as he made his way down to the tunnel, he had the satisfaction at least of believing he was going to sign off with a victory. The Wallabies led 28–22, and with Brisbane having been gripped by a heatwave, surely not even the All Blacks could muster the energy to pull off a late comeback when they had already given so much.

'We never said ... "I'm going to do this to work hard for Richie." ... And I think that's the beauty of his captaincy and his leadership — it was about empowering people to do things for themselves, not because of him, or let him down, or let the coach down. We all collectively, I wouldn't say followed, but respected and honoured and admired.'

—ALI WILLIAMS

A half-smile, more of a disbelieving smirk, ran across McKenzie's face when he saw All Blacks replacement first-five Colin Slade fail to kick out a penalty with two minutes remaining. Slade's mistake meant the All Blacks didn't have the attacking lineout on the Wallabies' five-metre line that they should have. Instead they were on defence, having to find a way to tackle their way back into possession. It was an impossible task and yet there were the likes of Charlie Faumuina and Patrick Tuipulotu throwing their enormous frames into contact to hit Wallabies attackers with everything they had. Brodie Retallick joined them in the trenches, eking out the last of whatever he had, while Kieran Read and Sam Cane scrambled to get over each tackle to try to legally win the ball.

It should have been hopeless, and yet a full minute after the final hooter, All Blacks midfielder Malakai Fekitoa crashed over for a try and Slade atoned for his earlier mistake by nailing the winning conversion. McKenzie's veneer of calm cracked. He couldn't believe that once again the All Blacks, against all the odds, had found a way to win a game they had no business winning. They had been outplayed for most of the test. They had been loose, sloppy even, for most of the match. But what they had was heart and commitment: a will to win that saw them, to a man, dig into their deepest places in those final four minutes. Their collective work ethic saved them as they salvaged the game not with skill and enterprise, but with graft and toil. They won because they had enough energy to win: enough will to keep going when the tank read empty.

If ever there was a victory testament to the training standards McCaw had driven, it was that 29–28 win against Australia in 2014. The All Blacks had drawn 12-all in Brisbane two years previously. That night they didn't have the ability to dig themselves to victory. In 2014, though, they were fitter, stronger and capable of giving more. They could apply themselves to the unglamorous chores of tackling, cleaning out and foraging for longer. Interviewing long-serving All Blacks conditioning coach Nic Gill in late 2014, he talked about how there had been a gradual process of increasing the squad's training load to the point where, across the board, they were individually 30 per cent fitter, faster and stronger than they had been at the 2011 World Cup. To reach those improved standards took courage and sacrifice, but he said it also required someone to consistently lead the way. 'Everyone has good days and bad days,' said Gill. 'There are days when athletes just feel a little off. Everyone except Richie, that is. He never has an off day. He seems to be able to push himself to the limit every time he trains.'

There was another difference between the All Blacks in Brisbane 2012 and the All Blacks in Brisbane 2014. A number of new, younger players had come into the side after the 2011 World Cup and were feeling their way into the international game in that first encounter. But by 2014 they were more experienced and more aware of what level of commitment was expected. And what had made them aware was seeing McCaw in action for themselves. The likes of young Aucklanders Steven Luatua and Charles Piutau had grown up idolising McCaw from the comfort of their lounges, and while they thought they had a handle on what he was all about, that changed after playing alongside him.

The awakening for Luatua came in Tokyo 2013. 'In that game against Japan I went to make an assisted tackle and I saw this black jersey come flying in. And I look … it is Richie. That happened a few times — he just flies in. That's the way he plays and it is inspiring. When Japan were trying to score in the last play, I was making a tackle in the corner and Richie came in over the top. I definitely wouldn't have been able to make it without him. You can be as fit as you want but that comes from the inside. The desire and the way he plays — that lifts us. It is pretty special being able to play alongside him.'

It was the All Blacks' 26–19 victory in Paris a week later when Piutau became aware that McCaw was playing at a different level to him. 'In the last few minutes of that game I noticed how many times he was making tackles and getting back up,' said Piutau. 'You hear so much about him, but to be alongside him, I definitely felt his presence.'

* * *

McCaw's work ethic was another pillar in his captaincy. He commanded respect through the way he played, through the way he conducted himself, and through the way he constantly strove to be the best at whatever he did. He was always the first man off the bus at training. On game day, he was first off the bus. It's where he always wanted to be. Where he felt he always had to be.

He was famously never late for any meetings. He was never involved in any off-field scandal. He was always well prepared for whatever task was at hand and every minute of every day he was working on something. He never let a moment pass him by and his conduct was impeccable.

He drove the highest standards across the board, worked harder than anyone else, and while it was inspiring, it was also hugely intimidating. Assistant coach Ian Foster noted in 2019 that McCaw never meant to intimidate any young All Blacks, but his reputation was such that it was almost inevitable new players to the squad wouldn't feel relaxed around the skipper. Even Kaino, a bruising hulk of a man, who played for years in the back row with McCaw, spent much of his early career feeling inadequate in comparison. The biggest goal in Kaino's career was earning the respect of McCaw and he didn't feel he did that until 2011 when he played every minute of every test at the World Cup.

At the same World Cup, star outside backs Cory Jane and Israel Dagg felt the shame of failing to live up to the expected standards. In the week of the quarter-final they ended up in a horrible mess after taking sleeping pills and energy drinks, which then led to them going out to the local pub where they necked a few beers obviously intoxicated. The story about their antics broke on the morning of the game and Jane — Dagg was injured and not playing — was a tearful mess afterwards. He had played brilliantly on the night. His work under the high ball was immaculate and his decision-making superb. He made good use of all possession that came his way and was the undisputed man of the match. But facing media in the mixed zone, the team's self-styled joker was blinking back the tears. What had upset him the most was knowing that he had let the captain down. He had failed his team-mates — but it was the fact that he had failed McCaw which really hurt. All McCaw said publicly was: 'I think if we're realistic about putting everything we can into winning this tournament, it is about making good decisions.' But as every child knows, a disappointed parent is much worse than an angry parent.

To be so driven required constant mental application and this, as Ali Williams says, was where McCaw stood out as different to previous captains. His physical work was underpinned by his psychological strength and he spent as much time working with mental skills experts Gilbert Enoka and Ceri Evans as he did working on his conditioning and skills. His ability to stay on task, to shift relentlessly from one job to the next, ticking each preparation box every day of every test week, left his peers in awe.

Mils Muliaina, who came into the All Blacks in 2003, saw his appreciation for McCaw rise to new heights in 2009. An injury to McCaw in Super Rugby meant that Muliaina, who captained the Chiefs to the final of Super Rugby in Pretoria that year, received a phone call from Graham Henry after the game. The Chiefs had been well beaten by the Bulls so it was a curious moment for Muliaina to be told he was going to captain the All Blacks in tests against France and Italy.

Making his life harder was that other senior players were also injured and the young side he captained in the first test of the year lost to France in Dunedin. It was an ugly performance, full of poor decision-making that signalled the general inexperience of the squad. It was in the build-up to the second test in Wellington that Muliaina discovered just how tough it is to be captain of the All Blacks.

'I've never experienced anything like that in my life,' he says. 'I remember rolling into Wellington after the first test loss and the management guys were like, "We're going to go to Parliament" and they were like, "Now, you've got to go now, you've gotta go and sort your speech out" and stuff like that. Fuck, I'd never spoken in front of anyone in my life. Here I was under massive pressure because we'd just lost the first test, having to then prioritise my week. How was I going to mentally prepare and tick my boxes? I was shitting myself over a bloody speech in Parliament and meeting the Prime Minister and then you're like that's Monday and Tuesday gone, Wednesday's your day off. Thursday, fuck, I'm shitting bloody bricks that I haven't got my own physical prep right and I'm supposed to be preparing a team. So how is my team actually going?

'And that's when I really got a grasp about why Richie was such a special leader. Because you have to be so focused on what you're doing because there is so much of everything else that you don't realise until you are in that position. And this was at a time when we were struggling. You don't begin to realise that there are going to be all these other expectations around your job as a captain and that's where I have total respect for the way Richie captained and the way the other captains have done their job. In some ways, once it was over, I was like shit I'm glad it's not my role. Perhaps maybe if I was prepped in that way, but I suppose the expectation was I would just pick things up and it would be okay.'

* * *

McCaw's work ethic and ability to uphold the highest standards in all aspects of his job wasn't unique. What set him apart was that he pervaded more deeply into the psyche of the team than any other captain. He inspired a generation of players to take greater responsibility for all aspects of their performance. He played 148 tests and led the All Blacks to two World Cup titles, but his real legacy was the culture of self-responsibility he instilled and the way he enabled his peers to truly see what it meant to be a high-performance athlete.

What he did was raise the level rather than reinvent the wheel, as captains throughout time have recognised that their quest to win trust, respect and admiration is all-consuming. All captains have recognised that they have an obligation to be exemplary when it comes to punctuality. To uphold dress codes. To be the first one on the training park and the last one off it. They have all recognised that they will be judged for the things they say, the way they treat others and the aura they exude.

Kirkpatrick's peers respected the way he quietly went about his business. Bryan Williams says that Andy Leslie earned the respect of his peers not just because of how he played at No. 8, but for the way he conducted himself. 'For being the man he is,' says Williams.

Shelford, given his military background, had the force of personality on and off the field to demand that standards were upheld. Perhaps as evidence of that, he can recall a year after he was dropped, how horrified he was to see how the All Blacks presented at the official World Cup dinner. 'There was this power struggle between the two unions and the two coaches Wyllie and Hart. And it didn't really work for the All Blacks. I went to the first dinner and the closing dinner and the All Blacks were terrible. They were pissed. They hadn't even ironed their bloody shirts and they looked fucking terrible. They were a completely separate team — split right down the guts.'

Anton Oliver, who felt marginalised as captain when John Mitchell took over as coach in September 2001, wrote in his biography that he was appalled at how quickly standards dropped on the end-of-year tour to Scotland, Ireland and Argentina. He recalled that after a heavy drinking session — driven and run by Mitchell — the squad gathered the next morning at Edinburgh Airport and he found himself staring at the sticky beer stains on the shoes of fullback Ben Blair. The All Blacks were in their No. 1s, flying the flag for the country, and there, plain to see, was the evidence of their excess on a young player's shoes. All around him players were dishevelled, certain to score poorly had they been on parade.

The importance of keeping standards was partly why John Hart was so keen for Sean Fitzpatrick to continue after the 1995 World Cup. He wanted Fitzpatrick not just because of his command of the No. 2 jersey, test experience and ability to guide the team on the field. He wanted Fitzpatrick's self-discipline and understanding of the All Blacks' values to guide others. Hart would be the first coach in the professional era and he knew that Fitzpatrick understood professionalism despite never having been a professional.

He knew this because he had seen how Fitzpatrick and others had conducted themselves as part of the great Auckland team of the 1980s. 'We used to have some simple rules,' says Hart. 'Three rules. Dress, on-field discipline, timekeeping. We trained at 5.30 at Eden Park. And I can still remember that at 5.29 David Kirk pulls up in his car. He is sprinting across to get into his gear. He's a doctor, he's been at the hospital, and his whole commitment was that you have got to be out there at 5.30. That was life skills. Those guys were all mature, living life, and that's why I was lucky to have Sean as my captain in the All Blacks.'

The impact of Fitzpatrick was felt by all those around him, and a huge reason the All Blacks only lost one test between 1996 and 1997 was the professional standards the captain drove. 'He was incredibly professional,' says former team-mate Justin Marshall. 'At the time I entered the environment he wasn't looking to finish but his knee finished him. His mind was still raring to go. He was still at the top of his game. The thing I noticed about him, was that he had reached the age where he was thinking hard about how he could stay ahead of the younger generation.

'In general he was a talented player who played the role differently. He saw how the younger players were coming through and it was a personal challenge that he stay ahead of them in the way he trained and the mind-set he adopted.

'He was one of the most dedicated trainers I have ever seen. I wouldn't say he was a gym rat by any means. He wasn't in there going nuts because he was all about looking after his body. Still getting good gains but looking after himself. It was when it came to team runs and training that his demands and expectancy levels were incredibly high. Mistakes for him were unacceptable.

He was of the mind-set that when we were doing those sorts of things, that was emulating a test match. That rubbed off on me. I have had criticism from a lot of my former team-mates — both at the Crusaders and All Blacks — where they have said, "Bloody Marshall, he's such an angry trainer." Wyatt Crockett told me that he dropped the ball at training once and the look I gave him, he said he was actually scared. What makes the All Blacks the world's best is that we train like we play. You don't just drop the ball and turn your back. I carried that right through my career and that was all down to Fitzy.'

CHAPTER ELEVEN

HEAT OF THE BATTLE

KURTLEY BEALE, HIS face stained with blood, boots the ball jubilantly into the crowd and then yells to the heavens as his Wallabies team-mates grab and wrestle with him to say well done. The veteran fullback has just scored under the posts to put Australia one point ahead in the second Bledisloe Cup clash of 2017. The crowd at Forsyth Barr Stadium in Dunedin can hardly believe it. A week ago, in Sydney, the All Blacks had scored 54 points in 54 minutes and here they are now, with just three minutes left, staring at defeat.

They haven't lost to Australia in New Zealand since 2001 but this feels like the night that will change. There is a determination about the Wallabies that says they want to make history. They look ready to finally close out a big test in New Zealand.

As Bernard Foley prepares to take the conversion, All Blacks captain Kieran Read is in the middle of the tight circle his players have formed. He's animated and intense, but not wild and angry. Visibly, at least, he looks controlled. His tone, as his team-mates will later reveal, is calm and assured. There is even an underlying confidence — certainly no one can detect any panic. The captain is not demanding more effort. He's not admonishing his team-mates for the tackles they missed in the build-up to Beale's try.

What he's doing is explaining exactly what he wants to happen next. He tells Beauden Barrett to kick off high and short — to make it contestable. He tasks himself with trying to win the ball. If he's successful, the plan will be to probe for space close to the ruck. To keep possession and keep going forward. If they do that, options will present themselves.

Barrett puts the kick-off precisely where he was asked and Read wins the ball in the air. The All Blacks probe left and right and they make it to the Wallabies' 22. Halfback TJ Perenara passes right to Richie Mo'unga, who flips it to Scott Barrett. The big lock cleverly delays a pass to Read, who is storming back on the angle and cuts through the defence. He passes to Perenara, who immediately releases to Beauden Barrett, who storms under the posts to win the game. It was brilliant rugby. Clinical rugby that was only possible because Read had given precise instructions about what he wanted. Under pressure, he was calm and controlled — made sure everyone understood their tasks rather than the consequences of not doing them. That calm allowed clear heads to make good decisions and the All Blacks were able to trust their skills and use them to win the game.

It's a big moment for Read. It's one of the few times in his captaincy that the team has been under real pressure so late in the game and his ability to cope with it has been truly examined. Every captain hopes they will react well in tight situations, but no one ever knows until they actually have to do it. The way Read responded leads many to draw further comparisons between him and previous captain Richie McCaw.

Many media analysts portrayed Read as a McCaw clone long before the former took over the captaincy in 2016. Superficially, at least, there were obvious similarities. They were both schooled outside Canterbury but gravitated to play their professional rugby there. They were both loose forwards, both their mothers were school teachers, and neither loved the fact that many of their team-mates, particularly in the forwards, didn't play in plain black boots.

Between 2012 and 2015 it was custom to see McCaw get off the team bus first at training, closely followed by Read. McCaw would be first out to start training, closely followed by Read. When an exercise required players to pair up, it was Read and McCaw. The general impression and prevailing view became they were one and the same: that they were similar people and therefore Read would be a similar captain.

It wasn't quite like that, though. They weren't all that similar as people. Read, having grown up in multicultural South Auckland, had a broader social range. He was naturally inclusive, better able to connect with younger players and those from a Pacific Island background. Read was married with three children and so more empathetic towards those team-mates with families and how they would be feeling being away from them on long tours. He was possibly more gregarious, equipped with a natural humour and greater sense of fun that made him more approachable, less intimidating. McCaw was more conservative, shy, quiet and less able to relate to those from different backgrounds. He wasn't a loner — he and team-mate Conrad Smith would binge-watch cerebral TV content such as *The Wire* — but he was comfortable in his own company.

Read never particularly liked that the media saw him as being so similar to McCaw. But there was one similarity he hoped would be acknowledged. Read had different ideas to McCaw about inclusion and how to engage younger players in the All Blacks, but on the field the former wanted to be like the latter. Read was a huge admirer of McCaw's on-field captaincy style. He liked the calm demeanour of McCaw, the way he communicated clearly and concisely under pressure and focused on the task. Read wanted to be a similar on-field presence and the 35–29 victory in Dunedin was a reassuring moment: conclusive evidence that he had that same ability to manage the troops through a crisis. But a year later, playing in Wellington against South Africa, it became apparent that Read was missing one part of the captaincy jigsaw — that he wasn't, yet, the same on-field leader as the man he'd replaced.

* * *

The All Blacks are precisely where they need to be to win the game. The hooter has gone and they trail South Africa by two points. But they are in possession and they are under South Africa's posts. The tryline is so close they can smell it. They are inches from it, and having scored two previous tries in the last 10 minutes where one of the All Blacks forwards managed to burrow over from close range, several attempts are made in the dying seconds to repeat the feat. But while the Boks are tired, they have held out for 13 phases.

There's no need for the All Blacks to be despondent, though, because the ball is safely at the back of the ruck. If TJ Perenara takes his time, he can fire the pass to Beauden Barrett, who will be no more than 15 metres from the posts. Bang in front. It's about as simple as it gets in the not so simple world of dropping goals, and three points is all the All Blacks need to win 37–36 and virtually secure the 2018 Rugby Championship.

But Barrett, playing in front of his home crowd, has had a shocker with the boot, missing easy kicks all night, and doesn't retreat into the pocket. Having previously discussed the prospect of dropping a goal when they had a scrum two minutes earlier, he's changed his mind. He and Perenara have assessed the situation and believe there is an overlap to exploit if they throw the ball right. So Barrett takes the pass from Perenara and in one slick movement flips the ball to Damian McKenzie, who is flying up on his right. For a split second it looks certain the All Blacks will score. McKenzie is just about through the giant gap that had been identified to exploit and all he will need to do is give the simple pass to Ben Smith, who will score. But just as that scenario looks inevitable, Boks wing Aphiwe Dyantyi manages to bat the ball out of McKenzie's grasp and it's game over. The All Blacks have lost.

In the post-game interviews, Perenara is asked about the last play and whether there is collective regret about the decision to run the ball. 'The call went out to take a shot [drop goal] there. We went to set for it, but we get a picture where we get a three-on-two and, for me, there's a lot more things that can go wrong in a drop goal than there can in a three-on-two situation. If we execute that, we're probably not having this conversation about the drop goal. But yeah, the decision to go for it, or the chat to set up for a drop goal, did definitely happen, but we get a picture that we back ourselves to score in. And, looking back on it, I think it's still the right call.'

A week later and his coach, Steve Hansen, disagreed it was the right call. He and the team had reviewed the loss, and in his view the biggest problem was game management. He didn't think he'd seen an All Blacks side fail so badly on that front since the 2007 World Cup quarter-final defeat to France. 'That's the last time I can remember a game that was so poorly managed, and it was because of the pressure of the scoreboard and the event. This time the same thing happened and we got too individualistic. All we had to do was take a big breath, maybe take a shot at goal in the sixty-sixth minute, then score a try, and that gives you the eight points you need to get in front.

'A dropped goal wouldn't be bad either, would it? We couldn't do one of those in '07 either because it's not the thing that the five-eighth at that time was used to doing. It's not one Beauden has done ... those things they stay with you because this time it really hurt.'

The loss was pinned on a collective lack of leadership. It was seen, by the players and coaches, as a failure to make the right decisions at the right time and it provided a window into the modern world of captaincy. Several questions arose in the wake of that loss, none more pressing than who exactly had ultimate decision-making authority on the field? When the All Blacks packed down the last scrum of the game under the Boks' posts, Read called for the goal to be dropped. But the decision was made to override that call and it was never made entirely clear by whom. Presumably Barrett, advised by his outside backs who had seen the opportunity to exploit if they kept the ball in hand.

It showed the dangers of the collective system, or at least the need for the captain to be explicit when something is an order rather than a request. The impression was drawn after the loss in Wellington that Read lacked authority as captain. Normally, he was an astute tactical judge; a bold and at times aggressive captain in some of the strategic choices he made. But not that night and it was hard not to wonder whether he lacked a little authority.

Allowing senior players the freedom to react and use their best judgement had served the All Blacks well since they had moved to their collective leadership model in 2004. There had been several times when players had made bold calls without the captain's approval. In 2014 the All Blacks looked destined to draw their opening game of the season against England until Aaron Cruden suddenly tapped a penalty to himself just as captain Richie McCaw was about to tell the referee they were going for goal. Beauden Barrett had seen space down the right, and two phases later Conrad Smith scored a try in the corner.

After the game McCaw talked about how the decision-making process was built on trust and respect and that his players knew they had a licence to back themselves if they saw something which they felt could be exploited. The modern game is dynamic, fluid and complex. It's a fallacy to imagine that the captain stands alone, constantly making big decisions that will swing the flow of the game. Test football in the professional age doesn't work like that. There's a broader game plan set by the coaching staff, in conjunction with the players. Everyone knows their role in that bigger plan and has responsibility to fulfil it. The micro decision-making as it unfolds tends to be the most important aspect of test football and this typically has nothing to do with the captain. The timing of a pass, the angle of the support run, the decision to hold the ball or kick ahead … these are the little things that usually sway the outcome.

The captain's influence sits at the macro level. It's more about assessing whether the strategy is being adhered to and delivering the intended results. It's about trying to assess whether the team is playing in the right places on the field; balancing their tactics appropriately. It's big picture, mostly, and the more experience a captain gains, usually, the more adept they become at sensing how the game is unfolding and what is required.

This was certainly the case with McCaw, who learned from his most public failure, which was the quarter-final loss to France in 2007. That night in Cardiff he didn't manipulate the big picture. The All Blacks didn't reset tactically when the French came back at them and for the last 13 minutes they repeatedly did the same thing — drive tight through the forwards — with no success.

It was a tactical misread. But there were two other specific findings to come out of that game. The All Blacks had been guilty of poor game management, according to the independent review of the World Cup failure, largely because McCaw had been left isolated by his senior leadership group. The review concluded that: 'We consider that on-field leadership and decision making was a factor in the loss in the quarter-final. Arguably, the team and its leadership group has only occasionally been tested to the same degree over the last four years. The trend, as witnessed in Melbourne earlier in 2007, was for the leaders to revert to type and let McCaw make the calls. We recognise that in the last

10 minutes of the second half, the All Blacks faced a dilemma. Whether to go for a drop goal without Carter or [Nick] Evans, or whether to continue to attempt to score through a try or a penalty.

'The team chose the latter. The rationale was that it had worked before in games in similar situations. In addition the drop goal had never been executed under pressure — something the coaches acknowledged could have been worked on more as a strategy. The coaches did, however, send a message out to the team with 10 minutes to go, to set up for a drop goal. The on-field decision was made to continue with the tactic of attempting to score a try or to get a penalty. In the dying minutes of that critical game, the leadership model failed to deliver what was its most important objective — decisions which give the best chance of winning the game.'

In 2008 McCaw leant more heavily on a better-equipped leadership group. He became expert at using those around him to help build a better picture about how respective games were poised. His intelligence flow was constant and that enabled him to better assess if, how or when things needed to change tactically.

He was no longer isolated or left to work everything out for himself and under pressure — the All Blacks became adept between 2008 and 2015 at making good strategic decisions. 'Richie was great at delegation,' says Ali Williams. 'It was more a case on the field of him saying, "Okay Kevy [Keven Mealamu], what do we need to do here?" Or "Dan [Carter], how are we playing?" And then Richie would say, "Boys, this is what I'm seeing. We need to do this, I'm going to do that."'

The second finding from the 2007 World Cup defeat was the need for the captain to be able to articulate what he wanted to happen. Language had to be concise, appropriate and specific, and leave individuals certain about what was expected.

McCaw became the master at precise on-field communication. The hours he spent working on his mental skills were mostly dedicated to the art of staying calm under pressure. Decision-making is not an emotional business. Captaincy at the highest level doesn't require any motivational aspect. The best leaders are those who stay composed, alert and able to think and respond under duress. This is where McCaw set new standards of on-field leadership. In conjunction with Gilbert Enoka and Ceri Evans, McCaw and the other senior leaders tried to understand the biology of the brain and how it responds to stress. Specifically, with Evans, they adopted his now famous red head/blue head model which enabled McCaw to identify when he was falling into an anxious, stressed zone (red head) and what he needed to do to get out of it and return to being calm, focused and living in the now (blue head).

During the 2011 World Cup final he could often be seen stamping his (non-broken) foot, which was his physical means of trying to stimulate the mental process of jumping from red head to blue head. In the same game, Read can be seen occasionally staring into the crowd, fixed on a point during stoppages in play. By the end of his career, McCaw was rarely a red head. As a blue head he could ask the right questions of his leaders and hear their answers. As a blue head he could digest and process the information, and most importantly, he was able to concisely and clearly communicate. He learned that he had to be prescriptive yet also economical with his instructions. He did away with pointless platitudes; there were no 'come ons' or 'we need to step ups'. It was all about the next task — what had to happen and who had to do it — and never again on McCaw's watch did the All Blacks drift like they did in 2007.

It wasn't just his vocal direction that transformed the All Blacks into a better tactical and strategic team between 2008 and 2015. His body language and demeanour were a big part of it, too. Cory Jane can recall an element of panic gripping the backline during the 2011 World Cup final. They were starting to bicker, he said, snap at each other for dropping the ball or not passing on calls. The tension was rising until McCaw gathered them in the final quarter and exuded such calm and poise that it was infectious. The edginess disappeared and Jane said that it was all down to the confidence everyone took from McCaw.

That was the same story in Dublin in 2013 when the All Blacks were chasing the game from 19–0 down and the clock was getting away on them. Each time a half-opportunity to score was blown or a little moment passed without the All Blacks taking advantage, McCaw would remain calm. His head was always up, his shoulders back, his voice steady and the message consistent. Halfback Aaron Smith was truly amazed at the serenity of the skipper and decided that if McCaw was so calm, then he should do his best to be, too.

McCaw was a different on-field leader in 2015 than he was in 2007, and perhaps the biggest difference is that by the time he led the All Blacks for the third time at a World Cup, there was no doubt in anyone's mind that ultimate decision-making authority lay with him. The whole business of steering the team was done collaboratively, but if a specific, potentially game-defining decision had to be made, everyone knew McCaw would make it. Everyone trusted him to make it and there would be no ambiguity as to whether he was asking or telling. He had an iron grip on the team — an ability to delegate, listen, digest and act but to also overrule and demand when he felt his own judgement was best.

McCaw's aura or presence was the intangible glue that bound the All Blacks between 2008 and 2015. His incredible work ethic, form, attitude and reputation all combined to make him a larger-than-life character who somehow pulled the best out of everyone around him on the field and ensured that the leadership team knew how to support him without impinging on his authority. The All Blacks in that period struck the near-impossible balance of having an empowered leadership group and yet also a powerful and authoritative captain who knew how and when to make a specific, non-negotiable demand.

The last part — the ability to demand something unequivocally — was something Read didn't have in Wellington against the Boks and it was not surprising that Hansen made the comparison between that game in 2018 and the 2007 World Cup quarter-final. Both games, to some degree, were lost as a result of the captain not having the ability, for whatever reason, to control and effectively manage the macro strategy of the game. And in both games the respective captains failed to impose themselves at a critical time and communicate forcefully that the team needed to drop a goal in the dying minutes.

There was one further similarity, which is that both games became watershed moments for the respective captains. Just as McCaw rethought everything about his captaincy after the loss in 2007, Read, too, extensively reviewed his role that night in Wellington. He became aware that he needed to be more assertive and demanding in future tests. He needed to develop that same force of personality McCaw had — that same ability to change tone and make it clear he wanted a specific action to be carried out.

When he was asked later in 2018 about whether he would have insisted that his side set up for the drop goal in the last minute, he said: 'Yeah, I would have. But it is a funny one because you pack down the scrum and the call was made to drop the goal. But it didn't happen but I also back him to make that decision because if D-Mac [Damian McKenzie] doesn't get the ball knocked out of his hands and scored the try we win the game. I think, though, if you look back and say if we are in this position again we drop the goal — especially in a game that really matters. We weren't mentally as strong as we needed to be and that was the biggest lesson we took out of it.'

* * *

Modern rugby has detailed and complex game plans, which make it hard to see and feel how the game is unfolding. There are so many parts to it and it is played at such speed and intensity that captains have it tough trying to process and determine their next move. In the amateur era the game plans didn't have anywhere near the same level of detail or complexity and the big picture was easier to read.

Rarely would anyone ever suggest that an All Blacks loss was caused by a tactical catastrophe or decision-making horror show by the captain. Other factors tended to more obviously determine the outcome: the quality of the set-piece work and the general aggression and accuracy of the forward pack. So much of rugby back then was determined by the physical battle: win the collisions and win the test. The French even had a saying — 'no scrum, no win'. Rugby was that simple back then.

The great All Blacks side of the late 1980s played brilliant rugby on what was an effective but limited game plan. They didn't operate, says captain Buck Shelford, with a suite of options or endless decisions to make. The plan was to get on the front foot with the forwards and then give the ball to the backs. If that didn't work, Grant Fox at first-five would kick more. 'Back in our day you had your No. 10, who was your driver, your conductor, and he would know the game plan,' says Shelford. 'I would turn around to Foxy and say, "What do you want?" Foxy and I had a really good understanding of one another. He would tell me when he didn't want the ball. He loved it when we were on the front foot. We had a lot of moves off the back of the scrum and by getting four or five metres over the gain line, we would be on a roll and the backs would love it because they were running onto the ball.

'He loved getting the ball like that compared with getting off set piece directly because he stood quite deep. He wasn't the sort of player to take on the defence but it worked really well. Sometimes he would say, "Give me the ball" and I would say no but that was how we managed things.'

When Graham Mourie was captain in the late 1970s he felt his job was to deliver the game plan that the coach had instructed, but to then adapt it accordingly as the game played out. 'In 1977 against the British & Irish Lions I wasn't actually the captain, Tane

Norton was. But we got an injury and Laurie Knight had to go into the front row. Laurie was No. 8, and [Lions prop] Fran Cotton graciously gave a bit of advice as he went in. "Don't worry, Laurie, I'll hold you up, put your shoulder here, lad." So the next scrum, I said to Tane, "Let's pack down a three-man scrum. These guys are so dyed in the wool they'll pack down eight against us and we'll

'You had to think on your feet as captain and I think from my perspective, my strengths were probably more game understanding and ability to make those tactical changes. We didn't have video analysis so you just had to go out there and sometimes it would take you 20 minutes to work out what the other guys were doing and how they were going to play the game.'

—GRAHAM MOURIE

score in the corner." So we packed down a three-man scrum and won the ball quite easily and unfortunately one of the other loose forwards dropped the ball when we would have scored.

'You had to think on your feet as captain and I think from my perspective, my strengths were probably more game understanding and ability to make those tactical changes. We didn't have video analysis so you just had to go out there and sometimes it would take you 20 minutes to work out what the other guys were doing and how they were going to play the game.'

CHAPTER TWELVE

REGRETS ...
I'VE HAD A FEW

EVERY CAPTAIN OF the All Blacks has learned that it doesn't take much to upset the balance of their tenure. One bad decision, one loss, one glaring error in a big game and a captaincy can be irreversibly tainted. History is cruel and definitive when it comes to judging All Blacks captains. There is no footnote in history: no asterisk that explains bad luck. It's black and white, recorded in wins and losses, and a captain is remembered as good or bad and rarely anything between.

History is also selective. People remember what they want and their judgement is coloured by what they see in the landmark moments. To fall on the right side of history — to be remembered as an All Blacks great — a captain needs to make a footprint in the nation's consciousness. And to do that, they need a defining achievement. They have to guide the team to a significant victory — be it a test series or World Cup. There has to be something major that can be held up as proof of excellence.

An outstanding win ratio is not of itself reason to judge a captain as great.

Take Andy Leslie, the gentlemanly captain of the All Blacks on the 1976 tour of South Africa. He won the Bledisloe Cup in 1974 and was unbeaten as captain when the team set off for the Republic. Once they got there, a combination of bad luck and suspect home-town refereeing derailed the All Blacks. The elusive first series win in South Africa escaped the All Blacks, and without it, Leslie has entered history as a good leader, a trusted friend to many and a thoroughly decent man. But his name won't resonate in the halls of the pantheon. He's not riddled with regret, but he's come to see where he could have played his hand differently.

'We got some bad calls,' he says. 'There were a few issues that we probably could have handled a bit better. When guys were replaced in those days you had to have doctor's certificates. I think it was the second test, a [Springboks] player got injured. He was replaced immediately when he was meant to go to the sidelines — to be checked by the doctor. You are handling that in the instant and perhaps I could have done it differently. We were also pretty upset in the last test where we thought a couple of incidents could have resulted in penalty tries. I could have dealt with a couple of situations better but you know, that's history.'

Leslie by no means sits alone as a captain with regrets. There have been plenty who have failed at critical times, and with ample time to review why, have reassessed what they would have done differently if they could be given their time again.

* * *

It wasn't hard to imagine that it was the World Cup rather than the Bledisloe Cup Reuben Thorne was holding aloft in August 2003. The All Blacks skipper was turning the public tide — making a nation believe in him as captain and his team as potential champions. A year that had started badly with a loss to England in Wellington was back on track after two wins against France and a clean sweep of the Tri Nations. The All Blacks had gained everyone's attention. When they won at Eden Park to take possession of the Bledisloe Cup for the first time since 1997, they were the new favourites to win the World Cup when it kicked off in October. So, when Thorne raised the silverware, it didn't require a leap of imagination to see that he could be doing the same with the Webb Ellis trophy.

If there had been a specific worry about the All Blacks after their loss to England, it was their lack of an iconic, commanding captain. Thorne didn't hold the public's confidence. He wasn't seen as a towering personality or the sort of domineering force the All Blacks would need to win the World Cup. But at Eden Park a lot of minds were changed and not just because the All Blacks won, but because of the role Thorne played in securing that victory.

At 21–17 up the All Blacks hadn't completed the job and the Wallabies had them scrambling. The pressure was increasing and the All Blacks needed a period of stability to get things under control. Which is what they got when Thorne took command of a malfunctioning lineout. The All Blacks had been coughing up possession from the touchline until Thorne decided it was his responsibility to fix things. He made himself the lineout target — rising three times in succession to secure critical possession. 'I had been in the All Blacks since 1999 and we had had so many close calls where we had just lost the Bledisloe Cup in the last second of the game or by one point and we just couldn't get the thing back,' says Thorne. 'We'd had a really good game previously to win the first test but to get the cup you had to win both. In that last quarter we needed to keep possession. The way our lineout system was set up, the best option to go to was near the front which was myself. I went for three in a row and there was one point I went to Keven Mealamu and said, "We're going to do something different" and he said, "No, go to yourself again." I said, "Righto" and we managed to win those balls and they were crucial at the time. They kept us with possession and we managed to close the game out.

'We had been trying to get our hands on that trophy for a long time and been through a bit of heartbreak. So to actually get it was really satisfying but also satisfying from a personal point of view that I played well and the team had performed well. We'd scored a record win in South Africa and we'd put 50 points on the Wallabies in Sydney. We had built nicely, so when we won that Bledisloe Cup things couldn't have gone better from my point of view.'

The headlines in the press the next day changed in regard to Thorne. One paper screamed 'Captain Invisible becomes Captain Invincible' and the All Blacks tootled off to Australia a few weeks later full of hope. Confidence rose when they demolished South Africa in the quarter-final, to set up a semi-final against the Wallabies in Sydney. This was the game they wanted.

They had scored 50 points on the same ground a few months earlier and eight minutes into the game they were pressing hard. First-five Carlos Spencer was running left, his backline queuing up. He could see Mils Muliaina would be unmarked if he skipped the pass. So he let it go. A long flat bullet pass ... that Wallabies centre Stirling Mortlock saw coming long before it was released. He grabbed it and cruised 80 metres to score at the other end.

It's early in the game, but it's still the killer blow. It's the try that opens everyone's eyes to the fact the Wallabies have readied themselves for this encounter and are smarter and more resilient than the All Blacks. For the next 70 minutes, that becomes painfully apparent to every New Zealander, and when Wallabies captain George Gregan famously stands over the prostrate Byron Kelleher, shouting, 'Four more years, four more years, boys', Thorne knows the game is up. The World Cup dream is over and this meek exit will be his legacy and defining moment as All Blacks captain.

History will not be kind when it comes to remembering his captaincy and Thorne, a good, decent man, will have the rest of his life to review what he might have done differently. 'I look back now after many moons at many experiences and there are certainly things that I would do differently,' he says. 'There were relationships I would have worked harder on. I look at my relationship with Carlos Spencer at the time ... we got on but we weren't close and the captain and the first-five should have had a stronger relationship. We should have been more connected about how we were approaching the game.

'If I could go back, I would work a lot harder on that particular relationship. Spend more time with him, get to understand him better so that we could work better together. On the field we were quite opposite, he was the sort of flamboyant showman who could do anything, whereas I was a head down sort of grafter. Yet off the field he was actually really quiet and so was I. We were different people that didn't have too many interests outside of rugby and I wonder whether if we had worked a bit better together, or been a bit closer, whether it would have benefited the team.

'I can also remember at one stage the senior players were paired up with some of the younger guys ... as a bit of a mentor, someone to talk to, whatever you want to call it. Mine was with Ma'a Nonu and again totally different people. I found it difficult to understand him and probably vice versa. Different ages, different backgrounds, different interests ... the whole thing. The All Blacks are a diverse group from around the country and one of the challenges is to bring that group together and create some sort of meaningful team culture where everyone gets on well and works well together. It's not easy. I was pretty friendly. I'm quiet, so perhaps some people mistake that for being a bit aloof or whatever but it's not the case. I was never unfriendly, but if I had known then what I know now about how teams operate, then it would be different. I think that would go right across all players and management.'

* * *

The phone in Justin Marshall's room rings. It's an internal call and when he answers, he's told to go to coach John Hart's room immediately. That doesn't sound good to him. Being summoned like this suggests bad news awaits.

The All Blacks are due to play Ireland in six days to try to maintain their unbeaten record in 1997. Marshall, who became the starting halfback the previous year, is desperate to hold his place, so as he makes his way to Hart's hotel room his mind is racing. 'I started thinking about where I had been the night before, because back in the day we were more social than they are nowadays,' he says. 'That was my major concern and I was trying to convince myself I hadn't done anything that would warrant me being in trouble. I was also aware they had started to monitor training, so I was going through in my mind all of the reasons and excuses I could bring out for some training inadequacies.

'So, pretty much I was shitting myself. I was feeling a bit sick in the gut. I walked into Harty's room very much prepared for bad news. He went through a process of saying, "How are you doing and how are you training?" And straight away I had my answers. And then he said, "You obviously are aware that we are having problems with Fitzy, he's struggling with his knee. We are going to be naming him in the side for the weekend, but should he not get through training, we've had a really good discussion about this and we would like you to captain the All Blacks."

'Honestly, when people say they almost fell off their chair, I literally did. And I didn't say anything, and he kind of just looked at me. When you crystal ball this situation, it's kind of like, "Oh thank you so much, I'm so proud and I'm very humbled." But the first thing that came out of my mouth was "What about the other guys?" If you go through that '97 side, you would think, *How the hell did he pick me as All Blacks captain?*

'I said, "I don't know if I can do it Harty because I'm not sure I've got enough respect in this team at such a young age. I don't feel like I'm the right choice because I wouldn't have the support of the players." And he said, "I've already spoken to them and they think you are a good choice. They think you definitely have the competitiveness: that every time you are going out and doing all that you can for this team and for your country. And you are in a position where decisions are easier to make because you can see a lot. Also we have been impressed with your maturity. So we've spoken to all the senior players, the leadership group and they support you.'"

Marshall's head was spinning as he walked back to his room. One minute he's preparing to be dropped or disciplined, the next he's probably going to captain the All Blacks against Ireland at Lansdowne Road. His promotion to the captaincy was confirmed three hours before kick-off when Sean Fitzpatrick's knee was too sore to get through even the light pre-game run-around.

It was an incredible moment for the 24-year-old to lead out one of the great All Blacks teams. Behind him in the tunnel were giants of the game — Zinzan Brooke, Olo Brown, Josh Kronfeld, Andrew Mehrtens, Christian Cullen, Frank Bunce and Walter Little.

Marshall was pumped. Even a few years ago such a scenario would have been unimaginable to him. There were a few darker moments in his past — drink-related incidents that had required police intervention. But here he was now, recognised by his peers — some of them legendary — as having the skills and maturity to captain the All Blacks. And it was peer approval that almost meant more to Marshall than being the captain. It was a big, big moment for him to be endorsed by the likes of Zinzan Brooke, Fitzpatrick and Bunce.

He was sharing a room with Brooke that week in Dublin and that proved to be invaluable as the veteran No. 8 was a fountain of good advice. He told Marshall to keep doing what he had been doing and to realise that the team was experienced and cohesive and mostly ran itself. The only real difference about being captain was that he would have to deal with the referee. Brooke's advice proved to be startlingly accurate.

Marshall did indeed find that the team ran itself. His job was much the same, until after the game — which the All Blacks had won 63–15 — when he had to make a speech at the after-match function. He didn't mind speaking publicly but 23 years later he still hates the fact he didn't do his research and thanked Nick Popplewell when Keith Wood was the captain of Ireland. But other than that, his captaincy stint was working well. A week later and the All Blacks won in Manchester against England more comfortably than the 25–8 scoreline suggests before they then thumped Wales 42–7 at Wembley. And maybe more importantly, he'd kept himself out of any kind of trouble off the field. 'I knew that even though it hadn't been said, that was the one thing they were really worried about me,' says Marshall. 'I don't ever hide behind my past. It had been an issue for me — being overly social and having that extra drink when I should be going home. It was at the forefront of my mind when I was named captain that I couldn't slip up in that area.

'I was confident I could do that but I was also conscious I didn't want to alienate my mates or change my personality just because I was captain. So I had to make sure I wasn't in that last group to leave the bar sort of thing. It was a bit of a mind-set change but to be honest I was absolutely fucked by the end of the week because of the extra work you have to do as captain. All the extra meetings, the extra media commitments, I wasn't used to that so it is quite emotionally draining when you are the captain. You can't exactly climb into half a dozen cans in the changing room because you have to front the media, then give a speech and sit on the top table and glad-hand a few people.'

It was only in the final match of the tour against England at Twickenham that Marshall's captaincy hit choppy water. The All Blacks played like they were feeling the effects of a long, hard season. 'Everything is going along rosily,' says Marshall. 'There was a bit of shit at Old Trafford that was outside my control ... you know, Norm Hewitt and Richard Cockerill coming nose to nose during the haka, but I don't know how I could have been expected to do anything about that. The second England game we didn't play well. I had a few run-ins with the referee who was Jim Fleming. England were being really negative at the breakdown as they obviously recognised that if we got any kind of quick ball we were going to cut them apart.

'So my forward pack were getting irate about it. They were saying to me, "Marshy, you have to go and talk to the referee about this." So I talked to him and he would tell me to go away and eventually it got to the point where I said, "You know what, Jim, if you don't fucking well do something about this, my forward pack will take the law unto themselves and then we will have a hell of a messy test match." So he marched me back 10 metres. As I was walking back, I said, "Look, Jim, I am just trying to tell you how it is my team are feeling and how frustrated they are." And he marched me back another 10 metres.

'We managed to draw the game which was a miracle but a lot of the fallout in the media, without fully knowing the circumstances of it, suggested I wasn't mentally strong enough or disciplined to be the captain. I wasn't on a personal agenda with Fleming. The senior players asked me to talk to him and when I started to think that he was going to cost us the test match — because he was a shit referee — I tried to talk to him. He marches me 20 metres and all of a sudden I am a shit captain. I win three games and a draw but when the team gets named in 1998, I am in it, but Taine is captain. There has been no communication. Nothing.

'I don't ever hide behind my past. It had been an issue for me — being overly social and having that extra drink when I should be going home. It was at the forefront of my mind when I was named captain that I couldn't slip up in that area.'

—JUSTIN MARSHALL

'I don't have a personal thing with John [Hart]. We still talk and we get on fine. But he didn't fly down to Christchurch and talk to me — review my experiences as captain. I thought he would talk to me about all that, about how I felt and whether I would consider doing it again and to lay out what he was thinking. But we didn't have any of those conversations that should have been had. I just read it like everyone else. That was really disappointing.

'I thought I could have been a much better captain but I needed to learn. Obviously, telling the ref he was doing a shit job and that we would enforce the law ourselves wasn't the right thing to do, but you learn from that. All I ever wanted to do was play and I never needed to be a captain. I never said it, I never mentioned it until now, but it did sting that John didn't talk to me and tell me why they were going with Taine. It didn't get dealt with and I was pretty much thrown to the wolves because I had to talk about it and I didn't know why I wasn't the captain.'

The hurt lived with Marshall throughout 1998. He had to find a way to integrate into the team after being captain, and while Randell was a close mate, there was a little bit of awkwardness that the role transferred from one to the other without anything being said. Harder still for Marshall was that he felt that had he been given more time, he could have grown into the role, learned from his experiences and become a good captain. Instead, his four-game stint has been recorded as a failed experiment — as an interesting concept that never quite worked. Seen through his eyes, it's an unfair assessment of the job he did and the potential he showed.

'To captain my country made me more focused as a player. I would have liked to have had more opportunity at it because I think it takes time to get your balance right. Sometimes Harty made rash decisions. For a methodical, hard-thinking man he sometimes doesn't think through things. He was very influenced by the media. He didn't want the attention of the media for doing things wrong. He was easily changed in his mind-set and I would have liked the opportunity to see how I would have gone with another year.

'You don't just go into that role and automatically find the formula. You need time to get your balance right and that balance is making sure that you are not emotionally fucked by the time it comes to kick-off. You have got to learn to push back a little and organise yourself to make sure you stay in a good mental place and don't get bogged down by it all. Ultimately, I loved it. I felt a huge lift in my game that I was leading the team and that I could grow into it and do a good job of it.'

* * *

By half-time of the 1999 World Cup semi-final, Taine Randell couldn't remember why at the end of 1998 he was unsure about whether he wanted to be All Blacks captain. The awfulness of 1998 was a distant memory as he and the All Blacks trotted towards the changing room at Twickenham, leading France 24–10. It wasn't all over but it so nearly was. France were still in the game, but only just.

Randell's career had taken a dramatic and welcome twist after he decided to stay on as captain in 1999. An inexperienced All Blacks side that lost five in a row in 1998 was looking like a different team. They had found an element of confidence and belief, and one blip in Sydney aside before the World Cup, were looking much more like an assured All Blacks side. Randell was growing into the captaincy. He felt more certain about his right to hold the job. He was playing better football and as a consequence he felt respect among his peers was growing. The All Blacks were in a better place than they had been 12 months previously and were 40 minutes away from making the World Cup final.

If they could make the final, Randell's tenure as captain would have to be reassessed. To get the All Blacks that far would claw back much of the reputational damage inflicted the previous year. It would change the picture — and if they could win the World Cup, that would immediately elevate Randell to a different stratosphere. He'd have a special place in history if the All Blacks could finish off France and then beat the Wallabies the following week.

But All Blacks coach John Hart was certainly not looking that far ahead when the team arrived in the changing room at half-time. 'I could show you my half-time speech,' he says. 'I wrote my notes on my programme and I said, "These guys will not lie down, we need to get them in the corners and give nothing away and finish them. Don't relax, just put them in the corner, keep pressure on, take every point and put them out of the game." And I watched it unfold. We didn't do any of that. To be fair, the French had 25 minutes of the most outstanding rugby and luck I have ever seen. The bounce of the ball and things that happened in that 25 minutes were unbelievable and I thought we were refereed really harshly on the offside. We lacked that ability to close it down. You know it's really difficult. You're sitting in the stand … I think the captain runs it once he's out there.'

It was indeed an incredible 25-minute blast by the French. They scored 31 points, while the All Blacks disappeared. No one had seen anything quite like it. The French, fairly quiet and unimaginative in the first half, were suddenly carving up the All Blacks. They found holes when they passed. They found holes when they kicked. Everything they did led to points.

The All Blacks were seemingly powerless. They had no means to win the ball or keep it. They watched hopelessly as the French dissected them — and maybe it wouldn't have mattered who had been captain that day. Maybe even the most demanding and authoritative figure would have been left dumbstruck — unable to impose himself and reset the team before the game got away from them. Maybe even the biggest personality and most astute, experienced captain would have been rendered useless by the French in those 25 minutes.

But the suspicion that Randell froze and failed to react will dog him for the rest of his days. 'I just didn't know what was going on,' he says. 'At half-time things were hunky-dory. We'd had a good year. We understood the pressure and what we were as All Blacks. And I was the most accountable, but it's hard to explain. It's just blank. Much of it is blank. There was no tears. There's just nothing, it meant that much.

'Until about the last five minutes, I was in a daze. Justin Marshall had been the All Blacks halfback and one of the toughest guys I know. He got dropped for that game and in hindsight that was a big mistake. When things are going well, anyone can play for the All Blacks, even an average player in an All Blacks team will look good. When things are going down, that's when you need your toughest guys, and not having Justin there, I think to this day that was the biggest mistake we made.

'There was a 15- to 20-minute period, and holy shit, I don't know. We were all wide eyes, not knowing what was going on. They'd kick a ball in between four of us and it would land in the middle and they would get it. I genuinely did not know what to do.'

A consolation try by Jeff Wilson pulled the score back to 43–31 but the All Blacks were out and the sensational collapse was going to be Randell's legacy. It's what he would be remembered for. Having started his captaincy with five consecutive defeats, he'd shown a depth of character to stick at the job in 1999 and transform the team. It had taken courage to stay in the role and he went into that World Cup semi-final a better captain than when he first started in the job. But when it mattered most, he didn't have a way to impose himself or be the heroic figure New Zealanders wanted him to be. He had no means to turn the course of that game and those 40 minutes in London swept him onto the wrong side of history.

* * *

There's been a flurry of texts and emails, a few panicked phone calls on the Tuesday before the All Blacks' World Cup semi-final against England in 2019. What sparked this mini-drama was the non-appearance of All Blacks captain Kieran Read at training. This is unusual — suggests there is a serious problem … hence the media's frenzied messaging of one another.

At lunchtime on 19 October, at the Conrad Hilton in Tokyo, All Blacks coach Steve Hansen, a veteran in the business of putting out media fires, tackles the whole business head-on. He doesn't wait for any of the 300 or so media packed into the room to ask any questions. He knows what is coming so he starts things off with: 'There is no issue. You didn't see him train because he was in the gym on the bike. He got a tight calf out of the game the other day, we just weren't prepared to put him on the track today — on a wet track.'

The following day, at the same venue, Read fronts the media — everyone looking for tell-tale signs of a limp as he makes his way to the top table. There is none and he is relaxed, friendly and good-humoured. He's going to play and his confidence is a huge boost for his team-mates as Read was superb in the quarter-final destruction of Ireland. It was one of his best tests in years and proof he had not only put his back surgery behind him, but of how well he had evolved his game.

Between 2012 and 2015, Read was used as a ball carrier and distributor closer to the touchline. The All Blacks wanted to use his speed, athleticism and offloading skills in the wider reaches. It worked. Read became recognised as one of the greatest — if not the greatest — No. 8 in All Blacks history. He deservedly ended 2013 as World Rugby Player of the Year and the sight of Read producing some kind of game-winning magic was the defining memory of that year.

By 2016, when he took over the captaincy, his role was reimagined. Hansen wanted Read to play closer to the action, use his size and power to damage teams tighter to the ruck, and to become a distributor in heavier traffic. Read's role was to wear teams down and then slip clever passes to support runners. It was also to use his bone-crunching defence to hurt opponents. Anyone tackled by Read felt it and he put doubt in ball carriers' minds — after half an hour or so, even big, hard men would be keeping an eye out for him. His performance against the Irish was one of the great, destructive shifts from an All Blacks No. 8 and his team needed another of the same calibre against an England side that were likely to be even more physical.

It didn't come. Not from Read and not from any of his team-mates. Instead, the All Blacks were strangely passive. England scored a try after two minutes and were never under pressure. They were more dynamic. They were more clinical, more brutal in the collisions. The All Blacks sat on their heels, seemingly spending the 80 minutes waiting for England to come at them. It was, frankly, weird.

Those who have watched the All Blacks closely in the last decade — even in the last four years since Read took over as captain — haven't seen anything like this. The All Blacks have, on occasion, played poorly in this period. They have lost six tests, but none like this. In Yokohama they offered almost nothing in the way of a fightback. That's what's weird.

When they lost their only game in 2016 against Ireland in Chicago, they roared back into life after an appalling opening 50 minutes. They were 30–8 down and then woke up. They scored three quick tries and reached the final quarter three points adrift and with the game just about within their grasp. They left it too late and it wasn't enough when it came, but the All Blacks' backlash did at least come that day at Soldier Field. It came in 2017 when they found themselves 17–0 down to the Wallabies after 20 minutes in Dunedin. It came when they were 30–18 behind in Pretoria in 2018; and it came the last time they had played England before the World Cup. At Twickenham in November 2018 the All Blacks were 15–0 down after 25 minutes and hanging on. One more score by England would have killed them off. But the All Blacks rallied, scoring 16 unanswered points for a victory that was impressive for its depth of character.

The All Blacks never roll over and play dead. There is always a period in any test when they find a way to be effective. But it didn't happen that night in Japan. There was a fleeting sense of a recovery looming when Ardie Savea scored a fortunate try off the back of an England mistake at the lineout to close the gap to 13–7. But the surge never came. That was not the catalyst for a recovery and the final 20 minutes ended with England as dominant as they had been in the other 60.

Accepting defeat wasn't the hard part. It was trying to understand why the All Blacks had been so passive, unable to impose themselves. They had been beaten up physically and their lineout had disintegrated. Tactically they were predictable and without variation — failing to do what they had done against Ireland the week before and send Read and Joe Moody crashing into the heavy traffic. Instead, they constantly tried to play wide and behind the gain line. It was a plan that England had no trouble thwarting and yet the All Blacks didn't mix it up.

Defeat left Read almost in no man's land in terms of placing his captaincy. He had been a superb All Black. A brilliant No. 8 — probably the best in New Zealand history; certainly the one with the widest range of skills. He would be signing off as the second most experienced captain in All Blacks history, his 52 tests in charge being one more than Sean Fitzpatrick managed and 87 per cent of them had been victories.

What Read's captaincy didn't have, though, was a defining achievement. There was no landmark victory for Read — no monument as such to acknowledge his greatness. And in fact, there were two failed expeditions that would come to sit large in the history books.

The first was in 2017 when the All Blacks drew the three-test series against the British & Irish Lions. It was a cruel series for Read as fate threw a couple of impossibly difficult situations at him. The first was a red card to Sonny Bill Williams 23 minutes into the second test. The All Blacks were hard on themselves after they eventually lost 24–21, believing they had become a little blinkered and narrow in their tactical approach when they were reduced to 14 men. Maybe they were, but no other team in the world would have been able to make even a game of things reduced to 14 men for that long and the All Blacks were a few minutes away from a draw.

Then in the third test, with the scores tied at 15-all, the All Blacks won a kickable penalty in the last minute. Referee Romain Poite gave it, the TMO, George Ayoub, even though he shouldn't have been consulted, agreed it was the right decision, but incredibly the French official was persuaded to change his mind by his assistant referee Jérôme Garcès. It was downgraded to a scrum in what remains to this day one of the most scandalous pieces of officiating in the modern game that has never been explained.

Without victory against the Lions or a successful World Cup campaign, Read's tenure will be one that forever generates questions — none more pertinent than whether he could have done more to change the course of the 2019 semi-final. It's a question he will no doubt ask himself for years to come, especially as the semi-final was played on his birthday. But as much as that defeat hurt and as often as it will pop up in Read's life given the association with his birthday, it's not going to haunt him. It will live with him, disappoint him, but despite its significance, he says it won't define him.

The day after the loss, Read, with tears in his eyes at times, and his voice a little shaky, provided the sort of perspective that gave an insight into why he was such a popular and respected figure among his peers. 'It's way bigger than the individual, it's bigger than myself,' he said of the defeat. 'The amount of positive messages that have come from people you care about, it helps. Also the fact it was my birthday yesterday, and to get back to the hotel room and there's cards from my kids waiting for me. It changes things … it puts things in perspective. It's a rugby game, people care, we care, you enjoy moments. I'm a dad and that's first and foremost the thing I want to be remembered by. It's all relative. My kids aren't going to love me less.'

CHAPTER THIRTEEN

SWINGING THE BALANCE

IT'S NOT ALWAYS apparent or tangible why certain All Blacks captains have been able to achieve greatness while others have failed. Sometimes luck has everything to do with it. There isn't a captain sitting in the pantheon of greats who would dispute that. All those All Blacks captains who have enjoyed a definitive victory of some kind to distinguish them from those who haven't, will admit that they were aided by some kind of good fortune. A lucky bounce of the ball, a refereeing decision that benefited them, or a random brain explosion by an opponent have often been the catalysts to a landmark moment for the All Blacks.

But luck is by no means the whole story. Not even close. No side can win a World Cup on luck alone. No side could win a Grand Slam or series in South Africa simply because they got lucky. There has to be more to it than that, even if it is not always easy to define or understand what conspired to deliver the pivotal and career-defining success.

Test rugby can seemingly be governed at times by an obvious and consistent set of happenings. The team that dominates the forwards battle often wins. The more physical side gains the rewards of their endeavour by being able to play with more space and time. It's often that simple. Other times, a test can swing on one moment of brilliance — players such as Christian Cullen, Jonah Lomu and Beauden Barrett possess incredible individual skills that can produce tries from anywhere. It can be deadlocked and then a fertile imagination combined with agility, acceleration and power sees one team break free.

Yet sometimes it's not possible to really know what swung the outcome of a test. There can be nothing obvious that pushed things one way or the other and it may be that victory is built on a series of good, but seemingly small, decisions or accurate plays. It might just be that all the component parts of the captain's influence — his work ethic, his reputation, his ability, his decision-making, and all-round command and respect in which he is held — combine to ensure that one team benefits from tiny percentage advantages that lead to them winning. In the biggest games, the tests that really matter, it is often a one per cent difference that separates the two teams.

Former All Blacks captain Taine Randell, who endured five consecutive defeats in 1998, has spent plenty of time thinking about what separates teams at the highest level. He feels that the difference is most often experience, be it the judgement of the captain, the contribution of the senior leaders, or the general ability of enough players to do the right thing at the right time. The best captains have found a way, be it through their force of personality, good judgement or good luck, to ensure that the one per cent difference swings in their favour. That's essentially what separates great leaders from good leaders — the ability to somehow wield enough influence to tilt the balance of fate. The great leaders win the tiny battles so that after 80 minutes they have edged ahead.

'What I've found even watching games since is the difference between winning and losing is so small,' says Randell. 'You could have one bad day of preparation manifest itself and, I know it's a cliché, but the difference is a genuine one per cent. I think what we've all found as New Zealanders is that experience makes up that one per cent. I think of that Durban game [All Blacks lost 24–23], if we had won that, it would have been a lot different, and you know, careers change on that one per cent. It can come down to one little piece of inexperience and you just know if we were a bit more experienced, you'd be calm, you'd convey calmness and you'd get a different result. We didn't have that. The opposition did. And as a young captain I was learning on the job.'

'You could have one bad day of preparation manifest itself and, I know it's a cliché, but the difference is a genuine one per cent. I think what we've all found as New Zealanders is that experience makes up that one per cent.'

—TAINE RANDELL

Even if we don't always know why, what we can be sure about is that certain captains have fallen on the right side of history: secured their reputation as a great on the basis they led the team to an iconic victory. Into this category goes Graham Mourie for being the first All Blacks captain to secure a Grand Slam of the Home Unions. David Kirk takes his place for leading the All

Blacks to the 1987 World Cup. Sean Fitzpatrick is the only man to captain the All Blacks to a series win in South Africa. Tana Umaga led the All Blacks to a series win against the British & Irish Lions in the age when the composite side has become the best-funded and -supported team on the planet. Richie McCaw won two World Cups.

And then there is Buck Shelford, who doesn't have a definitive landmark as such in his career, but holds his place as one of the great captains on account of the fact he never lost a test as skipper and for the way he lost the role. The legend of Buck has grown in the last 30 years, almost as if it is taken as read that the All Blacks would have won the 1991 World Cup had he been at the helm. The consensus is that he was denied his definitive moment by internecine politics and pettiness and hence he's been given an honorary place in the pantheon.

Who knows how the nation would feel about him had he captained the All Blacks to failure at the 1991 World Cup? His reputation as one of the toughest, most uncompromising, most driven men to lead the All Blacks would probably be dented. Instead, the injustice of his situation has enabled the aura to grow. The hyperbole has gone unchecked, the stories about him have been embellished and his tenure romanticised. It's why, 30 years since he was unceremoniously dumped as the captain who never lost a test, he is still in demand — be it to front public health campaigns, endorse products or talk to the media.

Buck is the exception to the rule. He is the only All Blacks captain to be considered great without having the landmark achievement to confirm it.

* * *

The one per cent factor is most easily seen and perhaps best put in context by comparing the All Blacks' respective Grand Slam tours in 1972–73 and 1978. In the former, the All Blacks were one point away from being successful. They had beaten Wales, Scotland and England but drew 10-all with Ireland. The draw meant Ian Kirkpatrick's captaincy not only came to an end, but was ultimately lacking the great achievement it needed to be defined as great.

He was a great player. A great All Black. A great man, even. But his captaincy, as a result of that draw in Ireland, doesn't meet the criteria to be considered great. A victory in Dublin would have immortalised Kirkpatrick and the 1972–73 All Blacks. Instead, they came home to discover there was a distinct appetite for change. A blind eye may have been turned to the heavy drinking on that tour and the domineering culture of the back seat, had the Grand Slam been won.

But in the wake of failure the mood was less tolerant, the behaviour of the senior players was put under the spotlight, and the tenure of Kirkpatrick came to an abrupt end when the All Blacks lost to England at home later in 1973. 'I don't know whether they made the right decision in picking the right captain following Kirky,' says Andy Leslie, who was the man who replaced Kirkpatrick as captain. 'But I think they made the right decision to take the responsibility off Kirky because following that he played magnificent rugby.'

The All Blacks didn't win the one per cent balance of fate in 1973, but they did in 1978 when they beat Ireland with a late try.

They beat Scotland 18–9, yet the scoreline is misleading in terms of the drama. Scotland snapped a drop goal late in the game to try to bring the scores level but it was charged down, leading to the All Blacks scoring a try at the other end. A fingertip diverted the course of history — the charge-down preventing the draw and the subsequent bounce of the ball delivering the victory. And then in Cardiff the All Blacks escaped with victory courtesy of a late penalty that will forever be contentious.

As is now written into folklore, All Blacks lock Andy Haden threw himself out of a lineout late in the game to try to win a penalty. The All Blacks were awarded a penalty, but not, according to referee Roger Quittenton, for that feigned act. The penalty was supposedly given because Welsh prop Geoff Wheel had tangled with All Blacks lock Frank Oliver. Either way, it was a lucky break, but perhaps the luckier break was the fact that Mourie didn't have to wrestle with any moral or ethical dilemma to determine whether to allow Haden to do what he did.

The genesis of Haden's plan had been formed earlier that week when players were idly chatting and it came to light that a former All Blacks team-mate, Ian Eliason, had been encouraged to fall out of a lineout in a provincial game against the great Colin Meads. The tactic in that context was designed to not only win a penalty but to deter Meads, a genuine enforcer, from being able to take control of lineout ball through a process of fear and intimidation. The idea stuck with Haden.

'So in the game Andy came up to me and said, "I'm going to do it,"' says Mourie. 'And actually I didn't click on to what he was talking about until he did it. Would I have condoned it? In retrospect once he did it I thought, *Shit, that's what he meant.*

I think if you look at it in the sense of the game, it's not the sort of thing you'd want to be seen doing in a test match.

'Given the opportunity, I may have said no but the reality was it took me by surprise, it wasn't something that had been planned apart from that conversation that had happened during the week. There's been a lot of other attempts by players to do similar things, just not as blatantly overt. Front-rowers that have gone down or deliberately skewed the scrum. But I guess in the end you respect the rules of the game and in hindsight I don't know what Andy would have done if I'd said no.'

However it happened, Mourie managed to swing the one per cent balance in his team's favour on that tour in 1978. He did it in Ireland, Edinburgh and then Cardiff to ensure he had his great achievement. If the impression was initially drawn immediately after the 1978 tour that luck had been the commodity on which Mourie had relied, that changed three years later. Luck had played a part, but it wasn't the defining quality of his captaincy. His standing in the game, command of the team and ability to influence games was more a consequence of his instincts and innate sense of what would be best for the team. Mourie was a captain, as he would prove in 1981, who knew how to do the right thing.

His decision to not make himself available to play the Springboks when they toured New Zealand in 1981 strengthened his standing in the public consciousness as a great captain. It gave a deeper insight into the depth of his intelligence and morality and why he was able to gain results as All Blacks captain. By actively boycotting the tour, he deepened the perception of himself as a cerebral captain. He had built a reputation as a deep tactical thinker and astute reader of the game, and in 1981 he took a moral stand that was not only selfless and courageous, but also illustrative of his wider sense of responsibilities as All Blacks captain.

Mourie was a man with a moral compass and his legacy was greatly enhanced by having the strength to enforce his principles. It was strengthened again when his team-mates asked the selectors to recall him for the tour of France later in 1981. Great All Blacks captains have to prove they are capable of extraordinary things, which is what Mourie did.

'It was a very tough decision to make,' he says. 'But it wasn't just the morality issue about South African political interference and the ability for people to be able to play, or not, in their national team. It was also the effect it was going to have on the game in New Zealand and the effect it was going to have on New Zealand rugby, so I think there were probably three zones there and in none of those three was I comfortable that the right outcome was going to be achieved by the tour proceeding. So it was a pretty clear-cut case from a moral and philosophical sort of presence but from an emotional side it was pretty tough to make that call.'

* * *

When David Kirk starts thumping the Eden Park turf in 1987, it's not out of frustration. It's elation, tinged with relief, because he knows the All Blacks are going to win the World Cup. He has just scored to push the All Blacks out to a 19–3 lead in the first World Cup final. He knows it's going to be enough to win and that victory won't only be for the men under his charge that day, it will be for generations of All Blacks teams.

'What wasn't lost on me was that I had followed the All Blacks since I was a young kid,' says Kirk. 'You always thought the All Blacks were the best team in the world and you had always been able to claim that, albeit the Springboks would debate that and the Lions had a wonderful team in 1971. But we never had the chance to prove it. So the bragging rights if you like, to be able to say that New Zealand were the best in the world, hadn't been available up until then. Being able to play the tournament and know that if we won it, we would be crowned world champions, meant that we were representatives of a whole history of All Blacks teams who had never been able to call themselves that because they never had the chance to play in a World Cup. When I scored my try, I hammered the ground with my fist knowing that's it, we have won the World Cup.'

He was right, from the next kick-off, Kirk broke free again and two passes later John Kirwan scored to make sure of the victory. Half an hour later Kirk climbed the steps at Eden Park to take receipt of the Webb Ellis trophy and immortalise himself in All Blacks history. His tenure wasn't long, but it didn't need to be for him to establish himself as one of the great captains. He was the first captain to lift the World Cup, and as it turned out, he would be the only New Zealander to do that for the next 24 years. Each time an All Blacks side went to the World Cup after 1987 and failed, the legend of Kirk grew. His place in history became more significant and the enormity of his achievement in leading a team to World Cup glory came to be better appreciated.

Kirk, who has a medical degree and also won a Rhodes scholarship to the University of Oxford, is easily the most academically gifted captain the All Blacks have had. He's also shown in his post-rugby life an incredible capacity to be resourceful and flexible, having worked for the world-renowned consultancy firm McKinsey, attempting to stand as a National MP, and being chief executive of Fairfax, the giant Australian media company. The more he's achieved in the corporate world, the more it has reinforced his standing as a great All Blacks captain.

What's maybe not been fully appreciated, though, is the road he had to travel to reach Eden Park as captain of the All Blacks. It would be easy to assume that intelligence was his greatest attribute as captain; that being articulate and bright were the keys to him being a great leader. Those qualities helped, but what enabled Kirk to drive the one per cent balance in favour of the All Blacks side he captained was his tenacity and resilience.

Like Mourie before him, Kirk took a principled stand to not tour South Africa with the Cavaliers in 1986. But unlike Mourie, his team-mates didn't see it as the same great act of sacrifice. Instead, those who had been with the Cavaliers wanted Kirk out when they returned. And they got their way. Jock Hobbs took over the captaincy for the tour to France in late 1986 and then Andy Dalton was appointed in 1987 when the former was forced to retire due to concussion. It was only the day before the first World Cup game that Dalton finally gave in and said he couldn't play after damaging his hamstring a few weeks earlier.

For Kirk, there was the initial disappointment at being axed in 1986 when he had done nothing wrong. Then there was the added frustration of seeing Dalton, who had toured with the Cavaliers, take over from Hobbs. It seemed odd for the All Blacks to dump so many Cavaliers as a means to cleanse the team and heal the rifts that had been caused by the rebel tour, and then appoint Dalton to the captaincy. It was especially odd given that Sean Fitzpatrick was playing the house down and looked every inch the best hooker in the country.

It was confused thinking but Kirk didn't take it personally and says he was neither bitter nor resentful that he was overlooked initially for the role in 1987. 'I am not a bitter and resentful person and I really wanted to make sure I was in the All Blacks team that won the World Cup. When they announced Andy as captain, I was happy — well not happy but focused on playing as best as I could. My next goal was to be number one halfback and start the matches and be part of a winning World Cup team.

'The thought of captaincy had dropped away. Someone had made a decision that I couldn't control so what was most important to me was playing well and being part of the team. So I was kind of over it in that sense. I didn't dwell on it. I still, if you had been able to ask me at the time, would have said it was the wrong decision, but it had been made and there was nothing more to be done. That is something you learn in rugby and in life — if you want to be successful and things have not gone the way you want, you have to get on with what is in front of you and try to execute as well as you can.

'I wouldn't say I was relieved or that a burden had been lifted either. Part of me was probably still frustrated but I was able to convince myself to let it go and not worry about it. So when Andy pulled out of that final training at Pukekohe, and Brian [Lochore] immediately said to me, "You will captain the side tomorrow", I didn't think, *Wow, this is amazing.* I just said okay and, who knows, Andy could have been coming back one week after that so it was one game at a time.'

* * *

When Joel Stransky's drop goal sailed through the posts in the 1995 World Cup final, it not only broke New Zealand hearts, but it also left Sean Fitzpatrick's reign as All Blacks captain in danger of being condemned as largely unsuccessful. He would be considered a great player. He was arguably the best hooker New Zealand had produced — a dynamic and mobile force who redefined expectations about the role. He was tough, durable,

'That is something you learn in rugby and in life — if you want to be successful and things have not gone the way you want, you have to get on with what is in front of you and try to execute as well as you can.'

—DAVID KIRK

athletic and obstinate — a great character, a great team man and a great personality. But his captaincy between 1992 and 1995 didn't have a defining moment to elevate it to greatness. The All Blacks had beaten the Lions in 1993 but they weren't a great team. That tour had descended into farce for the visitors when their midweek side lost by almost 40 points to Waikato and no one was going to overly celebrate the series win when it came.

If anything, Fitzpatrick's first four years as captain were more memorable for the losses than victories. The All Blacks had lost the Bledisloe Cup series in 1992. They lost a one-off test to England at Twickenham at the end of 1993 and a two-test series against France in 1994 before handing back the Bledisloe Cup that same year. It wasn't a great tenure results-wise, and when the All Blacks lost the 1995 World Cup final, that was the stark truth facing Fitzpatrick. The All Blacks won 67 per cent of their tests under Fitzpatrick between 1992 and the end of the 1995 World Cup. It was okay, but couldn't stand comparison with the likes of Dalton, whose record was 87 per cent, or Mourie on 79 per cent. And it certainly couldn't stand comparison with the 100 per cent record of Shelford.

Fitzpatrick needed a defining achievement in the wake of the failed 1995 World Cup bid. As brilliant as the All Blacks had been in the tournament, they hadn't won it. All their magic in destroying Wales, Ireland, Japan, Scotland and England counted for not so much when they weren't able to beat the Boks at Ellis Park, and it was that knowledge as much as anything else that drove Fitzpatrick throughout 1996. It was the need to make amends that saw him accept John Hart's invitation to stay on as captain and Fitzpatrick had one goal in his sights that year — to win the three-test series in South Africa.

'We knew if we lost the first test [in Durban] we were buggered basically, because we couldn't win two at altitude,' says Fitzpatrick. 'Then we targeted Pretoria, Loftus, because if we didn't win that we knew we wouldn't win at Ellis Park. It's like golf courses — if you play badly at a golf course, you don't like going back there, and less than 12 months earlier we had lost at Ellis Park.

'In 1995, when I look back, we did things we shouldn't have done in terms of the preparation for the game. It's all easy in hindsight, but we learned from that in terms of the way we prepared to play the Boks. We had a different attitude. There weren't many personnel changes, probably 12 of the team that had started the World Cup final were starting in 1996. One of our great fullbacks, Don Clarke, was living in South Africa and he had been in touch during the tour and as I walked off the field he had tears streaming down his face. He would have been mid-seventies, 80, I suppose, and he said, "Sean, thank you", and he hugged me — and in those days we didn't do a lot of man hugs, especially All Blacks — and he said, "I can go to my grave a happy man knowing that the All Blacks have beaten South Africa in a series in South Africa." Which sort of summed it up really.'

For whatever reason, Fitzpatrick couldn't swing the one per cent balance the All Blacks' way in 1995 but he did in 1996, and with it, became revered as one of the great All Blacks captains. In 1996 he played with the confidence and authority of a man who knew his destiny. He was in the form of his life — bold, dynamic, into everything and able to do it for 80 minutes. He seemed to have an almost hypnotic power over the various referees and he inspired his All Blacks to dig deeper than they ever had. They did the unthinkable, which was to appear to be in control of almost every minute of the first two tests. Under pressure, yes, but able to cope. Able to stay connected and certain of their roles. It was brilliant leadership from Fitzpatrick. Maybe the best sustained period of captaincy ever produced by an All Black.

If he'd retired in 1995 as he was considering, his tenure would have been seen as okay and those quiet moments of contemplation would have been filled with endless replays of that Mehrtens drop goal late in regular time sailing wide and regrets about the way the team prepared and how they performed. That series victory in 1996 changed his life as now he trades off his name, his brand having been built on his successful captancy of the world's best rugby team.

* * *

The statistics of Richie McCaw's captaincy are so impressive as to give no clue that he, like so many great captains before him, nearly fell on the wrong side of history. The one per cent balance nearly tipped the wrong way on the night he so desperately needed it to be his. His legacy is so ingrained, that many forget how fragile it once was.

Singled out in the wake of the 2007 World Cup quarter-final defeat as a captain who didn't make the right calls, McCaw, in true Hollywood style, sets his sights on making amends at the 2011 World Cup. He takes greater control of the team. He throws himself even harder into everything, especially his mental conditioning. He demands more of everyone around him. And each test he plays, he becomes a little wiser and better at the nearly impossible job of captaining the All Blacks. The wins build up. His reputation grows and, all the time, in his sights is the Webb Ellis trophy.

The dream, to win it on home soil, looks entirely possible, maybe even probable, when the All Blacks beat France in their pool game to ensure they will qualify for the play-offs in pole position. When they defeat Argentina in the quarter-final, even without star first-five Dan Carter, who rips his groin before the last pool encounter, the dream is still alive. When they comprehensively outplay the Wallabies in the semi-final, even with their third-choice first-five Aaron Cruden, who has had to replace the now ruled-out Colin Slade, the dream is still alive. The dream is just 80 minutes from being fulfilled.

All that stands in the way of McCaw is a French team that they have already beaten. A French team that also lost to Tonga and has reportedly fallen out with their coach. A French team that was lucky to meet an England team in even greater disarray in the quarter-final and a French team that saw Wales captain Sam Warburton sent off after 20 minutes of the semi-final.

But it's a French team that roars to life in the final. It's a French team that has worked out much of the All Blacks' tactical plan and a French team that is playing faster and with more intensity than they did three weeks ago on the same ground against the All Blacks. When Cruden is forced off after 30 minutes due to a knee injury, the All Blacks send on their fourth-choice first-five Stephen Donald — at which point no one can predict on which side the one per cent balance of fate is going to fall.

Given the way France are growing in confidence and cohesion, they look like they are going to find a way to win as they did four years earlier. That sense only heightens when captain Thierry Dusautoir scores a try after 47 minutes to make the score 8–7 to New Zealand. What transpired, though, was the greatest 30 minutes of individual resistance ever produced. McCaw, on his own, kept the All Blacks in the game. Whether he did it legally or quasi-legally is moot: he found a way to slow French possession, to occasionally steal it and generally frustrate them.

He's a lone figure in this regard. Team-mate Jerome Kaino is tackling his heart out and Kieran Read is scrambling to the far reaches of the field, but McCaw is hauling the team around on his back. He's a lone soldier out there — fighting battle after battle and somehow doing enough to win each of them. He's going to make the balance of fate fall on his side by sheer willpower. He plays with an almost demonic energy that says he can't accept that his dream will be broken. Not like this. Not after spending four years building towards redemption.

If the All Blacks had lost that night at Eden Park, McCaw may well have been destined to a different legacy — one in which he was a great captain most of the time, just not at World Cups. He needed that victory to remove the qualifier, the doubt, the stain, the whatever it would be called, as a result of being dumped out of two World Cups by the French.

If Fitzpatrick's captaincy during the successful 1996 series was the best sustained effort in All Blacks history, McCaw's 80 minutes in the 2011 World Cup final was the best single test performance by a captain. It earned the All Blacks that one per cent balance and it earned him greatness.

CHAPTER FOURTEEN

UNITED FRONT

JOHN HART ISN'T sure exactly what he will find in the changing room when he gets there, but he's braced for the worst. When they had left the shed at Twickenham to resume the second half of the 1999 World Cup semi-final the All Blacks were 24–10 ahead. They would be returning having lost 43–31, dumped out of the World Cup after the most extraordinary 40 minutes of test rugby ever played.

Hart, who took over as coach in 1996, knows the defeat has ended his career. His job is untenable now the All Blacks have crashed out of another World Cup in spectacular fashion. And he knows that his players will be mentally shattered — none more so than captain Taine Randell. The last two years have been incredibly tough for the young All Blacks captain. He was thrust into a job he wasn't ready for and didn't particularly want in 1998 and suffered an emotionally torrid time as the side lost five tests on the bounce. He wasn't strong-armed into continuing in 1999 but Hart knows that he and others put pressure on, that they were influential in persuading Randell to give it one more year.

And so, given the background and the circumstances, Hart is determined to protect his captain in what he knows will be a messy and prolonged fallout. He knows that the media will be savage. He is aware of how spectacular the second-half collapse has been and how powerless the All Blacks were to stop it. The optics were horrible and the leadership of the team is going to be questioned and Randell pilloried. Hart is media savvy, but he hardly needs to be to understand the maelstrom that is coming.

'I went into that dressing room at Twickenham and I've never seen such a mess,' says Hart. 'And Taine was beside himself. He was supposed to do the interview 10 minutes after the game. I had to go and do it because the captain was broken. And I respected that. It was really tough for him and there's no way I ever look at 1999 and blame him as captain. We just collectively didn't handle the situation. But that dressing room showed the effect and impact captaincy had on his life. It really came out at that time.

'It was very difficult. I was trying to take the pressure off Taine. I was very careful to protect Taine and always will. I think it's your role as coach. I knew he was struggling. I decided I'd resign over there so people could have my head rather than have it drag on, because I could see what was going to happen, everyone was going to be dragged into it. So it was best to make a clean cut.'

Randell says he wasn't so much shattered as shocked by the time he flumped into the dressing room at Twickenham. His head was spinning. Too much had happened too quickly and he couldn't process events in real time. 'I do remember [Prime Minister] Jim Bolger coming into the changing room afterwards with his brown belt and black shoes. That was a strange thing to remember.' But other than that, he was numb.

It was a state in which he could remain long after he returned home as the nation's ire was directed at Hart rather than Randell. The reaction to the All Blacks' loss was virulent in a way no one could have possibly predicted. Every All Black had a story about being the victim of some nasty response. Justin Marshall, for example, picked up his suitcase at Christchurch Airport to find that, presumably, the baggage handlers in Auckland had scrawled 'loser' all over it. But no one was more exposed to the venomous response than Hart. He was seen as the architect of the defeat, the man responsible for the failure, and of all the ridiculous and unacceptable things that happened in the months after that loss in Twickenham, the worst was when a racehorse owned by Hart was spat on.

But as hard as it was to be the focus of this anger, Hart was ready to get through it as he felt protective of Randell and obliged to shelter him from the worst aspects of the public and media wrath. Their relationship had never quite been on an equal footing, with both men knowing that Randell was not the captain of choice, but the captain by a lack of choice. There was always an element of a power imbalance as well — Hart being the corporate veteran and battle-hardened mastermind of the great Auckland era of supremacy and Randell being the fresh-faced scarfie, coming into the All Blacks straight from egg fights and other student antics in Dunedin.

They got on, they saw the game in much the same way tactically, and were each in possession of smart, inquisitive minds. Both were articulate, worldly and intelligent, and hence there was mutual respect, but Randell was the reluctant captain, far from being a giant of the world game. It sparked in Hart a duty of care element he'd never felt when Sean Fitzpatrick — older, wisened and supremely confident in the job — had been All Blacks captain.

'By shielding the captain, I put a huge amount of pressure on myself,' says Hart. 'I became public enemy number one. Taine hardly got mentioned in the aftermath. But I got crucified. And that was tough. That was as bad as my life has ever been. That was horrendous.'

Randell appreciated the gallantry of it all. He was grateful that Hart threw himself rather than his captain under the bus. Maybe it wasn't obvious at the time, but Hart's sacrifice meant Randell's reputation suffered only minimal damage and that he would be able to continue his All Blacks career, albeit not as captain. But Randell also felt that it was the rightful extension of their relationship. That it reflected the balance of power that had always been there. 'He got most of the blame,' says Randell. 'But I think in saying that, he was the face of the All Blacks. In the absence of a strong captain, he was the face. So it's only natural that he took the most blame. If you had a stronger captain, invariably the captain would be the one to really cop it. But I guess, in my second year, I was not a strong captain. I certainly got my fair share but nowhere near as he did.'

* * *

To some extent, John Mitchell and Reuben Thorne were cut from the same cloth. The former had been a giant in the provincial game in the 1980s and 1990s — a tireless No. 8 who made up for whatever he lacked in explosive pace and dynamism with relentless desire. Mitchell was tough and uncompromising on the field and a big believer in observing its traditions off it. He was the long-serving captain of Waikato, leading with his fearlessness on the park.

Thorne was much the same. A solid loose forward whose game was built on accuracy and work rate, he too captained the Crusaders with a similar quiet authority and, like Mitchell, he was happy that once the boots were kicked off, it was okay to have a few beers and enjoy the moment. They weren't two peas in a pod but they had a connection and presumably Mitchell saw something of himself in Thorne.

Having originally flirted with the idea of appointing Andrew Hore, by May 2002 Mitchell, made All Blacks coach in late 2001, had settled on Thorne as his preferred captain. They were kindred spirits, or close enough anyway, to form a working relationship that was perhaps economical with words but strong enough for the two to build mutual understanding of what each other wanted and needed. They were aligned rather than close, professional rather than familiar, but bound strongly enough to endure some tough periods in 2002.

Thorne never appealed to the masses as the heroic All Blacks captain they wanted and the media criticism varied from moderate to heavy throughout his first year in charge and for much of his second. It was potentially unsettling. It could have undermined his confidence in himself and his ability to do the job, but whenever he was under pressure Thorne received all the requisite feedback and support he needed from Mitchell.

When Thorne needed his coach, Mitchell was there for him. 'I had good support from my team-mates and they all backed me because I guess the people on the field know what you do,' says

Thorne. 'And the coaches were the same, they said, "Look, just keep playing well, we're happy with what you're doing." Those are the opinions that really matter to me, so that helped.'

When the All Blacks came to play the Wallabies in the 2003 World Cup semi-final, Mitchell and Thorne were united. They had plotted the path together to this point, and having beaten the Wallabies twice already that year, they had a shared confidence about the game. It wasn't overconfidence, just a shared appreciation that they had worked well together to bring the team as far as they had and that they were playing well. Their mutual respect for one another was obvious and they sensed the opportunity they had to make history.

Except it didn't work out like that. 'There's a few things about the game I remember,' says Thorne. 'We actually started really well. We had the Aussies on the ropes. We played a really expansive kind of game and we had them stretched, but to their credit they'd done their homework and they were able to close us down. Then of course Stirling Mortlock got that intercept, which, if he hadn't have caught that pass, we probably would have scored. That was the point where we thought, *Shit, we're in trouble*. We hadn't really been in that situation of being behind all season. We'd been dominant, we had scored freely against most sides. But their defence was rock solid. We couldn't crack them and they kept generating penalties to stay out of reach.

'A lot of people said, "You didn't have a plan B or you didn't adapt" or whatever, but we actually played quite differently in the second half. They'd shut us down when we tried to go wide so we tried to go through the middle. But when you start going through the middle it's actually a lot harder to score points. We couldn't, no matter what we tried, break them, so you've got to give them some credit for that.'

The relationship between coach and captain had strengthened throughout 2003 and Thorne felt they were connected strongly enough to deal with the inevitable media backlash that would erupt. He was surprised and saddened to find out he had been wrong. When the All Blacks lost that semi-final, the connection broke.

Mitchell, who had been under all sorts of media scrutiny himself, effectively disappeared. He knew his days in the role were numbered, as New Zealand Rugby chief executive Chris Moller had told media in the days after the All Blacks had been dumped out of the tournament that even had they beaten Australia and gone on to win the World Cup, Mitchell's contract may not have been renewed. There was dissatisfaction within the upper echelons of NZR about Mitchell's lack of respect for sponsors and external stakeholders. So, aware that he was now in a battle to survive, Mitchell ditched his captain.

'I felt isolated in terms of dealing with all that because John Mitchell pretty much pulled right back out of it,' says Thorne. 'It was kind of, "You're the captain, you deal with it." I don't think I was well supported, like a captain now who has so much more support around him and education on how to deal with those moments. At the time, you just get on and deal with it. You had a job to do and part of that was fronting the media on behalf of the team. That was just what I did.

'I don't recall the finger being pointed at me specifically, because I played a reasonable game. I scored a try and I don't think there's much more that I could have done personally. But there were questions around the team mentality and were we focused. I had to front that, which was pretty tough. I don't think we choked. We went into the game and we were outplayed. We did change tactics, we tried different things, and we were outplayed on the day. And that's the reality of World Cup rugby and we've seen that recently. No matter how well you play and prepare, there's 15 guys on the other side who can, on the day, knock you over. This whole thing that there was a history of choking and we couldn't cope with the pressure and choked ... that was tough to handle as captain.'

'It was kind of, "You're the captain, you deal with it." I don't think I was well supported, like a captain now who has so much more support around him and education on how to deal with those moments. At the time, you just get on and deal with it. You had a job to do and part of that was fronting the media on behalf of the team. That was just what I did.'

—REUBEN THORNE

There's an old-school code of honour about Thorne that prevents him from truly opening up about the hurt he felt to be abandoned by Mitchell. It wasn't just that he deserved a better response, it was the sense of betrayal that came with it. The sense that the two had never been as close or connected as Thorne had believed. It also opened up questions about Mitchell's understanding of team and unity, as it looked awfully like he ducked for cover in an attempt to save his own skin.

In the end, neither he nor Thorne were retained. Mitchell was replaced by Graham Henry as coach and Thorne as captain by

Tana Umaga. Thorne was also dropped from the squad in 2004, unwanted by Henry. 'I was initially really upset not to be back in the team but the captaincy was definitely in its own way a burden, particularly when you're a person like me with a shy personality. It does weigh heavy on you in that respect, yes. But I still wanted to be an All Black and I dearly wanted to be in the team. I thought I was still young and playing well and I wanted to get back in the team and beat the Wallabies and do all the stuff that we'd been doing previously, so the whole idea of redemption drove me.'

And Thorne did indeed win the reprieve he craved: he was rewarded with the redemptive recompense his decency and honour merited when he was recalled to the All Blacks in 2006 and retained as part of the squad that played the 2007 World Cup in France.

* * *

The coach–captain axis is an imperative relationship in the high-performance set-up. There has to be compatibility, mutual respect and honesty binding the two most important figures within the All Blacks. There also has to be integrity — a genuine desire on the part of both to protect and support each other. There can't be any false element, any sense that one man is actually secretly working against the other or not convinced about the abilities of the other.

If the coach and captain are on the same tactical page, it spreads confidence and certainty. The captain, after all, is essentially the coach's representative on the field. The captain is the guardian of the coach's tactical blueprint, the man entrusted to carry it out.

The captain is the builder if you like, the coach the architect. They have to hold the same vision.

In the amateur era the quality of coaching was variable. It wasn't the job it is now — there was no science behind it; no real means to review and adapt. There was an added problem, which was that quite often All Blacks squads were poorly selected. The coaching role was respected, but not the way it is now, and it wasn't necessarily catastrophic if the coach and captain didn't always have a meeting of tactical minds.

'In those days there was a coach of varying degrees of capability and education so I was pretty lucky with the first couple of coaches I had,' says Graham Mourie. 'Eric Watson was a Junior All Black and I had Ivan Vodanovich in NZ Under 21s so that was a pretty interesting experience. Eric had a clear picture of how his teams should play. I think the forwards all loved him apart from the Auckland forwards. He was Otago and you did the hard yards in the forwards — you had to hit the rucks and clean out, you had to be there. So it was very much the Otago style of play in those days. With Jack Gleeson, I think Jack had a very good philosophy of playing the game and I'd certainly think, like with Eric, the philosophy wasn't always shared by everyone on the team.

'You've got to appreciate that in those days the team did a lot of the coaching themselves. We tended to be heavily involved in setting the game plans. For me, the role of the captain was to make sure that the team went onto the field with a winning plan. You then executed the plan on the field — and in those days it wasn't just the coach that set those plans, because, for example, Eric was a forwards-orientated coach and Jack was a backs-orientated coach and stuff got basically left to the senior players.'

That's not the case now and hasn't been since the late amateur era. Sean Fitzpatrick says that under coach Laurie Mains he barely had a say in how the team would play. The relationship between Fitzpatrick and Mains had been strained and difficult for much of their first year together in 1992 because it wasn't underpinned by mutual respect. But even when things thawed after Fitzpatrick began to prove himself as both player and captain, it never evolved into an open, collegial, respectful relationship where the captain's opinion was sought and valued. 'He was a total dictator,' Fitzpatrick says of Mains. 'And he didn't give us any leadership. He sat us down and said, "Get out there. This is what you are going to do." I didn't like that at all. It wasn't the way I was brought up. I was brought up in terms of group leadership. But we weren't in a situation where we were capable of doing it so we were stripped back to the bones and told this is what you have got, boys. If you don't like it, get out of here.'

Fitzpatrick somehow made it work. Tactically at least, the two came to be on the same page. They shared a mutual desire to get fitter and play at a higher tempo. They shared the belief that the All Blacks could be lethal if they played wider and with more creativity — and that commonality was enough to glue them together tightly enough to command the team.

Fitzpatrick lived with the regime that Mains wanted but he much preferred the inclusive, collaborative style of John Hart who took over in 1996. It's worth noting that Fitzpatrick's success rate as captain when Mains was coach stood at 67 per cent. In the two years Hart was coach and Fitzpatrick captain, the All Blacks lost once and drew once in 28 tests. His ratio under Hart was 94 per cent and the last two years of his career were the best in terms of his form and leadership.

Shelford's success ratio as captain between 1988 and 1990 was 100 per cent, the only blip in 22 tests being a draw with Australia. That was achieved in the similarly dictatorial regime of Alex 'Grizz' Wyllie. But 'dictatorial' as it applied to All Blacks coaches of the late amateur era is not used in a derogatory sense. The players, by all accounts, didn't feel like they were suppressed or treated badly. They may not always have liked the control and influence the coach would have on the team, but they mostly accepted that was the way coach–player relationships worked. Shelford, a man steeped in the military having served in the navy for 15 years, was more than comfortable in an environment where a man with a higher rank gave orders and he followed them. A chain of command was how things got done and he saw his role as implementing the plan Wyllie had devised.

That was one of the key reasons he and Wyllie built such a successful partnership. The provincial divide probably would have split the team much earlier than 1990 had it not been for Shelford's strength of character and the strength of his connection with Wyllie. A weaker captain could easily have been bullied into changing the game plan on the field to suit either the Auckland or Canterbury players, but Shelford never lost sight of the chain of command.

But, as Shelford says, there was also warmth to his relationship with Wyllie. It wasn't only a sense of duty that kept them together. The two men liked each other, found common ground to chat about and enjoy each other's company. 'The way things were back in the day, your coaches were quite strict about what they wanted,' says Shelford. 'With the All Blacks, what Grizz said went. And he expected you to front every game. I suppose he coached with a little bit of fear factor. As he got older, I think that disappeared a little bit. But everything he said was gruff because of his demeanour more than anything else. It was just the way he is. I got on well with him. We had quite a few laughs on tours. We talked all the time.

'There was a lot of innuendo about him, what he had done off the field. But I never saw any of that. I thought he was astute and liked the game plans he would come up with. When players think they are above and beyond the game itself, you think to yourself, *Where is this going to lead?* Grizz was really onto that — not suppressing players' ability to play but telling them to stick to the game plan, that way everyone understands what we are doing.'

Since 2004 and the introduction of player-led environments, the picture has changed radically. The big change has been the growth in size of the coaching team. In Shelford's day, there was one head coach. At the 2019 World Cup, the All Blacks had 15 people in their wider coaching/management team. A game plan is not devised by the head coach alone and then managed and implemented on the field by the captain alone. That's not the modern world of test rugby.

Yet the importance of the relationship between the head coach and captain of the All Blacks has not diminished. It remains the key relationship and has an enormous bearing on the culture of the team. The way the captain and coach relate to one another tends to set the tone of the environment. It will often determine the mood of the squad, the way they relate to one another and other coaching staff. If they have an obvious rapport, a genuine give-and-take relationship where they can joke with one another, it pervades the team. Likewise, if that relationship is strained, tense and difficult, it pervades the team.

* * *

There's no question Steve Hansen is agitated that Graham Henry, whom he replaced as head coach of the All Blacks, is now working for the Pumas. It wasn't such a problem in 2012 as Henry's role 12 months ago was advising and guiding the Argentinian coaching team. But by September 2013 Henry's role had morphed into technical adviser, and in that capacity he would be analysing the All Blacks for weaknesses, passing on knowledge about the inner sanctum to help the Pumas win in Hamilton.

There were two distinct levels to why this was causing angst among the All Blacks. The first was that Henry was also operating as a full-time assistant coach at the Blues Super Rugby side. In his role there he had detailed knowledge about the respective strengths and weaknesses of three young Blues players within the All Blacks. Francis Saili was making his test debut at second-five against the Pumas; Steven Luatua would be winning his third cap at blindside; and on the bench was outside back Charles Piutau. The conflict of interest to Hansen's mind was untenable.

The second issue was that of hypocrisy linked to loyalty. As head coach, Henry had expressed his disappointment that the likes of Daniel Bowden and Jared Payne had left New Zealand for overseas contracts when they were on the cusp of making the All Blacks. It seemed hypocritical that Henry, having been All Blacks coach for eight years which culminated in World Cup victory in 2011, was then wearing a Pumas tracksuit and sitting in their coaching box plotting New Zealand's downfall.

As New Zealand Rugby chief executive Steve Tew said a few days later: 'We had an agreement with Graham and Argentina for a period of time that he would assist them as they tried to get competitive and comfortable in the Rugby Championship. We also saw some benefits in having him assist John Kirwan at the Blues particularly early on in his coaching career back here in New Zealand. So we have weighed that up and believe the benefits outweigh the risks. But it is something we will keep an eye on. It is awkward watching Sir Ted in the Pumas' coaching box, isn't it?'

Awkward was maybe not how the All Blacks players saw it. Their emotions ranged from disappointment to anger to dismay, with some even feeling an element of betrayal. They certainly weren't impressed, which is why, when Henry came into the All Blacks' changing room after the game, there were a few icy stares. Those who were there say that captain Richie McCaw dealt with that particular episode with such aplomb as to preserve his former coach's dignity while respecting the mood of his players. It was a diplomatic masterstroke by McCaw to avoid embarrassment and signified how the nature of his relationship with Henry had evolved.

When McCaw first captained the team as a 24-year-old against Wales in Cardiff, he says he didn't have a clue what he was doing. By his last test on Henry's watch — the 2011 World Cup final — he was a colossus of a captain, one of the game's great leaders; and as a result, his relationship with his head coach reflected that. For most of Henry's working life he'd been an educator, and when the game turned professional he had been the principal of a major boys' school. The authoritarian tone never left him. You could take the principal out of the school but not the principal out of the man.

Between 2006 and 2010, McCaw became the head boy of Henry's regime. By 2011, though, from the outside at least, it appeared as if Henry's assistants, Hansen and Wayne Smith, and the other specialist coaches, were doing all the hands-on coaching. The players were spending more time with Hansen and Smith, while Henry focused on the bigger, tactical picture. It became a running joke that Henry, known to everyone as Ted, had become almost clueless about the technical intricacies being applied on the training ground. It wasn't meant as an insult or to undermine his authority, but as an appreciation that he had become one of the great strategist coaches of his time with an unrivalled ability to devise a game plan and know how to adapt and evolve it through constant analysis. It was also meant to signify the trust and confidence that Henry had in his coaching staff — particularly Hansen and Smith, who had both previously been head coaches of test sides. Henry was big picture — his assistants fixing the detail to make it happen.

But while there was good-natured ribbing that Henry was removed from the working detail of the team's training plans, it did also indicate that to some extent he had become a little detached from the players. It cast him less as grumpy, well-intentioned principal and more as a much-admired but slightly wayward favourite uncle. Henry had command of the team, but it felt almost as if McCaw came to outgrow him in the end. The captain, by 2011, had become the more influential figure in driving the team.

* * *

It's apparent from his body language that Hansen wants to interject. Kieran Read is to his left, answering a question about whether the All Blacks, who have just lost the 2019 World Cup semi-final 19–7 to England, turned up with the right mental attitude. It's a question that came after Hansen had said earlier in the press conference that at half-time he had challenged his team to be hungrier in the second half.

Read, who has a nasty cut above his right eye, is barely holding it together emotionally. He's obviously been on the brink of tears since the final whistle, might even have had a few moments where they slipped down his face. The question was: 'Kieran, Steve mentioned before … he said, "We needed to get hungry and desperate before it was too late." From your point of view, from the players' point of view I suppose, did the team turn up with the right attitude tonight?'

Read responded by saying: 'Yeah, I think we did. You've seen how hard we worked out there. Definitely the boys really wanted it. I think with the detail of the match it didn't go our way but the work rate and how much we really wanted it was there.'

Hansen, having waited not so patiently for Read to finish, jumps straight in: 'I'd just like to clear that up,' he said with a not so neutral tone. 'I think it's quite a disrespectful question to suggest that the All Blacks turned up not being hungry. They were desperate to win the game. Because I asked them at half-time to get hungrier doesn't mean to say they didn't turn up pretty hungry. There's a big difference and if you want to spend some time outside I'll give you a rugby education on that one. But to turn up and say an All Blacks team comes to the semi-final of a Rugby World Cup with the amount of ability and the history it has behind it ... that's not hungry, that's a pretty average question.'

The exchange generated clickbait stories around the world. But of course, as is always the case, the clickbaiters missed the real story which was that Hansen's reaction revealed how protective he had become of his captain. He was the lioness protecting the cub and it wasn't the first time that year either. After the All Blacks had drawn with South Africa then lost to Australia in consecutive tests before the World Cup, there was growing media criticism of Read. It irked Hansen, mostly because he thought it was unwarranted and unfair. He felt Read was playing well, doing everything that he was supposed to.

More significantly, Hansen felt that Read had grown immeasurably as the leader since taking on the role in 2016. The coach had seen his captain become more demanding of others in 2019. He had seen him take greater control at training. He had seen him become bolder and more authoritative in his decision-making on the field and yet, almost conversely, he had also seen Read empower and embrace the new generation of youngsters in the team such as Sevu Reece and George Bridge. And Read had managed to do all this after enduring back surgery in early 2018 that was major and potentially career-ending.

There had been some evidence prior to the defeat in Yokohama that Hansen was losing his patience with the media's line of questioning around Read's performances. The All Blacks played Tonga in Hamilton a few days before departing for Japan, and after the 92–7 demolition Read was asked about whether he felt his form was improving. Hansen rolled his eyes theatrically, which led to him being asked why. 'I'm just pretty disappointed with some of the questions you're asking. Most of them you could answer yourself. Ask us something that we can actually talk about that would be invigorating for the fans to read.'

Hansen was always aware that Read had the unenviable task of following McCaw into the job. That was never going to be easy — to replace the greatest captain the All Blacks had ever known — and the coach was careful to never, or rarely, make comparisons or even publicly mention McCaw between 2016 and 2019.

When Hansen took over as head coach in 2012, McCaw was already the most experienced All Blacks captain in history. He'd already won a World Cup and so Hansen's challenge as coach was to instil within McCaw a belief that he still had much to achieve. That he still had much to learn. If McCaw had outgrown Henry in 2011, there was a reversal of that power balance when Hansen took over. He would be the boss in every sense. He would be across everything that happened. Hansen would be hands-on at training.

But it wasn't a return to a dictatorial regime. Far from it. The leadership group would be as strong, if not stronger. They would have the same input into game plans and off-field protocols. Hansen knew the importance of allowing the captain's experience, reputation, inherent commitment and passion to drive those around him and he wanted to help the captain grow his influence. So there was room for debate and discussion. Everyone could be challenged and heard and it worked. Hansen became the Alex Ferguson figure he wanted to be: he had the same sort of power as the great Manchester United manager held for decades and yet there was ample room, too, for McCaw to grow into the greatest captain the All Blacks had ever known.

Integral to this mutual growth was the trust that existed between coach and captain. Hansen learned the art of giving the public an honest appraisal of tests without betraying his players and he was expert at shielding his captains from criticism. McCaw knew he could rely on Hansen's support and the security of that was the foundation for growth. And because both men knew where their boundaries lay and because Hansen was by nature more laid-back and less intense than Henry, coach and captain developed a relationship that was relaxed, friendly and at times comedic. They had an easy rapport, and when it was time to be serious, they had an equally intense desire to succeed. Their comfort with one another lightened the vibe.

The senior players in particular said the team environment post-2012 became less intense than it had been — that Hansen's ability to relax when it was time to relax gave everyone more breathing space to enjoy themselves. Veteran wing Cory Jane, ahead of the 2014 test with the USA, noted that players had greater licence to be themselves and enjoy the moment, yet the team was still winning, still on track to become the most dominant in history. He was happier, he said, enjoying his rugby more as a result.

However true that had been between 2012 and 2015, it became more so after 2016. Hansen had a similar rapport with Read as he did with McCaw. The biggest difference between the two captains, however, was Read's greater inclusivity. He was a more welcoming character, better connected with the younger players and more receptive to new ideas. Greater emphasis was placed on players being encouraged to be themselves and that applied directly to the way Read and Hansen interacted. The coach had more of a protective arm around Read, gave him space to find his feet in those first years of his tenure. They had that same ability to poke a little fun at each other and that same security that their relationship was embedded in trust.

'I was fortunate to have two fine men captain the All Blacks in my time,' said Hansen a week after he returned from the 2019 World Cup and signed off as coach. 'There was Richie. Great player, single-minded, very focused with what he wanted to do with his own career and how he wanted the team to be. Richie was a phenomenal player right to the very end. He had the engine that allowed him to do stuff that you just couldn't imagine other people being able to do. I watched him playing and you'd think, *Shit, there are two Richies out there.* He was very demanding.

'Then there was Reado, another fine gentleman. Very focused on what he wanted to achieve as an All Black and also what he wanted the team to achieve under his leadership. He was very much about uniting the team. He was great at building relationships with everybody across the board. He was one of the finest lineout exponents and really drove that part of our game for a long time. Again, softly spoken but demanding in his own way. Both of them very fine captains and good mates.'

CHAPTER FIFTEEN

PLAYING THE VICTIM

THERE'S NO OTHER job in New Zealand, in rugby, that comes with such a mix of adulation and hate. But that's life as All Blacks captain. It's a post where the occupant is revered in New Zealand and often despised, certainly not liked much, everywhere else. It's long been this way, but the vitriol directed at All Blacks captains has intensified as the legacy of the team and the profile of the game has grown. Success has bred jealousy and jealousy has clouded the judgement of many of those determined to beat the All Blacks.

The determination to beat the All Blacks is relentless around the world. They are the benchmark, the scalp everyone wants. It doesn't matter who the world champions are, a victory against the All Blacks will be seen as the greatest achievement in the game. Plenty of international sides have been in the midst of an appalling run of form and then been transformed into something unrecognisable when they have played the All Blacks. It is rare indeed for any team to have a bad day against the All Blacks. Somehow the sight of that black jersey, the prospect of, maybe, beating the legendary All Blacks, sees otherwise mediocre rugby teams become giants for 80 minutes.

A bad season can become a good season by beating the All Blacks. A victory against the All Blacks can save coaching careers and rejuvenate fading players. A victory can change a player's life. It's that big a deal. The Scots have never managed to beat New Zealand. Ireland took 111 years to do it, and when they did, every player involved had the certainty of knowing they would hold a treasured place in Irish sporting history. Wales haven't beaten the All Blacks since 1953 and the last time France did it was 2009. When the prize is an All Blacks victory, emotions run high. Passions can spill over into something else and all perspective can be lost.

It's a sign of respect, probably, that over the years All Blacks captains have often been demonised. The rest of the world has found it easier to attribute the All Blacks' continued brilliance to something dark and sinister rather than believe it might be hard work, innovation and collective ingenuity that has kept New Zealand at the top of the table. And this narrative reads best when the All Blacks captain is painted as the devil incarnate. At some stage in their respective careers, every All Blacks captain of the last 50 years will have experienced a period of vilification or victimisation.

Tana Umaga was vilified by foreign fans and media for his role in invaliding British & Irish Lions captain Brian O'Driscoll out of the 2005 tour. But two men in particular, Sean Fitzpatrick and Richie McCaw, endured endless and relentless opprobrium about the way they played and the things they allegedly did. No other captains have been the subject of such ire, which may be testament to their respective longevity in the role and globally recognised brilliance in performing it. They sparked a fury in others that was off the scale at times. They are among the captains New Zealanders have respected the most, but on foreign shores they cast a different shadow.

'The South Africans loved to hate him,' former All Blacks coach John Hart says of Fitzpatrick. 'I think it was in the second test of the 1996 series that Springboks captain Gary Teichmann got his head split open and he came off. I got a ring from the African manager Morné du Plessis afterwards to say that they were really disappointed at what had happened and that they blamed Fitzpatrick for it. So I said, "Oh, can I come back to you?"

'So I went with Jane Dent [media manager] and watched the video of the game and there's Teichmann on the ground and there's activity and it turns out it was friendly fire. One of his own guys kicked him in the head. And I couldn't see Fitzpatrick. So we played it over and over again and then we let it go on and there's Fitzpatrick out on the wing where he used to play quite a bit of the time.

'Well the media got to hear about this because Morné must have said something. So the next day I demanded an apology and I've still got the photo that they put in the paper with me standing next to Fitzy with a halo on his head. Players hated playing against him but he was just fantastic to play with.'

Being the focal point of opposition anger suited Fitzpatrick. He loved it despite the fact it saw him subjected to serious physical assaults throughout his career as captain. But he never reacted when the cheap shots landed. He'd take it all — absorb whatever punishment came his way, smile, sometimes even wink at the perpetrator, and give the impression he was possibly indestructible. Nor did he ever say anything. There was no whining from Fitzpatrick.

There was also the verbal taunting from opposition fans everywhere. He was called every name imaginable. He had fans chuck whatever they could find at him and boo and hiss his every move. Nothing but smiles and waves flowed back. Few captains have been so content to be cast in the role of pantomime villain. 'I loved it,' says Fitzpatrick. 'It was a way of taking pressure off the team. It took their [opposition] focus off, you know. I loved playing South Africa especially. In those days we didn't warm up on the field, but I always wanted to go onto the field just to annoy the hell out of the fans. They would go nuts. I would be walking into the stadium and they'd be throwing things at me and I'd turn around and be waving at them and it was all part of it, trying to silence the crowd. We enjoyed playing offshore as an All Blacks team. We liked hostile environments.

'I remember when Allan Border, the former Australian cricket captain, came to New Zealand and I met him at a function. He said he used to get booed and jeered everywhere he went and he said, "Sean, that is a mark of respect."'

* * *

It has gone midnight when the phone rings. The Nokia brick doesn't recognise the number, but a female voice on the other end, English, possibly Home Counties, says: 'Alastair would like to talk to you — can you hold for a second please?' She doesn't wait for a reply, which is convenient as it avoids having to ask who the hell Alastair is. Thankfully, when Alastair does take control of the phone, he's good enough to let slip his second name, which is Campbell, and suddenly it all clicks. It is the British & Irish Lions media team who are ringing and head honcho Alastair Campbell speaking. Campbell, is of course, world famous as he was former British Prime Minister Tony Blair's spin doctor for the best part of a decade. He has a fearsome reputation and famed ability to shape and manipulate the news which is why British & Irish Lions head coach Clive Woodward hired him for the 2005 tour to New Zealand.

It's an unusual move for rugby and politics to merge like this but Woodward is one of those guys who is always looking for a point of difference and is willing to try just about anything. The thing about the Lions is that it is hard enough for them to keep harmony in their camp having been drawn from players from four countries that spend most of their time plotting to take each other's heads off in Six Nations matches. Just as difficult to manage is their travelling media contingent which tends to run on national lines and sees injustice in every selection. It's a full plate long before having to deal with the All Blacks, tour games and a hostile New Zealand press pack, and so Woodward wanted Campbell alongside him, putting out fires, twisting narratives and creating distractions.

That Campbell is on the phone so late after the first test is not a surprise as the situation is tailor-made for him to work his influence. He's in his element as the first minute in Christchurch produced an astonishing incident which saw All Blacks captain Tana Umaga and hooker Keven Mealamu lift Lions captain Brian O'Driscoll from the side of a ruck and drop him on his head. The impact was enough to dislocate O'Driscoll's shoulder and end his tour.

The truly astonishing part, though, is that the incident was not seen by any of the match officials. If it had happened in today's game, the TMO would have picked it up, intervened and both Mealamu and Umaga would have been sent off and subsequently banned for a considerable time. Seen through the eyes of the Lions and their army of fans, the All Blacks captain was allowed to illegally injure the British & Irish Lions captain and get away with it. This is not conjecture, it is precisely what Campbell is saying on the phone. He's calm and matter of fact about it, but there's a determination in his voice that suggests he will be spinning this until the Lions have justice or Umaga's head on a stick, which they may see as the same thing. And sure enough, he finishes off by saying there's a press conference at the Christchurch Town Hall at 12.30 am where the Lions will be making their position clear.

In case it wasn't clear enough, the Lions wanted to reiterate their position later that same day in Wellington. Their mood had only soured by the time they reached the capital as, by then, citing commissioner Willem Venter had dismissed the Umaga incident as 'nothing to see here', but had somehow found evidence of Lions lock Danny Grewcock biting the finger of Mealamu at the bottom of a ruck.

It is ludicrous that Umaga's obviously dangerous act, committed in full view, has gone unpunished and yet something which happened under a throng of bodies has been discovered and punished. There's anger in the Lions camp that Grewcock will be banned for six weeks while the arch-villain Umaga will be free to lead his side in the second test in the capital. Again, this isn't summation, it's precisely what is being said by Woodward.

He's not hiding his rage, or his belief that the Lions lost 21–3 in Christchurch largely because of the O'Driscoll incident. The sense that Umaga is on trial is impossible to miss, especially when Woodward effectively suggests new evidence has come to light and shows the world's media the incident from what he says are new camera angles. He has big screens everywhere and a pointer in his hand, but the slow-motion footage from the so-called new angles looks to show much the same picture as before.

He must realise he's got nothing new, that he's not going to force the judiciary to reopen the case as it were, and so what's driving him, presumably, is a desire to smear Umaga's name. His goal is to damage the All Blacks captain's reputation and get in his head before the second test. Woodward wants Umaga to feel isolated, attacked, because if the Lions can instil fear in the All Blacks captain and a sense of dread, then it may pervade the team.

The UK media can hardly believe their luck — they have a story that is writing itself and it could hardly be bigger as the main character is the All Blacks captain and he has been cast in a role almost too villainous to believe. No one revels in an injustice quite like the British, and their media know how to pin blame for a defeat on anyone other than their own. As Woodward winds things down at the James Cook Hotel, it's apparent his mostly British audience are on message and fingers throughout the room are just itching to start typing, so Umaga can be plastered on newspapers across the UK and Ireland as public enemy number one.

* * *

The All Blacks lead the series 1–0 yet they are under siege and their captain is a figure of hate for the 25,000 or so Barmy Army Lions fans in New Zealand. It's unusual, possibly unprecedented, for an All Blacks captain to find himself in such a position on home soil. Plenty of All Blacks captains have been targeted by offshore fans in foreign lands, but Umaga knows that he will face the prospect of being on his home ground for the second test and half the crowd will boo his every touch. Wellington is his home yet it doesn't feel like that in the build-up to the second test.

The British media, already in a frenzy courtesy of Woodward, are taken to another level of ire when O'Driscoll expresses his bitterness at his fate and the lack of action taken against the perpetrators. 'I have worked so hard for so long to get to this and to have it taken away by a cheap shot leaves a nasty feeling. I just cannot put it into words. I am angry because it was such a cheap shot.'

The days after the first test were a trying time for Umaga. The judicial system had exonerated him, and while that had enraged the Brits, what was he to do about it? He was innocent according to the people empowered to actually determine that and yet guilty in the court of public opinion and seemingly still required to prove his innocence.

The media attack, he could live with. Woodward spouting off, he could understand. But O'Driscoll's response caused a problem. 'Drico was a well-liked player so it didn't help that he was outspoken,' says Justin Marshall, who spent much of that week in Wellington in counsel with Umaga. 'I remember talking to him about this during the week and that was the thing he was really struggling to cope with. He understood Woodward and his

PR machine doing what they were doing and he didn't really give a shit about what they had to say. But when O'Driscoll came out and said Tana was a dirty player and had intentionally tried to injure him, that hurt. When any player comes out and calls you a cheat and says you have tried to injure them, that strikes a raw nerve and that was what was really upsetting Tana that week.'

There had been mutual respect between the two captains until then. A breakfast organised by adidas at the start of the tour on Auckland's waterfront saw O'Driscoll and Umaga sit together, relaxed, chatty, answering media questions. At one point, the TV3 comedy duo Bill and Ben obtained the respective autographs of each captain only to reveal to them they had actually signed a civil union certificate. Both men found it hilarious.

For Umaga, there was a deeper sense of betrayal about O'Driscoll's public denigration. The All Blacks, rightly or wrongly, had long been believers in omertà — the Mafia code of saying nothing in the wake of foul play whether they had been victims or perpetrators. Test rugby was a tough place where tempers could flare and judgement be compromised. It was a full-blooded affair and that made it entirely possible for things to happen that shouldn't. As much as tests were governed by the officials, they were subject to the law of the jungle, and if everyone accepted that, then teams could spend 80 minutes knocking the living daylights out of one another and have a beer at the end with no hard feelings or any desire to run off to the press and squeal about what may have happened at the bottom of a ruck.

In the pre-professional days, when there was enormous scope for teams to operate outside the scrutiny of the law, if something still rankled, the expectation was that teams would say nothing publicly, enjoy the company of their opposition but plot privately on how to exact revenge. Action, not words, would be used to right any wrongs and a natural justice would prevail. It wasn't necessarily an eye for an eye, tooth for a tooth sort of system, but the All Blacks knew that if one of their own transgressed on the field, they would be a legitimate target at a later date. As Buck Shelford says: 'The guys didn't complain because you always knew there was going to be another game around the corner when you could get payback. A lot of teams had a call and if the shit goes down then we all get in because that way the referee can't send off half a team.'

When cameras intruded into the professional game and the tolerance for off-the-ball incidents lowered, the code of omertà remained. Taking revenge was no longer an option, so instead there was a greater reliance on the officials and judiciary to administer justice. In both eras, the All Blacks captain, in the unwritten laws of this code, held particular responsibility to observe the demand for silence. To complain publicly was a sign of weakness. It suggested the All Blacks lacked the tools or resourcefulness to look after themselves. There was also the worry that it would come across as excuse-making, or worse, remove rugby's best means of differentiating itself from soccer where players could writhe in fake agony, throw themselves on the ground when they hadn't been touched, and gesticulate to the point of intimidating referees if things hadn't gone their way. All Blacks from all generations have appreciated Oscar Wilde's observation that football is a game for gentlemen played by hooligans while rugby is a game for hooligans played by gentlemen.

Above all else, there was the optics to think about. What would it look like if the All Blacks captain was dubbed a whiner?

A serial moaner when things didn't go the way of his team? No All Blacks captain wanted to carve out that reputation and they made the assumption that a similar mind-set would prevail amongst their opponents. Fate was going to throw slings and arrows and whatever came had to be stoically endured, hence the sense of betrayal of the code and of the game itself when O'Driscoll opted to verbalise his disappointment and brand the act with such emotive language.

As Umaga would reveal in his autobiography about the immediate aftermath of the first test in 2005: 'The sustained personal attack they launched against me was hard to believe and even harder to stomach. You don't want to take it personally but it's almost impossible not to when another player, a guy you had some respect for, attacks your character in the most direct and damning terms.'

Having sat mute through the Lions' sustained attack, Umaga broke his silence on the Wednesday before the second test. There was a press conference at NZ Rugby headquarters, and if the performance by Woodward had bordered on surreal, the situation turned yet more odd when the entire All Blacks squad came out with Umaga and stood behind him, arms folded and rigid expressions making the whole business look like it was a convention for disgruntled nightclub doormen.

The mass presence was the result of the unprecedented media scrutiny and the advancing storyline which saw the Lions jump from focusing on just Umaga to branding the entire All Blacks team dirty. 'It got to the point where we had to have a couple of meetings to try and take the focus off what was happening in that regard,' says Marshall. 'We had to deal with the external media pressure that was going on Tana. We also had to go to a parliamentary reception that week with the Lions players which was really unpleasant because there had been a little bit of ill feeling about it. When we started to get it as a team, that was a good thing. They said we had targeted O'Driscoll as being one of the danger players of the tour. That had an impact on the whole team rather than it being all on Tana.'

Somewhat predictably, the conference failed to deliver Umaga's head on the spike. The British journalists asked the same question as many different ways as they could muster and all they got from Umaga was a confirmation he was sorry about what had happened to O'Driscoll but not sorry for his part in it. These things happen was the gist, so it would be best, suggested Umaga, that everyone move on. There was no admission of guilt, no acceptance by Umaga that there had been any malice or intent in the tackle.

Umaga had no intention of responding to O'Driscoll publicly. He wasn't about to get caught up in a war of words or fight this particular battle in the media. O'Driscoll may have been happy to whine, but Umaga wouldn't respond in kind. It wasn't the way of an All Blacks captain, and however tempting it may have been to say something, to question why the Lions were so determined to attack him and the team, Umaga was always going to resist it. There was an obligation to front a voracious media pack, but no compulsion to actually tell them anything, and so all that really happened is that Umaga hardened his resolve to make his most telling statement on Saturday night.

Having his integrity challenged like that armed Umaga with a ferocious desire to clinch the series with a statement performance.

Here he was under scrutiny in a way no All Blacks captain ever had been and not once had he wavered, staying resolute throughout the most intensely personal attacks. Umaga and his team had fixed on the belief that the best way to alleviate the pressure — the only way to quieten the critics — was to deliver a world-class performance.

'We got together during the week as a team,' says Marshall. 'And we said, "Right, what we can't do is get angry. We have to get disciplined. They are going to be foaming at the mouth. They are going to be aggressive and they are going to try to unsettle us. What we need to do is upskill ourselves and be faster on our feet, accurate with our passing, so they don't have the chance to get physical with us." That was a good focal point for us to get away from the aggressive side of it, otherwise I think Tana would have imploded and then exploded. I could see it was weighing him down and what you don't need with a captain who leads with his actions is him having his head down and his shoulders hunched.'

In other teams, perhaps the captain would have capitulated under similar pressure. But the institution that is the All Blacks seemingly makes it clear to those asked to be captain that they have a responsibility to be unflinching and resolute. Umaga, be it through intuition or the power of the office he held, felt this powerful need to respond with what he did on the field and not what he said in a press conference. He seemed to be filled with a conviction that his only obligation in the wake of the first-test scandal was to play with the authority, control and impact that had won him the captaincy.

While everyone who saw it will always remember the All Blacks' 48–18 victory as the game in which Daniel Carter announced his arrival as a world-class No. 10, it was also the night when Umaga proved his value as a captain. He knew the Lions would look to run at him. He knew there would be verbal assaults, little moments off the ball, and a mostly British crowd willing him to be exposed. He stood up to everything. He smashed every red jersey that came his way. He faced every verbal abuser and gave them a smile and a few choice words back and he tracked Carter for 60 metres to collect his pass and score the All Blacks' first try of the game.

Under siege all week and portrayed as a New Zealand version of Stalin, there was Umaga 20 minutes into the game, big toothy grin, coasting towards the posts. When he flopped over the tryline it seemed to sap the last vestige of hope to which the Lions were clinging. Their resistance collapsed after that score, as if they realised that they were dealing with forces they could never comprehend. Umaga's refusal to buckle and his ability to absorb all the pressure and turn it into an almighty performance said everything about his strength of character, but more about the power of the captaincy to instil almost superhuman qualities.

'He scored the first try in that test and he played the house down,' says Marshall. 'When you are the captain you can't hide yourself away all week. As captain you are expected to front. That's where captaincy is mentally challenging. You can't hide away and say, "Who gives a shit about what they are saying about me?" You have to go out, sit in front of the media and know they are going to hammer you. And that's where captaincy really brings out the true qualities of a player and a leader and I think the way Tana responded that week, with the way that he played, there wouldn't have been many players who could go through that type of scrutiny and play like that.'

Umaga defined his captaincy with his defiance in Wellington. He was the rock around whom the All Blacks built their performance, and even the Lions, as bitter as they were, must have had some grudging respect for the way Umaga came out and played in the second test.

'As captain you are expected to front. That's where captaincy is mentally challenging. You can't hide away ... You have to go out, sit in front of the media and know they are going to hammer you. And that's where captaincy really brings out the true qualities of a player and a leader'

—JUSTIN MARSHALL

* * *

All Blacks coach Steve Hansen is on edge. It might be the relentless heat and stuffiness of the hotel in which the All Blacks are staying in November 2012. It's in Edinburgh's Old Town and much of it is subterranean — dark and moody corridors winding into hidden rooms and mezzanine floors. Ironically, given the hotel is literally across the road from the birthplace of John Knox — the founder of the Presbyterian Church — management have scant regard for frugality or suffering and have the heating cranked. The heat doesn't help, but Hansen's mood has turned because he harbours a natural wariness about what may happen now that the All Blacks are north of the equator.

His first year as All Blacks coach has been sensationally good. The All Blacks crushed Ireland 3–0 in June before enjoying a clean sweep of the Rugby Championship. Media predictions that the

All Blacks would border on shambolic with Hansen at the helm have proven laughably wide of the mark. So too has the widely held claim that Hansen would be gruff and prickly with the media. Relations have been cordial, bordering on convivial. But that was before the All Blacks travelled north and now Hansen is tightening up: he's a little more guarded, less inclined to dig out a snappy one-liner at press conferences.

He doesn't trust that the All Blacks will get a fair deal from the officials or judiciary when they play in Europe. He's equally, or perhaps more, concerned that the all-powerful UK media will find a reason — any reason at all — to begin what he thinks will be an orchestrated campaign to portray the All Blacks as thugs and further influence the officials. He was assistant coach in 2005 and saw the Umaga–O'Driscoll incident escalate to the point where the All Blacks were berated by customs officials when they arrived in Ireland later that same year.

Hansen, in his eight years as assistant, had also seen Daniel Carter suspended for a week in 2009 at the behest of an International Rugby Board executive. Carter had avoided an on-field sanction for a high tackle against Wales, but after the game Wales coach Warren Gatland fumed to the media that international referees were intimidated by the All Blacks and gave them a better deal. Instead of warning him about bringing the game into disrepute, the IRB intervened and demanded that Carter be banned for one week. This intervention wasn't made public, but various members of the All Blacks management group saw the exchange between the official and the citing commissioner at the after-match function in Cardiff.

But what is troubling Hansen the most is that for the last

decade he has seen his captain, Richie McCaw, subjected to a litany of deliberate, violent acts, many of which had gone unpunished. His captain had somehow become fair game and oppositions were hell-bent on targeting him. And in the northern hemisphere it seemed as if they were allowed to illegally target him with impunity.

The list of atrocities committed against McCaw was incredible, but he was at least afforded a degree of protection if they were committed in the southern hemisphere. In 2006 he was picked up and tipped on his head by Wallabies wing Lote Tuqiri at Eden Park. Tuqiri was banned for six weeks. In 2010 McCaw was kneed in the head by Jamie Heaslip in New Plymouth which resulted in the Irish No. 8 being red-carded. A few tests later, Springboks lock Danie Roussow was yellow-carded in Wellington for punching McCaw in the back of the head. In September 2012, playing against the Boks in Dunedin, McCaw was 'cleaned out' by prop Dean Greyling. It was a horrific challenge which saw the captain's head thrown back after Greyling drove his shoulder into it at full speed. The yellow card and subsequent one-week ban was a punishment that did not fit the severity of the crime, but it was at least a punishment. And in Brisbane the following month, Scott Higginbotham head-butted McCaw — an act that was missed by the officials but picked up by the citing commissioner and led to a four-week ban for the Wallabies No. 8.

It was apparent that the violence against McCaw was escalating. His influence as both a world-class, ball-stealing openside flanker and charismatic and inspirational captain was growing and the All Blacks, since September 2009, had barely lost. McCaw's influence didn't need to be explained and there was an increasing sense that the better he became, the more justified others felt in physically assaulting him.

Obviously, it was a source of frustration for Hansen that for the better part of a decade his captain had been illegally targeted and yet there remained a global determination to portray the All Blacks as a dirty side. The deeper concern for him ahead of the first test of the 2012 northern tour was that McCaw would be set upon by the Scots, Italians, Welsh and English, all of whom would feel they could do so almost with the support of the game's officials and judicial officers.

The last time the All Blacks had been in the UK, in November 2010, a damaging precedent was set. In the test against England, McCaw was pinned at a breakdown when England's reserve hooker, Dylan Hartley, threw himself at the All Blacks captain. Hartley's forearm smashed into McCaw's face in full view of referee Romain Poite, yet the French official awarded England a penalty for a supposed offside infringement. Hartley also escaped sanction when the incident was cited, but All Blacks hooker Keven Mealamu was banned for four weeks for striking English captain Lewis Moody with his head. The inconsistency was galling and the injustice simmered bitterly within the All Blacks who didn't want to reveal that they believed Moody had deliberately provoked Mealamu by saying something unforgivable about the All Black's six-year-old niece who had been tragically killed in an accident the year before.

In the final test of 2010 McCaw was knocked off his feet by Welsh No. 8 Andy Powell. It would have been a great tackle but for the fact the Welshman collected McCaw's head in a collision that would have been an automatic red card today. The All Blacks skipper was shaken by the contact, taking a few goes to get back to his feet. But he was more surprised that having seen what happened, referee Alan Lewis awarded Wales a scrum. And to deepen the sense of conspiracy, there was a shocking lack of desire by the IRB to investigate an incident in the last minutes of the 2011 World Cup final when McCaw was eye-gouged by French midfielder Aurélien Rougerie.

The problem, as Hansen saw it in Edinburgh, was that the northern hemisphere had little or no respect for the All Blacks captain. He feared that while McCaw was a target everywhere in the world, he was particularly so in the north where it was almost true that immunity and possibly even fame would be granted to those who assaulted him. It was an intolerable state of affairs for the world's best team to take to the field unsure whether their captain was going to receive the appropriate protection from the match officials. No other captain in world rugby had to deal with a situation like this and it created an element of uncertainty within the team about how much policing of their own they should do.

In Edinburgh, Hansen came across as disappointed that when Greyling had nearly broken McCaw's jaw, the All Blacks forwards hadn't rushed in to let the Springboks know that what had happened wasn't okay. But before the All Blacks played England in their last game, McCaw says over a coffee in London that he has every confidence his team-mates will stand up for him if something similar happens again. It's obvious the issue has been discussed and that in itself says something. How many other teams need to have a strategy on how to protect their captain if and most likely when he is assaulted? And how far is too far?

Because the last thing the All Blacks need is for players to be sent off for exacting retribution.

The hardest bit of all, though, is that McCaw feels honour-bound to observe the code of silence and is adamant he doesn't want to be a captain who conveys weakness by complaining. Every time he has been subjected to off-the-ball incidents he has said nothing. The closest he came to breaking ranks was in 2010 after Hartley wasn't cited. 'I don't like to be bitching and moaning about it, that's not the way I am, but all players would like to see a level of consistency,' he said. 'With that incident I'm surprised he wasn't up. I don't know whether the ref saw it or not but I certainly made it known to him that I'd been hit. I don't like people to take cheap shots — that annoys me.'

That was the extent of McCaw's moaning. More than a dozen times he was subjected to acts that met the red-card threshold and he absorbed it all, said nothing about it. His self-restraint was beyond remarkable and it was driven, as he said, partly because stoicism was his natural thing, but more so by a need to project himself as a captain who could not be intimidated or beaten into submission. His refusal to condemn those who attacked him or plead to the game's administrators for greater protection deepened the respect in which he was held by his peers and further enraged those who felt the need to chop him down.

The temptation to say something in retaliation never seemed particularly strong in McCaw. He appeared to have inordinate faith that those who perpetrated violence against him would get their just deserts, be it through the judicial system or unofficial channels. And he also had this conviction that his captaincy would be stronger and more effective if he could somehow turn the other cheek.

* * *

Having seen their beloved team lose three times in New Zealand in June, a jam-packed Twickenham is confident that England will beat the All Blacks in their fourth encounter of 2014. That faith is starting to fade shortly after half-time when the All Blacks, albeit clumsily, exploit a three-man overlap to set McCaw over the tryline and give the visitors a 21–14 lead. The fact it's McCaw who has landed this damaging blow has exacerbated the mood swing among the 82,000 present from optimistic to poisonous.

Twickenham has never been overly hospitable to the All Blacks but it is particularly hostile in November 2014, and most of the venom is being spat in the direction of McCaw. It's less than a year until the World Cup kicks off and the English, as hosts, sense they need to beat the All Blacks at least once in 2014 to set themselves up psychologically. Their fans also seem to believe they need to do their part in unsettling the defending champion All Blacks and that the best way to do that is to subject McCaw to endless booing and jeering with cries of 'cheat' reverberating around the ground every time he's near the ball.

The lack of respect for the All Blacks captain is appalling and it is coming off the back of the increasing media agenda in the UK to label him a cheat. Throughout his career, McCaw has been dogged by accusations — from players, coaches and media — that he bends and breaks the rules to suit whatever purpose his team needs. *The Times*, *Telegraph* and *Guardian* had all devoted their Saturday coverage to writing different versions of the same thing — that if referee Nigel Owens is prepared to penalise McCaw's inevitable cheating then England have a great chance of winning. McCaw is a massive source of frustration to everyone other than the All Blacks and New Zealanders, and by 2014, with the All Blacks looking so imperious, the English fans can't see him for the legendary player he is and are sold entirely on this vision of him as the devil.

The shame of it is that it will be the last time McCaw plays on English soil before the World Cup and the Twickenham crowd, in their blind rage, have missed one of the great openside performances of the age. McCaw was outstanding in the 24–21 victory, and 10 minutes after scoring the critical try, he pulled off a turnover where the entirety of the English pack tried to budge him and yet he remained on his feet having entered the ruck legally and won his side the penalty. It was brave and brilliant — the sort of act every aspiring No. 7 in England should have been shown to inspire them — and yet the crowd were incensed. McCaw could have punched an old lady and it would have been better received, and the anger wasn't confined to the cheaper seats in the stadium.

As McCaw pulled off his incredible match-winning turnover, the enraged fan sitting in front of the royal box and All Blacks coaches is now incandescent. He's wearing red jeans, a pink shirt, a Burberry jacket and checked cheese-cutter — a near parody of the stereotypical toff. No doubt his Range Rover is in the car park at the back of the stand and his luncheon included a drop of something to fire him up as he spent the first 60 minutes hurling abuse at McCaw. Now he has turned to face Hansen, who is metres away, and is screaming with the compulsory lisp and plummy accent: 'Wichie McCaw is a horrible cheat and you must do something!'

Hansen is less amazed and more saddened that his captain is being treated like this. He could sense the mood was volatile even before the kick-off when Prince Harry, just a few seats away, was booming out England's adopted anthem, 'Swing Low, Sweet Chariot', during the haka to drown it out. But it's a new low certainly when McCaw is named man of the match and no one can hear his on-field interview because of the booing. Actually, the real low came an hour or so later at the after-match function when RFU president Jon Dance is understood to have opened proceedings by saying: 'I'm just going to come out and say what everyone is thinking, England deserved to win that game' — the inference clear enough that the supposed illegal work of McCaw had made all the difference.

CHAPTER SIXTEEN

CHARMED LIFE

LONG-TERM SUCCESS IS not the only reason the All Blacks, and in particular, some of their captains, have induced anger around the world. That the All Blacks continue to win as often as they do, and find ways to take test matches that weren't really theirs to take, is only part of the reason so many outside of New Zealand demonise its best players and specifically the captain. What also fuels the anger is the unquestionable sense that the All Blacks, and their captain in particular, live something of a charmed life.

New Zealanders don't like to tackle this issue. It's one that gets kicked for touch. Of course it does. Suggesting that it's one set of rules for the All Blacks and their captain and another for everyone else casts the whole sport into disrepute. It belittles the integrity of test football. But there have been so many grey-area incidents as not to leave fans and media around the world wondering whether referees and match officials are in thrall to the All Blacks — intimidated by the reputation, somehow fixed in their own minds that the All Blacks, and their captain, are above reproach. If they have won the ball at the breakdown, it's more likely than not to have been legal, because they are the All Blacks. Their legacy is built on excellence, not cheating, and hence referees have perhaps assumed legality on behalf of the All Blacks when they shouldn't have.

The team has been protected by its reputation, and the captain, particularly the long-servers — the big names such as Shelford, Fitzpatrick, McCaw and Read — have been able to push their luck further than most. Referees were a little bit scared of them, a little bit in awe, and possibly, when it came to 50:50 decisions, or 55:45 decisions, the All Blacks captain stared long enough and hard enough to win the outcome they wanted.

In the last 30 years there have been incidents that can't really be explained — critical moments when the All Blacks have escaped censure or been the beneficiaries of such outrageous good fortune that it has been impossible not to wonder whether their aura — their status — has enabled them to escape rightful judgement. There are, of course, other moments in history when the All Blacks have been unfairly treated, or subjected to an injustice that has hurt them. These are often raised as the means to diffuse the argument that says New Zealanders have the golden ticket of immunity. The third test in the British & Irish Lions series of 2017 is the most obvious case. At 15-all with two minutes left, the All Blacks were awarded a penalty by referee Romain Poite. It was the right call. But after a shambolic consultation with the other officials — which should never have happened — Poite reversed the decision, denying the All Blacks the easy three points or indeed the right to use the advantage they were playing under before the penalty. It cost the All Blacks the series — forced them to accept a draw — and in reviewing the game a few weeks later, it is believed World Rugby referee boss Alain Rolland dismissed the horror incident at the end by saying: 'Wrong decision but right result.'

Still, for every time the All Blacks have been unlucky, there are perhaps two counter incidents when they have been lucky. In 2009 in Cardiff the All Blacks led Wales 19–9 with eight minutes left when the home side made a stunning break. Reserve halfback Martin Roberts took a pass from wing Shane Williams, and at the same instant he gathered the ball, Dan Carter made a thumping tackle. But Carter's initial contact was high, around Roberts' chin, and there is no question that such a tackle would have resulted in a red card today. Even in 2009 when high tackles weren't on rugby's list of heinous crimes, it was still a good candidate for a yellow card. But referee Craig Joubert said he didn't see it well enough to administer a yellow or even a penalty.

Warren Gatland, Wales coach at the time, was fuming at the lack of action taken. He was incensed by the decision to not punish Carter. When he was interviewed by the BBC on the field after the game, he said referees were intimidated by the All Blacks. By the time he addressed the rest of the media, about half an hour later, he'd calmed down, but only a bit. 'It was a head-high tackle. A guy makes a break in the 22, and if that had happened at the other end then it would have been a penalty and a yellow card,' said Gatland. 'We don't ask for any favours, just a few calls to go our way. It's trying to change referees' opinions about not wanting to referee upsets. They don't want to be involved in upsets.' When Gatland was asked whether he was suggesting that referees are biased towards New Zealand and in awe of the All Blacks, he smiled and said no. But his assistant coach, Shuan Edwards, jumped in and said: 'They should have played the last 10 minutes of the game with 14 men. It was a high tackle and you see players get yellow-carded for that, you see players red-carded for that.'

If the Welsh thought they were hard done by in 2009, they could hardly believe what happened in Cardiff three years later. In the opening minute of the test, All Blacks hooker Andrew Hore viciously swung his arm into the side of Welsh lock Bradley Davies' head as the two men tracked to a ruck. Davies was unconscious before he hit the ground. It was a nasty, violent assault that, in any era, should have been a straight red card. The All Blacks should have been playing 79 minutes with 14 men but, once again, Craig Joubert didn't see the incident and the TMO back then had no power to intervene. So Hore stayed on and the All Blacks won 33–10 in a clinical and otherwise hugely disciplined display.

Davies, however, was stretchered off and taken to hospital where he suffered short-term memory loss and couldn't play for weeks. Hore was cited and banned for eight weeks, which was reduced to five on account of his previously good record and, in actuality, meant he would only miss two games. Wales assistant coach Rob Howley was presumably speaking on behalf of his nation when he said: 'It was an absolute disgrace. Situations and incidents like that have no place on the rugby field, and it had a huge impact on the game. You don't traditionally think the All Blacks want to do things like that. They are a good enough team not to so we were very surprised by the actions of the player.'

The whole business — the act, the lack of detection on the field, and then the perceived soft punishment — left not just the Welsh angry, but seemingly every rugby fan in Britain. Two days after Hore had been disciplined, All Blacks doctor Deb Robinson was making her way down in the lift to breakfast at the team hotel in London. She'd had a horror last few days as a virus had ripped through the team and she had been attending to their sickness round the clock, while suffering herself. She looked tired, vacant almost, as the lift descended, and she didn't seem to notice that the well-dressed businessman standing next to her has suddenly seen that she's wearing an All Blacks tracksuit. He takes a second look and then the indignation sweeps across his features and the blood rushes to his cheeks. He turns to Robinson and gets right in her face to yell: 'You are a fucking disgrace! What happened in Cardiff was a fucking disgrace and you should be ashamed!'

He seems all the better for getting that off his chest and takes his leave, swinging his briefcase as a child might their school bag. Robinson is stunned, but she's too tired to be bothered by it, and besides, she says she's heard worse, been subjected to worse, and shrugs it off knowing that this sort of blind rage comes with the territory. There is also the problem that there is not much she can say in reply to Mr Angry. He was of course wildly out of line to have carried on as he did, but what exactly could Robinson say in defence of Hore? He had left his management team in an indefensible position and enhanced the widely held belief that the All Blacks can commit the unthinkable and get away with it.

But arguably the Hore incident was by no means the most glaring example of the All Blacks not being held accountable. That happened in 1987 and once again Wales were the victims. In the semi-final of the World Cup that year Welsh lock Huw Richards and Gary Whetton began trading somewhat ineffective blows that were really more for the sake of appearances than thrown with any intent. One had annoyed the other so they were going through the ritual of 'sorting it out'. It most likely would have come to nothing in regard to sanction, but for the fact Buck Shelford intervened and knocked Richards unconscious with a punch to the head. Incredibly, when he came to, Richards was sent off and Shelford, studiously keeping his head down and skulking out of the official's eyeline, managed to get off scot-free.

History is littered with these unexplainable moments. Richard Loe enhanced his reputation as an enforcer in 1992 when he recklessly and deliberately smashed his forearm into the face of Wallabies wing Paul Carozza. The referee was within touching distance of the incident and yet apparently didn't see it. Jamie Joseph was able to stamp viciously on the ankle of England debutant Kyran Bracken in 1993. Everyone at Twickenham saw what happened but not the officials. Ali Williams avoided any sanction in 2003 when he was accused of stamping on the head of England fullback Josh Lewsey. In 2008 Brad Thorn picked up John Smit and dumped him on his head. It was a dangerous spear tackle, sparked a massive brawl and inflicted a groin injury on the South African captain that forced him out of the next test. It looked like a red-card offence, but it was ruled a penalty only by the officials, with Thorn subsequently being cited after the game and banned for a week. 'Just imagine [Springboks lock] Bakkies Botha doing something similar to Richie McCaw,' Smit fumed when he arrived back in South Africa. 'World rugby would have come to a standstill.'

In November 2016 World Rugby issued referees with an edict to adopt a zero-tolerance policy towards high tackles. With 33 minutes left of the test between the All Blacks and Ireland in Dublin, Malakai Fekitoa was guilty of a high tackle on Simon Zebo. It looked bad in real time and didn't improve on the big-screen replay. It's a red card all the way but referee Jaco Peyper decided only yellow. If he'd been sent off, the All Blacks would have been in trouble, leading as they were 14–6. But Fekitoa returned after his 10 minutes to score the winning try and rub salt in Irish wounds.

Three years later and Springboks coach Rassie Erasmus elected himself spokesperson for the rest of the world when he said, unequivocally, that the All Blacks had enjoyed a decade of good refereeing fortune on the back of their continued excellence. He was speaking ahead of the Springboks' opening World Cup clash against the All Blacks, and while it was a patent attempt to put pressure on the match referee Jérôme Garcès, he did seem to mean what he said. 'It was a well-known fact that when it was really tough and teams were under the pump some of the 50:50 decisions just went New Zealand's way because they deserved that for being number one so long.'

What's most interesting to ponder is whether various All Blacks captains have been able to exploit this blind spot: play on the edge of legality, or perhaps even beyond, gambling that they hold such an esteemed place in the game that they will get away with it.

* * *

The British & Irish Lions lost the plot in 2005 when they made accusations about Tana Umaga being a dirty player. They lost credibility when they suggested the All Blacks were recognised as a filthy team. They couldn't substantiate either claim and they lost the ability to be taken seriously when they expanded their argument from specific to general. But what if they had focused purely on the incident that took place 43 seconds into the first test? What if they had been calm, controlled and fixed on simply demanding an explanation from citing commissioner Willem Venter about why he didn't feel Umaga had any case to answer?

Umaga was categorically not a dirty player. He was a tough defender but always legal. He was a hard hitter but never outside the rules, and in 2003 he showed his sportsmanship when Welsh No. 8 Colin Charvis was out cold on the field in Hamilton and Umaga placed his opponent in the recovery position. So the wider allegations of thuggishness were never going to stick, but why did the All Blacks avoid any penalty or subsequent sanction for the O'Driscoll incident?

The evidence as it related to that incident was irrefutable. O'Driscoll was picked up by Umaga and Keven Mealamu and tipped beyond the horizontal. There was no duty of care shown by either All Black once they realised O'Driscoll was in a dangerous position and the Lions captain was dangerously dropped on his head.

It's feasible that the officials could miss it, but the TV cameras captured it clearly enough, and even back then — when there was a higher threshold for cards and citings — it still seemed worthy of a significant ban. Umaga responded brilliantly to the pressure he was under in the wake of that incident and proved his character and class in the second test of the series, but that doesn't change the fact he should never have been playing in Wellington.

Those who remain adamant it's pure fantasy — the stuff of wild conspiracies — that All Blacks captains are occasionally granted licence to operate outside the law should think about this. In 2005 Umaga tip-tackled O'Driscoll out of the Lions series and was not punished either at the time or by the citing commissioner. In 2011 Wales captain Sam Warburton tip-tackled French wing Vincent Clerc 17 minutes into the World Cup semi-final at Eden Park and was red-carded. The two incidents were almost identical, both happened in huge games, and yet the All Blacks captain was exonerated and the captain of Wales sent off in disgrace.

* * *

About half an hour into the second Bledisloe Cup test of 2016 it had become apparent that referee Romain Poite was refusing to engage with Wallabies captain Stephen Moore. The French official wouldn't entertain Moore on any level. Any attempt by the Australian to seek clarification about any decision was shooed away. Poite wasn't going to offer even the most basic courtesy and Moore was left powerless to say anything or strike any kind of cordial note with the referee.

In contrast, Poite was happy for All Blacks captain Kieran Read to ask questions and seek confirmation about why certain decisions had been made. There was an easy rapport between All Blacks captain and referee that night in Wellington — a respect between the two which afforded Read the opportunity to discuss things that were troubling him on a night when there were ample off-the-ball incidents. It's unlikely that the different treatment of the respective captains had any bearing on the result — the All Blacks won 29–9 — but it incensed Wallabies coach Michael Cheika that Read and Moore were not afforded the same rights.

'I was bitterly disappointed, to be honest,' Cheika said. 'I'm on record with the referees' boss Alain Rolland about the treatment to our captain and our players, by Romain Poite, and also by Nigel Owens over this last year. I'm not quite sure why, but there was a time in the game [tonight] in a break in play when the national captain of Australia [Moore] was asking the referee, "When might there be an opportunity for me to talk to you?" And he absolutely ignored him.

'He's got the whistle, I understand, but there's a place where the captain has an opportunity to speak to the referee. The referee may not like the captain personally, that might be his prerogative, but he has to afford him that opportunity if he is affording it to his opponents. I don't know if it's subconscious or not, but it's there and it's got to be dealt with because it can't be that the opponents can say everything to the referee.'

It's inconceivable that an All Blacks captain would ever be dismissed by a referee the way Moore was. The position commands too much respect and that's essentially the nub of the issue for everyone else — whether that respect is extended too far at times.

The Scots certainly thought so in 2017 when they were chasing a historic victory at Murrayfield. For the first time in decades, they were competing as an equal with the All Blacks, putting them under pressure and looking capable of actually doing it. The All Blacks led 22–10 with eight minutes left, but were obviously tiring having played 20 minutes with 14 men due to yellow cards. The Scots were proving hard to subdue and after a prolonged spell in the All Blacks' 22 they won a penalty advantage five metres out. Jonny Gray picked up and was advancing towards the tryline when Read, still lying on the ground after making a tackle, illegally slapped the ball out of the Scottish lock's hands. It was a cynical, professional foul and automatic yellow card. Except somehow the English referee Matthew Carley missed it.

All the video replays suggest Carley was staring right at the incident and was barely two metres from it. Did he really not see it? Or did he simply not fancy the idea of yellow-carding the All Blacks captain when the game was still in the balance? Was he afraid, as Gatland said many referees were in 2009, of being involved in an upset? Or was he able to convince himself that what he saw was legal and legitimate because it was the All Blacks captain who did it?

Whatever the reason, the outcome was that Read stayed on the field for the final eight minutes and made his presence felt. Scotland did close the gap to 22–17, and in the last play of the game came within five metres of scoring. If they had been playing against 14 men, would they have found the extra metre of space they needed to score?

We'll never know, but the Scots had their views a few days later. Scotland assistant coach Dan McFarland said: 'That was just cynical wasn't it? It should have been a yellow card, quite possibly a try, and quite possibly a penalty try. I can see that [all those options] would be something for discussion, but that's not up for discussion now is it? That's how they play. They're very streetwise, they're very clever.'

And the most streetwise and clever of all were Sean Fitzpatrick and Richie McCaw. Those two were on a different level when it came to manipulating referees and finding extraordinary favour. Fitzpatrick could spend a full minute crawling around the wrong side of a ruck and somehow successfully plead his innocence when he popped up for air. He was the master at interfering with the opposition's possession and even better at persuading the referee he hadn't been doing anything wrong. It was no wonder the South Africans loved to hate him — he was just so good at playing on the cusp of legality and getting away with it.

A bit like beauty, cynicism is in the eye of the beholder. Read illegally knocking the ball out of an opponent's hands is cynical from one perspective, and from another it's clinical decision-making. The rest of the world says Fitzpatrick and McCaw were relentless cheats, but the argument is just as easily made they were savvy; that they were street-smart, better at managing referees than their opponents. The French were angry at the way McCaw played in the 2011 World Cup final and they were angrier still that referee Craig Joubert didn't penalise the All Blacks captain once in the second half. The French felt McCaw was guilty of all sorts of infringements — coming into rucks from the side, not staying on his feet, handling the ball on the ground. They were playing for a penalty and it never came — which rendered them incredulous given how destructive McCaw was managing to be.

But the French players weren't the referee and McCaw kept doing what he was doing because Joubert ruled the captain was within the laws. Again, why should the French version be considered the right way to view what happened? Was McCaw guilty of doing anything other than expertly working out his boundaries and exploiting them to the full?

'I made a conscious effort, I'd always have a beer with the referee after a game, and I wanted to know the laws I suppose. So very similar to Richie, if you know the rules as well as the referee, you're not going to get caught out, they respect you. And yeah, it was probably also about annoying the other players, the other captain.'

—SEAN FITZPATRICK

All Blacks captains may well have enjoyed a charmed life to some extent over the years, but whatever good fortune came their way, they can say they earned it. 'It was a philosophy really,' says Fitzpatrick about his management of referees. 'If he likes you, a 50:50 call … it's going to go either way, especially in those days. But yeah, I made a conscious effort, I'd always have a beer with the referee after a game, and I wanted to know the laws I suppose. So very similar to Richie, if you know the rules as well as the referee, you're not going to get caught out, they respect you. And yeah, it was probably also about annoying the other players, the other captain.'

CHAPTER SEVENTEEN

CAPTAINCY IN THE DIGITAL AGE

THE INSTANT WAYNE Barnes signals the end of the match between Ireland and New Zealand in November 2018, the online torrent will begin. The All Blacks have been beaten 16–9, effectively toppled — not in actuality but in perception at least — as the world number one team. Ireland have finished a tremendous year with a tremendous performance. They deserved their first win against the All Blacks on Irish soil. Pick a facet, any facet, of the test, and Ireland had the edge in Dublin. They were more physical, more alert and more accurate.

This won't sit well in the online world, where faceless and nameless keyboard warriors vent all sorts of nasty stuff in lieu of reasoned analysis. The weird thing, though, is that the mainstream media have come to take their lead from social media: journalists and editors, paid to have perspective, balance and good judgement, have convinced themselves that the Twittersphere is a valid source of information and fair reflection of the public mood.

Some media organisations have almost come to see the angry musings of disgruntled fans as the news — reporting it verbatim as if 'Bob from Mosgiel' is the authority on all things rugby.

It takes barely 12 hours for an All Blacks defeat to become definitive proof of a crumbling rugby empire. It takes even less time for those involved to be written off as finished, useless and absolutely not the future — and as for the captain, on this particular occasion, he was facing calls for his head almost even before he'd made it back to the changing room. This is how things are in the digital age: frenzied and febrile, almost rabidly destructive when the All Blacks lose and equally triumphant and overhyped when they win.

It's a blame game when they lose, a quest to isolate and smear those deemed to have been responsible; and when the All Blacks win, it's a race to see which individuals can be built up way beyond where they should be. After the loss in Dublin, captain Kieran Read found himself at the centre of the Twitterstorm. He was the man most widely blamed for the defeat — both for his lack of leadership and because three minutes after the break he charged down an ill-advised chip kick by Irish wing Jacob Stockdale. If Read had then gathered the bouncing ball he was in the clear, and if he didn't have the legs to go the 50 metres, Jack Goodhue on his right would have. Either way, it was a certain try if he gathered the ball. But he knocked it on and that one act came to be seen as definitive proof that he was old and past it — not the right man to be at the helm of the All Blacks. It was a high-profile and costly error, but it didn't mean anything more than Read was guilty of lifting his head to see where Goodhue was before he had safely gathered the ball. The reasoned, balanced view is rarely heard these days, though.

The All Blacks coaches weren't happy with the team performance or result, but they weren't distraught about it either, and they certainly weren't worried about Read's form. The captain had endured major back surgery in January and the experts had been clear it would take maybe as long as 18 months for him to regain full mobility. In Dublin, he was probably at about 95 per cent capacity and the coaches saw everything they wanted to see from him. He was still running hard in the last minutes of the game; still making himself available to carry the ball. He was vocal, his body language strong and confident. He was making tackles, covering the ground and doing what the team needed. It was a strong performance but one that perhaps reflected he was missing that small element of dynamism and athleticism due to the surgery.

The coaches were prepared to be patient with their captain, confident that he was doing an indispensable job even at 95 per cent fit. And so this created what is now likely to be a near-permanent state of contradiction between internal and external assessments of the All Blacks. Throughout history, there have been times when the All Blacks coaches and selectors have seen things differently to the media and public. But the mass use of social media and its contagious nature has widened that divide. An All Blacks captain now can expect to be patted on the back and told he's doing a great job by his coaching team, and yet see and hear nothing but negativity and criticism everywhere else.

This fact wasn't lost on Read a few days after the defeat in Dublin. He's happy to meet for a coffee and talk about the loss, his form, the season gone and the one that lies ahead. 'No, I am not to be honest,' he says, when he's asked whether he's aware there have been some harsh commentaries about him that were labelled by

All Blacks coach Steve Hansen as 'ridiculous'. 'I literally do not read the media. And that is how I best operate. There is no point getting into all that. That is just natural for the New Zealand public [to react after a loss] and a New Zealand media outlet that in some ways are just wanting to make a headline, create some clickbait, and we understand that and it can be frustrating but I kind of stay away from that. You lose in this black jersey and you know it is coming. And to be honest, whatever comes your way is the least of your worries — well it is not the last of your worries, but what you are feeling is so much worse than what anyone could be writing about you. When you lose in the All Blacks jersey no matter who it is against it hurts and it stays with you.

'Everyone is their own person and uses it [social media] in different ways and I am not judging on that. But what you can't be doing is allowing that to affect your mood. For me, it is a great tool to use to connect with the fans, but I pay zero attention to what is being plugged my way. But I think for a young kid it is hard because they maybe take more heed of that than an older player. The guys are different now. They are coming through at a different age. It is 12 years since I came through and these guys are growing up in a completely different age to the one that I grew up in.

'The pressures of social media are real — that is another part of this whole puzzle you have got to grasp with these guys. It can be tough but it is also pretty rewarding, because you can see what it means to them all, and in terms of the black jersey, it hasn't lost any of its aura and mana. Everyone is playing for the right reasons.'

If there was any doubt that All Blacks captains now have to spend as much time dealing with the virtual world as they do the real world, it evaporated at the World Cup the following year.

After the All Blacks won their opening game against South Africa, footage emerged, on the social media account of a South African journalist, of Read seemingly 'taking out' Springboks flanker Pieter Steph du Toit. The incident was missed by the officials, but even if it had been seen, the outcome was likely to be no more

'You lose in this black jersey and you know it is coming. And to be honest, whatever comes your way is the least of your worries — well it is not the last of your worries, but what you are feeling is so much worse than what anyone could be writing about you. When you lose in the All Blacks jersey no matter who it is against it hurts and it stays with you.'

—KIERAN READ

than a penalty to the Boks. It had no material impact on the game, no real news value, and yet it came to dominate the media agenda for much of the time the All Blacks were preparing to play their second game against Canada.

This is now standard fare. It's almost a given that in the 48 hours after a test, someone, somewhere in the world, will release slowed-down footage of an incident and then spark a social media storm. Once that erupts, the mainstream media will latch on to it, bringing it into their domain to generate an easy storyline when they put it to the All Blacks and feed off their reaction. It's a cycle of endless nothing, feeding a news beast that lives off empty calories. It could be a massive distraction for a captain if they let it be, or if it is allowed to be, and it's the relative strength and skill of the head coach that will determine the ability of any virtual drama to infect the squad and damage the captain's standing.

Typically the skipper doesn't front the media until the day before the test and the whole virtual bubble is one that needs to be burst by the head coach and assistant coach when they are on media duty earlier in the cycle. At the World Cup, head coach Steve Hansen was expert at shutting down storms in teacups, dealing with the social media furore around Read's supposed off-the-ball antics by saying: 'I haven't taken too much notice of it, quite frankly. You could go and get shots of anything if you want to and create something. There's a judicial system that's been in place for a long time with rugby and, whether you like it or not, they've been pretty staunch on what they've been about. So if it gets past those guys then move on. We're not judged by social media.'

Hansen's last comment about not being judged by social media is one that every All Blacks captain of the foreseeable future is going to have to remember and repeat to an emerging generation of players who seem to forget that fact. Or don't know it. Anyone who spends time around the All Blacks will quickly become aware that the players live on their phones. They are never without them, and some of the younger, less experienced players can't resist trawling to see what the world is saying about them.

It's a dangerous place for vulnerable egos to live, but it's addictive and some players can't stop themselves from lapping it all up — high as kites when the Twitterworld loves them, sad, withdrawn and unsure of themselves when the internet decides otherwise. A big part of All Blacks captaincy in the digital age is keeping players' minds in the real world and only focused on listening to those whose opinions matter. In his final year in charge, Read was as much an agony aunt as anything else.

* * *

Anyone who has been All Blacks captain will say the profile of the role has always been high. Back in 1974 Andy Leslie knew, after being named captain, he'd have to be that little bit more conscious every time he was out in public. The job came with higher expectations, and people from all walks of life would suddenly know who he was. The profile of the job now, however, is significantly higher.

It says as much about New Zealand as it does the success of the All Blacks that, arguably, behind the Prime Minister, the next two most widely recognised figures in the country are the captain and coach of the national rugby team. Booker Prize winner Eleanor Catton can do her weekly shop without a single soul recognising her, while part of the reason Richie McCaw took a six-month sabbatical in 2013 was to limit the mental fatigue he was feeling at not being able to have a quiet beer with his mates without being bombarded for selfies and autographs. The job comes with a suffocating volume of fame and recognition that can be mentally exhausting.

Another major change has been the birth of the so-called supercoach. Back in Leslie's day there was no science behind coaching. It wasn't a discipline in its own right. Now it's an industry, a serious career where the salaries are big, and in some cases, bigger than those offered to the best players. The head coach has to be a media personality and a figurehead. The rise of social media has created an unprecedented culture of blame, but it's not all aimed at the players or captain, as the higher profile of the head coach has brought them into the sights of the trolls. To thrive in modern test football, the All Blacks need for their captain and coach to be united. They have to have a relationship that can endure the external pressure without any cracks appearing for the media to prise open. That relationship will also set the tone for the rest of the squad — give them a sense of whether they are in a strong, united environment or one that is riddled with tension.

The increased scrutiny and profile, the changed media landscape and the growth of coaching teams means that the job of being All Blacks captain in 2020 looks, in many respects, nothing like it did in 1970. The commercialisation of the sport has also had a significant impact. The captain doesn't necessarily have more sponsors' functions or engagements than anyone else, but he does have to do such things as front adidas store visits in foreign lands; regale AIG insurance brokers at their various offices; and take part in the various TV commercials to promote the association with the All Blacks.

And then there are the endless meetings that take place throughout the test week. The scale of those would be unrecognisable to All Blacks captains of even 15 years ago. The captain gets drawn into everything — meetings with the coaches, with the senior players, with his positional unit, with the sponsorship team. It goes on and it has to fit around the increased physical conditioning, mental skills practice and collective strategic work that is all part and parcel of the test preparation.

On the field, it has changed, too. The volume of tactical decisions that have to be made is greater than it has ever been because rugby has become a more complex and detailed game.

But the responsibility is shared. The All Blacks captain remains the chief decision-maker on the field, but it's too much to expect one player to be well enough placed to determine everything that must happen. Instead, the majority of decisions are made on the recommendation of other senior leaders, or those in key strategic positions such as halfback or first-five. It's definitely not the one-man job it once was, and the captain's role on the field is not to come up with all the answers himself, but to know to whom he should turn and to whom he should listen and when.

As much as the job has changed over the years, there remain areas of commonality. The All Blacks captain still has to be demonstrably tough. The expectation that they will be able to endure what others can't, or won't, has not lessened. Nor has the code of omertà. An All Blacks captain's days will be numbered if he takes to bleating about things in the press. It would be career suicide for an All Blacks captain to do anything other than stoically shrug to any questions relating to any personal attacks that may be launched. Silence is the only way to initially deal with controversy — then performance. Talking is still best done on the field and even the cyberworld can't exert enough pressure to extract any kind of whine out of the All Blacks captain.

A modern extension of this concept is playing for 80 minutes. With 23 players in match-day squads, there's typically a flurry of personnel changes made in the second half of a test match. Front-row forwards typically play no more than 60 minutes these days. Some teams are comfortable that their captain can be a 60-minute man. The Wallabies spent a few years playing the final quarter of big games without their skipper, as Stephen Moore was a hooker who didn't go the distance. England did the same when Dylan

Hartley, another hooker, was captain in 2016 and 2017, while the Boks were comfortable taking Siya Kolisi off well before the end of World Cup games in 2019.

This fad — if it is a fad — will never reach New Zealand. The All Blacks captain will, unless he is injured, be on the field for the duration of every test he plays. That's a non-negotiable demand of the role and the major reason why, in 2017, when Read was injured for the final test of the year, Sam Whitelock was chosen as captain ahead of Sam Cane. 'It was going to be either him or Sam Cane, and Whitelock — bar injury — is probably going to play 80 minutes,' explained Hansen. 'That was the deciding factor in the end.'

Just as true now as it always has been, is that form is a captain's best weapon. When the captain plays well, the All Blacks typically play well. Respect, be it internal or external, is best earned through performance. A captain can be forgiven a few poor decisions if he has otherwise been among the best players on the park. McCaw is recognised as New Zealand's greatest captain for multiple reasons, but none more compelling than the brilliance he produced in the No. 7 jersey. He signed off as the All Blacks' greatest player and greatest captain — the two being inextricably linked.

As much as form is about establishing the right to be picked and proving the best choice in the respective position, it is about appeasing the public need to believe that the All Blacks captain is capable of superhuman feats. It's like Reuben Thorne says — he was a good, steady player, but that wasn't what the public and media wanted. The All Blacks captain has to have more explosive qualities — that magical gift to pull off the extraordinary and seemingly possess the ability to do the impossible.

And, maybe, the most important quality the captain must possess is the ability to detach himself from the pressure and from the everyday grind that comes with the job, and appreciate the moment. There's no job quite like it and those who have done it say it was such a rush, such an all-consuming position that they only came to realise how much they enjoyed it and what it all meant after they were no longer the captain. 'Basically, I'm an All Black captain for the rest of my life,' says Taine Randell. 'You're an All Black forever and I'm an All Blacks captain, and as difficult as the time was, if offered the same opportunity to go through the same pain, I'd do it again. It is only afterward, in retrospect, you get an appreciation of what you've done. It wasn't an overly successful time but I was there and I did it and I'm really proud of the fact that I did it.

'You're an All Black forever and I'm an All Blacks captain, and as difficult as the time was, if offered the same opportunity to go through the same pain, I'd do it again. It is only afterward, in retrospect, you get an appreciation of what you've done. It wasn't an overly successful time but I was there and I did it and I'm really proud of the fact that I did it.'

—TAINE RANDELL

'It is immensely stressful and it's one of those things, you're so motivated at the time, you're so focused as to the exclusion of everything else. And you sacrifice. You'll have these former All Blacks who'll say, "Enjoy it, you'll never know how good it is." And you're focused on what's happening that week. You're too busy for anything else and so you miss the appreciation. Only afterwards you realise how awesome an experience, opportunity it was. And as I say, given the same circumstances, would I do anything different? Nah.'

It's a relentless and demanding job which can often feel thankless and hopeless and yet can also be the most rewarding post a New Zealander will ever hold.

PLAY IT AGAIN, SAM ...

SAM CANE IS making his way through the Docklands in London, hoping to find a barber. He's paying little attention, so didn't see the taxi pull up on the kerb beside him until All Blacks coach Steve Hansen jumped out of it with surprising speed and agility. Hansen wants a quick chat, to break the good news that Cane will be starting the All Blacks next game, against Namibia at the Olympic Stadium. Cane's stoked as he came to the 2015 World Cup knowing he would barely play: the 23-year-old was competing for the No. 7 jersey with All Blacks captain Richie McCaw.

But McCaw, having played two days earlier against Argentina, would, along with the rest of the team that started against the Pumas, be sitting out the Namibia game. The adrenaline is starting to surge through Cane as Hansen turns on his heel to take his leave. But the coach suddenly stops and says, casually, over his shoulder, almost as if it had slipped his mind, that Cane will also be the captain.

Cane would have been less surprised if Hansen had told him he would be playing at first-five and not openside flanker. Captaincy was never something Cane had considered. Even when, at just 21, he was elevated to the All Blacks leadership group in 2013, Cane didn't see himself as a likely captain. He had certainly never imagined that captaincy would be thrust upon him at the 2015 World Cup.

He arrived in England having played 25 times for the All Blacks — the majority of his caps, though, had been won off the bench. The omnipresence of McCaw had restricted Cane to 11 starts and he didn't feel that was enough football to have earned the role. He didn't feel that he had a portfolio of world-class performances to justify his elevation.

Also, he didn't consider captaincy was in his make-up, didn't imagine that anyone would look at him and disagree. But obviously Hansen did. He took the view that Cane, despite having been afforded only limited game time, had played strongly for the All Blacks. He had won the role on quality rather than quantity of performance Hansen explained to the media the day after he had broken the news to Cane.

'The most important part of leadership is playing well and he does that,' said Hansen. 'I don't think he's ever played poorly for the All Blacks and he has got a tricky job in the team following the skipper. Whenever he gets his opportunity, he plays well. He's got a good rugby brain. He's happy to voice his opinion and lead by example. He has the ability to cope with the pressure that comes with being an All Black. When he first came in, he was only a baby and not a lot of people knew a lot about him. He coped with that well. He coped with all the criticism early in his career from the media because they didn't know him. But he never deviated off the game plan. To me that is mental fortitude — to stay on task when everything around you is imploding.'

Cane found the session as illuminating as everyone else. He even turned to look directly at his coach after the question was asked whether Hansen had known from the moment he had picked Cane that he was one day going to be the All Blacks captain. 'I could sit here and say that I did,' said Hansen. 'But it would be bullshit. I just thought he was a pretty special player. It's an overwhelming place to come into the All Blacks and special players sometimes don't make it. But sitting back and watching him, he had the mental fortitude to cope with it quickly and he thrived in the environment. And after a while we thought he was capable of being a leader so we brought him into the leadership group.'

The elevation to the captaincy sent Cane's career path on a new trajectory. From being a little-known understudy to McCaw he was now seen as the heir apparent to the heir apparent. It had been clearly signalled that Kieran Read would be taking over the captaincy in 2016 when McCaw stood down after the World Cup, but Cane was the new front-runner to take over from Read when that time came.

* * *

Almost five years after Cane led the team against Namibia, he was confirmed as the All Blacks' successor to Read. The announcement was made on 7 May 2020 via a video link on Sky Sport's *The Breakdown* programme. Cane, like the rest of New Zealand, was at home, subject to the strict isolation rules forced by the outbreak of Covid-19. Cane had actually been told of his appointment two months earlier. New All Blacks coach Ian Foster had asked him in February to lead the team in 2020, but to keep the news quiet until nearer the beginning of the test programme. Identified as the heir apparent to Read in 2015 and confirmed as captain in 2020 — Cane's journey appeared to have run as expected. Except it hadn't at all.

'I don't think [Sam Cane has] ever played poorly for the All Blacks and he has got a tricky job in the team following the skipper. Whenever he gets his opportunity, he plays well. He's got a good rugby brain. He's happy to voice his opinion and lead by example. He has the ability to cope with the pressure that comes with being an All Black.'

—STEVE HANSEN

His confirmation as captain in 2020 ended up surprising many as Cane's career had hit multiple speed bumps since 2016. The most significant of which were the rise of Sam Whitelock as an alternative contender as All Blacks captain, the emergence of Ardie Savea as a world-class openside flanker, and a broken neck for Cane. By late 2018, everything appeared to have conspired against Cane.

Whitelock, who had captained the Crusaders to the Super Rugby title in 2017, was chosen to captain the All Blacks in the final test of that year when Read was injured. Hansen explained it had been a straight choice between Whitelock and Cane, with the former winning out on the basis he was destined to play the full 80 minutes. But when Read was still unavailable for the June series against France in 2018, it was Whitelock who was again given the captaincy, suggesting that he, rather than Cane, was seen as the likely long-term successor to Read.

In early October that year, Cane fractured vertebrae in his neck following a run-of-the-mill collision with Springboks flanker Francois Louw. There was nothing untoward or illegal about the incident — both men were doing their job at a breakdown, but Cane didn't get up after they had collided. He was in agony, but somehow, with the permission of the All Blacks doctor, managed to get to his feet and walk off the field at Loftus Versfeld in Pretoria. He had major surgery a few days later in South Africa and was told that had his neck not been so developed and strong, he most likely would have been paralysed.

He would initially be looking at a six-month recovery programme, half of which would require him to be in a neck brace, and then he would be reassessed to see if he could return to play. Best-case scenario was that he would play again in April 2019, but if the bone didn't heal the way it was forecast, he could miss the World Cup and possibly even never play again.

While Cane worked through his recovery, Savea suddenly blossomed as a world-class openside flanker. Regular game time was the making of him and he grew in confidence, grew in influence and authority. By the time Cane had recovered and the All Blacks played their pre-World Cup tests in 2019, Savea had to be included in the starting loose trio. His form demanded inclusion; and as the tournament developed, it became clear that, should it come to it, Savea would be picked at the expense of Cane.

Both men started the critical opening test against South Africa but a stuff-up by the match officials saw Cane denied the chance to return to the field in the second half after he had passed a head injury assessment (HIA). Against Ireland in the quarter-final he was replaced at half-time by Scott Barrett. Cane had produced a storming performance but the coaches, having seen the team take a commanding lead, wanted to change the tactical approach in the second half and felt injecting Barrett would best serve their plan.

Cane was starting to look like he was fading in importance and that impression intensified when he was not named in the starting team to play England in the semi-final. Barrett, a specialist lock, was picked at blindside flanker and Savea at openside, with Cane on the bench. The coaches wanted to increase their lineout options and were willing to sacrifice the bruising defensive work of Cane and his qualities at the tackled ball to have it. Cane did not appear to be the heir apparent to Read the day the team to play England was announced.

But while many saw the events between late 2018 and 2019 as Cane regressing as a possible All Blacks captain, soon-to-be-promoted assistant coach Foster felt differently. He could see how adversity strengthened Cane, and the best evidence of that came in the last week of the World Cup when the All Blacks had to pick themselves up after losing to England and play the dreaded bronze medal match against Wales. That was the week that Cane established himself as Foster's preferred choice. That was the week Cane displayed the mental strength, desire and awareness that Foster, should he indeed win the head coaching job, would be looking for in his captain.

Most of the squad were mentally broken by the defeat to England. Their World Cup dream had ended and yet they still had to find the resolve to don the black jersey again in five days and uphold its values and traditions. It was the ultimate test of character and Cane was in the thick of it. His team-mates, including the most senior, said he was the man who set the standards during training that week. His energy and passion were infectious and he got around his peers and demanded they produce something they could be proud of.

He led the way with his work ethic in the build-up and during the game. His tackling was phenomenal. He hit the Welsh hard and unsettled them. He was seemingly at every ruck, picked off a few turnovers, and was always on hand to carry the ball. The All Blacks won 40–17, and as they trooped up to receive their bronze medals there was a realisation within management and among the players that it had been a mistake, a big one, to not pick Cane to start against England.

Of all the lessons learned during that failed World Cup campaign, none was more painful than realising too late how much the team needed the influence of Cane. If Foster was unsure before the World Cup who he would choose as his captain, he wasn't by the time he arrived home. Cane had shown himself to be incredibly tough, standing up and walking off the field with a broken neck. He'd shown his resilience and appetite for hard work in the way he had rebuilt his body and recovered so quickly. He had delivered quality performances between 2012 and 2015, and world-class efforts since 2016. Even at the World Cup, despite his game time being curtailed, he'd been superb. The decision to replace him against Ireland and bench him against England was tactical and not related to his form. And besides, tactical or otherwise, the coaches knew it had been a mistake. Cane, through a circuitous route, had proven unequivocally he had to be a starting player — and as he was only 27, that could easily remain the case for the duration of the next World Cup cycle.

All that pushed Foster towards Cane. The kicker was Cane's ability to connect with the likely squad Foster intended to select. Foster felt Cane had an easy rapport with younger players: that he was able to embrace them yet not befriend them; that he was accessible, yet not smothering. Cane also had the respect of his senior peers and wasn't afraid to hold them to task. Cane had long been in possession of these qualities, but they had intensified since he had broken his neck. Foster had seen the change — he'd seen how Cane had returned to the game with an increased appetite to make every moment count. Cane had a depth of gratitude that few could replicate and an increased desire to relish the remainder of his career, and he gave an insight into that when he was happy to be interviewed the day before the World Cup quarter-final against Ireland.

'I just feel really lucky,' he said. 'There was never a time during it where I was like, "Why did this have to happen to me?" I wasn't angry. I had done that cleanout a thousand times before and that had never happened. But I wasn't angry at rugby. I was just thankful that it wasn't worse and realised it was a genuine accident and these things happen. I became really appreciative of the people in my life who are there to help and support you. Although rugby is a massive part of my life and has been for a long time, I realised I was going to be okay if I couldn't play again.

'It doesn't define me and knowing how close I came to facing a different future, I would have been okay with it. Once my rehab process got under way and the Chiefs season kicked off, and particularly when they were struggling, that's when I really wanted to get out there and play again. I realised how much I love the game, training and competing and being around the team. Even though there is all the pressure on game day, I never forget to enjoy it. I say to myself to smile and enjoy the little moments.'

ACKNOWLEDGEMENTS

A SINCERE THANK-YOU to all those who took the time to talk to me and give the book the insight it deserves. I want to acknowledge and thank publisher Alex Hedley, whom I suspect performed a Jedi mind trick on me when we met for coffee to first discuss his idea. I was adamant I wasn't interested and yet, by the time I finished my latte, he had me hooked. Whatever success this book enjoys will be down to him and his team at HarperCollins who do magical work. And finally, to my family, who spent much of the lockdown forced to read and critique every chapter, thank you for your honesty, love and support.